Grand Tour

DIARY OF AN EASTWARD JOURNEY

BY PATRICK BALFOUR

ILLUSTRATED WITH PHOTOGRAPHS TAKEN BY THE AUTHOR,
MANY OF WHICH ARE UNIQUE

HARCOURT, BRACE AND COMPANY

NEW YORK

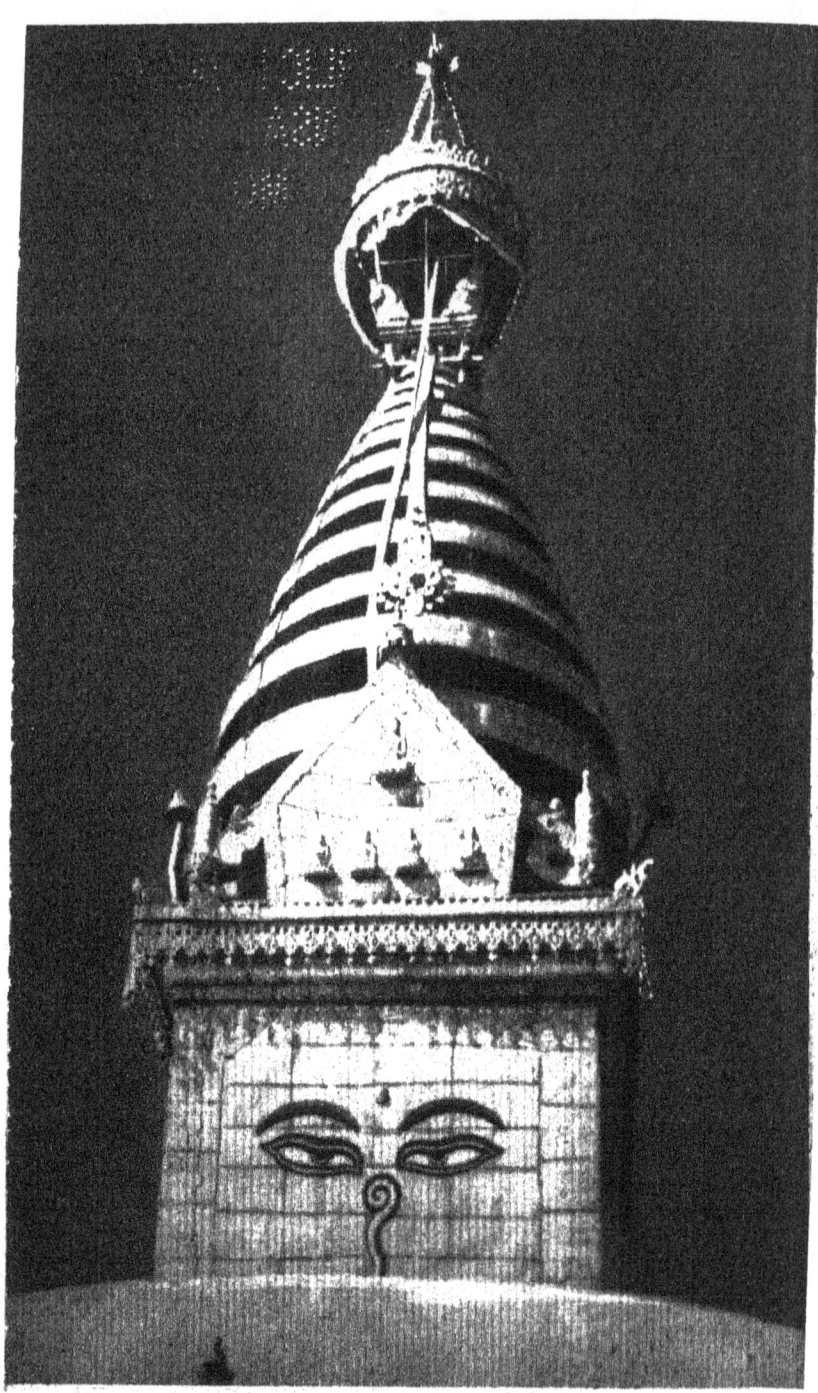

The Eyes of the Temple of Swayambunath, Nepal

To
O. C. C.

PREFACE

THE Grand Tour to-day is both more and less than it was in the eighteenth century. More, because not merely Europe but the world is the traveller's oyster; less, because, covering a greater breadth of country in a similar length of time, his impressions must needs be less profound. Rangoon is as near to us as Rome to our forefathers, and, aeroplanes apart, hardly a port in the world is above a month's journey from London. The steamship, the motor-car, and the railway train enable us to put a girdle round the earth in fifty days. Hence our Grand Tours have acquired a new character.

This is the account of a superficial journey. I am almost ashamed to tot up the number of countries which I contrived to visit in the space of a mere six months. The atlas is a notorious seducer. Step by step it leads the traveller on, covetous as a collector, insatiable in his accumulation of geographical experience. There is a certain defiance in the physiognomy of a map, challenging a raid on its complacent pastures of yellow and mauve and pink; and since to-day all too few countries are "off the map", the traveller no longer requires the jaws of an intrepid adventurer wherewith to gratify his roving appetites. Often he sacrifices a staple dish to variety of diet; but even hors d'œuvres can make a sustaining meal. It is arguable, moreover, that, short of spending six months in a single place, it is possible to discover as much about it in six days as in six weeks. I have a sneaking sympathy with the rubberneck tourist in that I would prefer to spend even six hours in a country than not visit it at all!

Hence those who require from a book of travel an exhaustive analysis of the countries traversed, with detailed investigations of a political, antiquarian, historical, or anthropological nature, will be pained by this book's inadequacy; and those who are already familiar with the East may be irritated by its assumption that they know as little of it as the writer.

PREFACE

Whereas in the past the Grand Tour was undertaken with the avowed educational intention of improving the mind, to-day we travel from a variety of motives, more negative than positive. Travel is primarily an avenue of escape, both actual and spiritual, from the complex liabilities of modern life. But though the pursuit of knowledge may be incidental to this instinct, it remains implicit in every voyage. The field of every traveller's interests is perceptibly widened by what he sees, and, if this book succeeds in stimulating in the reader some fraction of that curiosity to know more of the East which his journey aroused in the writer, it will not have been written in vain.

Places are as good company as people : sometimes better. As often with people, their appeal depends neither on visible qualities nor on intrinsic interest, but on their atmosphere, which can always be recalled by pressing the button of their name but is generally indefinable as taste or smell. It is in a modest attempt no less to inform than to communicate in words some echo of the many "atmospheres" with which this journey has enriched the memory of my senses that I have placed it on record.

I have to thank many friends and acquaintances, too numerous and widespread to name, for hospitality such as only remote countries know how to dispense, and particularly my friends of the British Navy for the delightful privilege of travelling in one of His Majesty's ships. Specifically I must thank His Highness the Maharaja-Marshal of Nepal for his gracious permission to visit Nepal and the innumerable facilities afforded me in his unique country ; the Royal State Railways of Siam for every courtesy and assistance ; Mr. Anker Rentse, of Kota Bharu, for information on the mythology of Kelantan ; Mrs. John Betjeman for help with the Nepalese chapters ; and "Colonel Christmas" for the opportunity to visit India in so delightful a fashion.

Not to mention the sandwichman, who started the whole thing.

P. B.

All the photographs, with the exception of the royal Rolls-Royce facing page 123, are my own, and some have already appeared in *Harper's Bazaar*, the *Sphere*, the *Field*, the *Evening Standard*, and *Town and Country*, New York.

CONTENTS

CHAPTER   PAGE

PREFACE - - - - - - - vii

PART I
Motoring to India

I.	ENGLAND - - - - - - -	15
II.	STILL ENGLAND - - - - - -	24
III.	FRANCE - - - - - - -	34
IV.	ITALY - - - - - - -	44
V.	AT SEA - - - - - - -	49
VI.	CYPRUS - - - - - - -	55
VII.	SYRIA - - - - - - -	60
VIII.	IRAQ - - - - - - -	72
IX.	PERSIA - - - - - - -	84
X.	PERSIA (*continued*) - - - - -	94
XI.	AFGHANISTAN - - - - - -	112

PART II
Further East

I.	INDIA - - - - - - -	133
II.	NEPAL - - - - - - -	143
III.	NEPAL (*continued*) - - - - -	154
IV.	INDIA - - - - - - -	172
V.	INDIA (*continued*) - - - - -	188
VI.	THE ANDAMAN ISLANDS - - - -	205
VII.	MALAYA - - - - - - -	216
VIII.	MALAYA (*continued*) - - - - -	232
IX.	MALAYA (*continued*) - - - - -	244
X.	SIAM - - - - - - -	259
XI.	SIAM (*continued*) - - - - -	271
XII.	INDO-CHINA - - - - - -	285
XIII.	INDO-CHINA (*continued*) - - - -	300
XIV.	SIAM, SUMATRA, HOME - - - -	314

LIST OF ILLUSTRATIONS

THE EYES OF THE TEMPLE OF SWAYAMBUNATH, NEPAL	frontispiece
DOVER, AND CALAIS	46
OSTUNI: VILLAGE IN APULIA	47
CTESIPHON, AND IN THE BAZAARS OF KHADIMAIN	84
THE GREAT PERSIAN PLATEAU	85
A PERSIAN BRIDGE	92
TILING IN THE TOMB OF KHOJA RABI, MESHED, AND BY A PERSIAN STREAM	93
VILLAGE IN KHORASAN, AND IN THE SHAH'S PALACE OF GULISTAN	96
CARAVANSERAI IN KHORASAN, AND RUINED MOSQUE AT TUS	97
MINARETS OF THE MUSALLA, HERAT, AND AN AFGHAN DAWN AT FARAH	112
IN THE AFGHAN DESERT: OURSELVES, AND SOLDIERY	113
AFGHANS	116
AFGHANS	117
AFGHAN VILLAGE, AND A FORT AT GIRISHK	124
HALF-WAY THROUGH AN AFGHAN BRIDGE	125
INTO NEPAL	144
WOMEN COOLIES IN NEPAL, AND NEPALESE CHILDREN	145
DURBAR. SIR FREDERICK O'CONNOR WITH THE MAHARAJA AND RULING FAMILY OF NEPAL, AND GARDEN PARTY AT KATMANDU. THE MAHARAJA ESCORTS THE KING	148
MALLA ELEPHANT, KATMANDU, AND DRAWING WATER IN PATAN	149
THE GREAT GARUDA, KATMANDU	156
DARBAR SQUARE, PATAN	157
PALACE IN DARBAR SQUARE, BHATGAON, AND DARBAR SQUARE, KATMANDU	160
WINDOW IN PATAN, AND MAHABUDDHA TEMPLE, PATAN	161

LIST OF ILLUSTRATIONS

NEPALESE ROOF SUPPORTS	164
SWAYAMBUNATH: A TIBETAN BY THE GILT STATUE OF TARA, AND PRAYER WHEELS	165
PASHPATI: SACRED MONKEYS, AND BURNING GHAT	172
HINDU HOLY MEN: NEPAL, AND BENARES	173
BENARES: BURNING GHAT, AND BATHING GHAT	176
TAJ MAHAL, AGRA, AND HUMAYUN'S TOMB, DELHI	177
DELHI: NEW—COUNCIL HOUSE; OLD—EIGHTEENTH CENTURY OBSERVATORY	192
OBSERVATORY, DELHI	193
ABORIGINAL WOMEN, ANDAMAN ISLANDS	212
COCKFIGHTING IN MALAYA, AND ON THE KALANTAN COAST	213
KALANTAN SHADOW-PLAY: RAMA, THE HERO-KING; HANUMAN, THE MONKEY GOD; AND A SACRED CLOWN	220
CASUARINA TREES AT SINGORA	221
AUDIENCE HALL, GRAND PALACE, BANGKOK	272
WAT SUTHAT, BANGKOK, AND TEMPLE GUARDIAN IN GRAND PALACE, BANGKOK	273
MARKET SCENES AT CHIENGMAI, NORTHERN SIAM	288
LAO WOMEN, ON THE MEKONG RIVER	289
HEAD OF SIVA, BAYON, ANGKOR THOM	292
BAS-RELIEF BAPUON, ANGKOR THOM, AND HEADS OF SIVA, BAYON	293
TOWERS OF THE ANGKOR WAT	300
CAMBODIAN PEASANTS, AND BRIDGE AT PRAH KHAN, ANGKOR	301
CAMBODIAN DANCERS, ANGKOR WAT	308
MOAT, ANGKOR WAT, AND FUNERAL PROCESSION AT ANGKOR WAT	309
RACIAL TYPES: SIAMESE AND ITALIANS	316
RACIAL TYPES: TIBETANS (IN NEPAL), AND AFGHANS	317

PART ONE
Motoring to India

Chapter I

ENGLAND

QUITE a crowd had collected in Pall Mall. A cinema camera bestrode the top of a van; a couple of operators tinkered with its mechanism and a boss shouted cryptic directions from the street, contemptuously indifferent to the gaping populace. Clubmen emerging from lunch winced at so unseemly a congestion in their neighbourhood—but stopped to look. Friends who chanced to be passing snatched the kudos of coming to see us off. "How nice of you," we said, "to bother!" Other friends discovered with surprise that *we* were the centre of those goings-on outside the R.A.C.

"Where on earth are you off to?"

"India."

"*India?* Not in that pompous Rolls?"

"In that pompous Rolls."

I strode about, hatless, trying to look important. Manfred was being efficient about the car.

The Press photographers eyed us, but waited, sensing bigger fry to come. A reporter begged my pardon, but was I Colonel Christmas? I was not. Spectators hurried from the corner of Lower Regent Street on the premature assumption that we were a street accident, and concluded instead that we were a gangster film. A florid woman said: "You know, I was going on this trip originally. But my husband..." A pink-faced, spectacled young man introduced himself as a member of the expedition.

"My name is Quinney. Where's Christmas?"

"Christmas," I said importantly (and optimistically), "is coming."

Manfred's head emerged from the tool-box.

"There's no jack," he said, "and no hammer."

"We'd better wait till Christmas comes."

The florid lady turned to Quinney. "You know, I was coming on this trip originally. But my husband . . ."

Then there was a stir in the crowd, and eyes turned right. Christmas was coming.

Colonel Christmas, at the wheel of what the detective stories call a "long, grey touring-car", made his way with a harassed expression through the crowd. The "tonneau" overflowed with sinister and unshaven individuals who shouted, "Make way there! Make way!" On the running-board an enormous stove, some five feet high, steamed and sizzled and so obscured the Colonel's view that he had difficulty in steering to the kerb. A policeman, as though anticipating an explosion, encouraged the crowd to "Stand back!"

"Coo!" said the crowd, "Blimey!" and, "What's he doing with the bathroom geyser?"

The reporters (who were in the know) muttered, "Char-coal," advanced towards the car, but were driven back by the heat.

Colonel Christmas sat in the driving-seat, dazed, shock-headed, but benign, and tried (or did not try) to cope with a hundred people at once.

"Where are the jack and the hammer?"

"There's a jack and a hammer in the car."

"No."

"Oh."

Mrs. Christmas appeared. She was thin and smart in black and scarlet, and a cigarette drooped from her thin scarlet lips.

"The jack and the hammer. The man said he'd put them in the car."

"He hasn't."

"Drat him!"

The crowd redoubled on the arrival of the Colonel and his geyser. People put their heads out of the windows of passing taxicabs, rapped on the glass, stopped.

"Anyone hurt?" said a hopeful little man at my elbow.

Christmas was buttonholed by a lean gentleman with a set expression who asked a good many questions.

"That's Waters," said Mrs. Christmas.

"Who's Waters?"

"He's on the trip too."

"Now then, Colonel Christmas," shouted the cinema operator. "If you don't mind just one moment . . ."

But at that moment the crowd's attention was diverted towards a dark-skinned figure in robes and a turban making his way towards the cars. Christmas and Mrs. Christmas greeted him ceremoniously, then lined up for a photograph. At the last moment a distinguished Persian scholar who happened to be passing got into the photograph too, and they all stood pointing to the geyser.

"You all feel very grand and important now," said someone, "but you'll be nobody at all by the time you get to Croydon."

A reporter urged me to look there, old man, could I tell him something about this charcoal outfit? I could not. Quinney said: "Don't you think we might try and start putting the luggage on?" But there were no straps. The Indian princeling took his leave. "Don't you think we might try and start putting the luggage on?" I suggested to Mrs. Christmas.

"There are no straps," said Mrs. Christmas.

"Will there be some?"

"The straps were left behind at the house. I expect they'll turn up." She lit a cigarette.

The Persian scholar and an ex-diplomat from Teheran looked critically at the more pompous car and murmured things about "clearance". Sombre, erect and cumbersome, she was like an old-fashioned dowager: Belgravia, not Asia, was her spiritual home.

"They may get as far as Ancona," said the diplomat.

"Fontainebleau," said the scholar.

Colonel Christmas was making a speech into the talkie machine.

"I am endeavouring to motor to India on charcoal, because if people in India can be induced to use home-produced charcoal instead of imported petrol, the country and the government will benefit. I foresee no difficulties with my gas-producing plant. Charcoal can be easily obtained, and it is ever so much cheaper than petrol. I calculate that twelve pounds of charcoal is equal in power to one gallon of petrol. The charcoal costs twopence and the petrol approximately two and sevenpence. Thus to run my car on charcoal would cost fifteen times as much as to run it on petrol."

To which surprising computation the Colonel added: "We are now leaving for Dover."

He let in the clutch and left abruptly for Ealing, where the works were. Just in time Manfred called him back. He had forgotten to collect the triptyches, permits, papers, and so forth, without which we could not leave England to-morrow.

"Good lord!" said the Colonel, and hurried into the R.A.C.

Manfred took control of the situation. "We can't do anything until we've got straps for the luggage and a jack and a hammer. We'll go and get them."

"All right," said Mrs. Christmas. "Step on the gas."

As we went, the florid woman was saying to Mr. Waters, "You know, I was going on this trip originally. But my husband . . ."

We got the straps, which were too small, and a jack, which did not fit the Dowager; went back, forward, hither and thither, got other straps, another jack, and returned to Pall Mall as the lamps were being lit and an autumn dusk settled on the London streets. The tumult and the shouting had died. The crowd had gone. Pall Mall looked strangely empty. Only a patient knot of women and hangers-on awaited us in the premises of the R.A.C. Quinney, they explained, and Waters, had taken most of the luggage and left for Dover by train. (Later they were to grow quite accustomed to motoring to India by train.) Mrs. Christmas left for "several cocktail parties", saying, "See you at Dover to-night." Such as remained of the luggage was packed into the Dowager. Two women disengaged themselves, with many embraces, from the group on the pavement, and proved to be our travelling companions. We settled ourselves in the car and were off.

Polite, tentative questionings broke the silence. "Have you travelled much?" "Did you know the Christmases before?" "Are you meaning to stay out in India?" "Did you manage to see *Nymph Errant* before you left?" Fog descended on the outer suburbs, but Manfred's immaculate driving had us soon on the Dover road, heading for India.

Only a fortnight before, I had returned from Scotland

on the night express with no clear plans for the winter. London, like the majority of its inhabitants, does not look its best in the early morning. Paris and Berlin are light sleepers and early risers. However early, their cafés are awake (if, indeed, they have ever slept), and in the streets are people hurrying to their work. But London is a sluggard, a city in which the traveller who values first impressions should at no cost arrive before breakfast. Till nine o'clock she has a bleakness all her own.

As I drove through the empty streets, after a sleepless night in the train, a chill of depression caught me. The blank squares of Bloomsbury, which in the daytime have a pleasant air of cosmopolitan studiousness, seemed singularly inhospitable. Shaftesbury Avenue, deprived of the vital vulgarity of its crowds, was naked to indecency. The closed shops were unmasked by the cold morning light in all their drab ugliness. Laid bare, Piccadilly's excrescent buildings stood out with unwonted defiance. I found myself wondering why it had never been admitted that this, architecturally, is the ugliest street in the world (with the possible exception of Princes Street, Edinburgh).

The day was dreary. It was that transition season of the year when summer has gone but autumn has not yet come. The country has an exhausted, used look. Its greenness is rusty, dead. Where the leaves have begun to turn they look untidy, like crumpled pieces of brown tissue paper which somebody has dropped among the green foliage. The weather is neither warm nor cold: the days are neither long nor short.

The chill of early-morning London was still with me at midday when I boarded an omnibus in the Strand. The omnibus swung from Pall Mall into Lower Regent Street; and then I saw the sandwichman, ambling towards Waterloo Place.

The inscription on his sandwich was peculiar:

TO INDIA
BY ROLLS-ROYCE CAR
FOR £34
LEAVING OCTOBER 18

—and an address in Paddington. Now India was the last country in the world which I had ever desired to visit. For some reason its prospect had always repelled rather than attracted me, and in the normal course I should have passed the sandwichman without a tremor. But London was at its worst, I had alighted sleepless that morning from the Scotch Express, my view of the immediate future was a blank, and I felt called upon to make some decision regarding it.

Of course, I concluded, there must be "a catch somewhere". There always was in advertisements. The applicant would be expected, first, to invest £2000 in some dubious mechanical enterprise. He would be asked to put down a good-conduct deposit of £200, with which the advertiser would then decamp. He would have to provide his own Rolls-Royce. The advertisement was a hoax. Endless probabilities swam before me. But there could be no harm in trying. I answered the advertisement and thought no more about it. That night I went early to bed.

I must have been asleep a good two hours when the telephone bell rang by my bedside. It was long after midnight. I swore, and lifted the receiver.

"It's Colonel Christmas speaking," said a voice.

"Who ?"

"Our route to India is as follows." My interruption was disregarded ; the voice proceeded to an unbroken recital of names which, to my still semi-somnolent consciousness, meant little beyond a hazy assumption that they belonged to places in Asia. I managed to get a word in. "Supposing," I suggested, "we meet to-morrow and discuss it ?"

"Twelve o'clock," said the voice, "at my club ?"

"That will suit me perfectly. Your name again ?"

"Christmas—Colonel Christmas." Adding, as an afterthought, the name of his club, the Colonel rang off.

By now I was wide awake. In a moment I was out of bed in search of an atlas. Poring over the map of Asia Minor, I cursed my lack of concentration on the telephone and traced a dozen possible routes for the Colonel to have chosen. But all, as far as I could see, must include Persia. And the prospect of Persia was in itself sufficiently attractive to give me another wakeful night.

Next morning I determined on caution. Crooks, I knew,

had a notorious partiality for military rank, and it was in a defensive frame of mind that I approached my rendezvous with the Colonel. But the moment I saw him I was disarmed. It would have been hard to imagine anyone less like either a Colonel or a crook. He had a vague air and a gentle, melodious voice. His hair and moustache were grey and untidy; his clothes were haphazard; his large blue-grey eyes had a dreamy look but twinkled when he smiled; and he had a quiet sense of humour. He must be a man of about forty-five, and tough beneath the childlike charm of his manner and appearance: the kind of man who could never pass unnoticed.

He was, he explained, in the Foreign and Political Department of the Indian Civil Service, and was returning from leave to Peshawar, where he had been appointed to a new post. He made a point of never returning to India by the normal route, and this time he proposed motoring to Brindisi, thence taking a boat to Haifa, in Palestine, crossing the desert to Baghdad, and proceeding through Persia via Teheran and Meshed to Baluchistan, and so to Quetta. He had bought a Rolls-Royce car for his own use in India, because of the notorious excellence of their engines. He was trying out a new invention by which it was possible to run motor-cars on charcoal instead of petrol at approximately one-fifteenth of the cost. As passengers he had his wife and another man and woman. Now he was proposing, if he could collect enough additional passengers, to buy a second Rolls-Royce for the journey. Why he took it into his head to do this I never quite fathomed. Someone, I believe, had told him that you could sell Rolls-Royces to maharajas in India at an enormous profit, provided you could get them out there (though it was hard to imagine that any motor-car could be worth anything to anybody, far less a maharaja, after covering five thousand of the roughest miles in the world). Perhaps he felt that there was safety in numbers. But I think it was simply that he got into the spirit of the thing, carried away by his own enthusiasm.

The £34, naturally enough, covered no more than a seat in the car. But on the Colonel's computation the entire journey, including food, hotel accommodation, and etceteras, should not cost more than a similar amount, of which the exorbitant steamer fare from Brindisi to Haifa (£19 second class for a four days' journey, for the Lloyd-Triestino Company has a virtual monopoly of the route) formed by far the biggest proportion. From the first I thought the Colonel optimistic in his estimate and mentally increased it by another £20. But, even so, to get to India, overland, for under £100 seemed a good enough bargain.

The situation as it stood was this: that if, within the next few days, Colonel Christmas could find a minimum of three, and preferably four, extra passengers, he would buy a second car. His advertisements hitherto (he had advertised in *The Times* as well as on the sandwich-boards) had not been fruitful. Two applicants, curiously enough, had proved to be relatives of his own; but they were both doubtful starters. One woman had stipulated that she should have breakfast in bed each morning and never on any account be asked to start before ten a.m. One reply bore only the laconic, and presumably rhetorical question: "What's all this about?" Another, which appended a telephone number, seemed more hopeful; so the Colonel rang up. Could he speak, he asked, to Mr. Wiggins? Oh no, was the surprised reply, Mr. Wiggins could not possibly speak on the *telephone*. The Colonel explained his business, to which the voice replied that it was sorry he had been troubled. Mr. Wiggins was stone deaf, well over eighty, and had been bedridden for fifteen years. "But he's a great one for the newspapers, and it keeps him nicely occupied answering all them advertisements in *The Times*."

My mind was made up on the spot. All the tiresome businesslike questions I had prepared went out of my head. With such a man as Colonel Christmas there could be no question of anything so sordid as references and contracts. He could count on me, I said, as a certain starter. Meanwhile, I would do my best to recruit other passengers.

During the next few days, from no suspicious motive but from pure curiosity, I tried to discover some more about Colonel Christmas. I found that mention of his name gave rise, as a rule, to merriment. "Well, I'm damned! Another of Christmas's crazy schemes! Charcoal! Typical of him. I'd give anything to be coming with you. You couldn't have tumbled on a better man." The Colonel, I gathered, had spent a great part of his career in Persia, where he was a famous figure. He had been imprisoned there during the war and survived a series of astonishing privations. The stories of his adventures and escapes would make a book in themselves ; but Christmas could never be induced to write it. But though I found plenty of people to tell me about Colonel Christmas, no one seemed able, if inclined, to accompany us to India, and time was getting short.

Then I thought of Manfred. Manfred is what is technically known as a "man of leisure", and inhabits a villa in the south of France. But there is nothing leisurely about Manfred, who is always ready to do almost anything at a moment's notice. Moreover, two of his three favourite occupations are travelling and driving a motor-car. What could be a happier coincidence? I had heard that he was due in London, where he usually spends the winter months. I rang him up. Manfred answered the telephone.

"Come to India," I said.

"Come to lunch," said Manfred.

I came to lunch.

Manfred came to India.

That afternoon I telephoned the news to Colonel Christmas. That afternoon Colonel Christmas bought a large Rolls-Royce, second-hand, for £300.

Hence the Pall Mall pantomime.

Chapter II

STILL ENGLAND

WE did not wait for the Colonel and his wife, who were hardly likely to reach Dover before midnight. I retired to bed in an ample room whose commode, not inappropriately, contained only a spanner.

At about eight o'clock in the morning, I was awakened by a battering on my door, and Colonel Christmas entered, black and dishevelled. He had only that moment arrived from London; he had left before midnight, but all the way down the charcoal gave endless trouble. Eight hours is certainly excessive for a journey normally accomplished in two and a half, and it did not need a mathematician to calculate that at such a rate we would be a long time crossing Asia. Christmas therefore had decided to abandon his charcoal plant, and a young man from the works, agreeing that there was something wrong somewhere, promised to take it back and refund him his money. (This, in point of fact, his superior afterwards refused to do.) Sorry as we were for Colonel Christmas, that his pet ewe lamb should have failed him so early in the proceedings, Manfred and I could not help being faintly relieved. For it was obvious that the "stove", even if it had worked, would have caused endless trouble at every frontier, and that we should have been continually held up on suspicion of smuggling explosives. Besides, it was better that it should fail us at this stage than in the wilds of Central Asia. On the other hand, its failure was likely to involve us in some delay. The thing had to be removed: then the engine had to be reoverhauled and readapted to petrol; and this, if we knew anything about garages, would take time.

There was another mishap. Driving down the evening before, we had noticed ominous bumpings in the neighbourhood of the Dowager's off rear wheel. Accustomed only to

Belgravia, she was clearly outraged at being torn from her native element. But if the perfect surface of the London-Dover highway was too much for her springs, how (if, indeed, she ever got us there) would she stand the trackless desert ? The offending spring was examined and proved to have gone entirely. There was nothing for it but to telephone London for another to be sent down by train.

Christmas was anxious. We had just a week to catch our boat at Brindisi, with the risk of forfeiting our passage money if we did not, and the loss of even a single day was a serious matter. He began to talk of driving day and night to reach Brindisi in time. He had had only three hours' sleep in the last three nights, but after swallowing some coffee he was off again to work on the car. Mrs. Christmas had gone to bed. The other ladies, Mrs. Mock and Miss Gumbleton, took the delay in good part, though Mrs. Mock had put on her seasick plaster that morning in anticipation of crossing the Channel, and would have to endure its discomfort (and forgo, moreover, a bath) until such time as we might make Calais. Notwithstanding, they went off happily together to buy hats—woman's unfailing emollient in misfortune.

Mr. Waters remarked, "They talk about the weak camel that holds up the caravan. But both the camels are now lying down," and started to spread his map on a table. "When I go on a trip of this kind," he added, "I always believe in acting on the hypothesis that I am running it myself." Quinney and he pored over the maps together, while Manfred and I, with a girl of Manfred's who had come from Canterbury to see him off, set out to make the best of Dover, and found it a good best.

Dover, in travel literature, has always been unfairly neglected. Hardly a traveller, it is true, fails to give it a mention—whether contemptuously, in reference to its "depressingly English" aspect, or sentimentally, in reference to the whiteness of its cliffs. But it figures simply as an inevitable point or symbol in a journey, and has never, so far as I am aware, been credited with a personality of its own. No one would willingly stop a day or two in Dover, as he might in Hamburg or Marseilles. But whoever is forced to stay there discovers, to his surprise, an enchanting town. Dover, unlike Folkestone, has never been successfully "developed" as a seaside resort. Thus its beautiful Regency sea-front, its perfectly proportioned crescents and terraces, its narrow back-streets with their pleasing, boarded houses of the period, survive unimpaired by the pretensions of Edwardian hotels, and the place has a forgotten, symmetrical air. As you near the eastern end of the town the rugged, primitive architecture of the cliff, towering like an ever-present white menace over the houses just at its feet, contrasts agreeably with their sophisticated dignity.

Dover has an atmosphere of its own. The perpetual coming and going of the Continental boats gives it vitality and a feeling of romance, but since the travellers pass it by it retains a quiet integrity, unsullied by the scum of passengers which ships eject into many a demoralized port. Moreover, a town cannot be so close to the Continent without imbibing a certain Continental flavour. Dover is friendly, unofficious, free-and-easy, do-as-you please, nicely calculated, if he would only stop there, to break the foreigner's fall before he is swallowed up in the aloof, bewildering turmoil of London.

We felt free, as though across the Channel: our friends and creditors had written us off the map. Dover was to us a foreign town.

We found an oyster bar, with Whitstables at three shillings a dozen, kept by a buxom lady who assured us that the oysters enjoyed being opened. Her father had had the shop for seventy-two years, and his father before him. We found an Italian restaurant where we lunched off jugged hare, a perfect zabaglione and chianti. There was a Swiss waiter, with a partiality for backchat, who told us he was Irish with a mistress in Valparaiso, and if you go to Italy Mussolini he give you jolly good hiding.

From time to time we visited the garage to see how work was progressing on the cars. The stove looked bigger than ever now that it had been detached from the running-board (in which it had burnt a large hole). The Grey had been reduced to such disintegration that it was hard for the un-initiated to conceive how she could ever go again. From underneath her protruded an elegant suède-shoed leg, and an agreeable baritone sang: *"Ple-ease lend your little ear to my . . ."* abrupt cascade of expletives. "The dogs are nowhere near each other. There's a dog broken off. *Ple-eas,*" it sang again, emerging to disclose Old Etonian braces and a suit of filthy borrowed overalls, *"lend a ray of cheer*—I fail to see how these brakes can ever work—*ti-tum tell me that you love me*—hell!"

The garage was full of enthusiastic amateurs whom Christmas had somehow picked up on the way, and they were all doing things to the car, while mechanics stood around contemplating its inside with the contented appreciation of surgeons in an anatomical museum or art-connoisseurs in the Tate.

The companionship of machines is a delight which has always eluded me. There are people—and Manfred is one of them—who can be happy for hour after hour in a garage, doing nothing in particular, lulled by the proximity of cars into a kind of ecstatic trance from which no outsider's conversation can arouse them. If you venture to make them a remark they regard you at the third time of repetition with a look of detached surprise, as though you were a contemptible human strayed into the house of the gods. They seem affronted that you should dare interrupt their mystic communion with the infinite. In me machines kindle no spark. I am embarrassed in their company, as in that of horses and children, and can think of nothing to say. Their stupidity when I am forced into practical contact with them enrages me.

"Come on," I said to Manfred, "we can do no good here."

Someone was now driving the Rolls at full speed, backwards and forwards, over the Old Etonian's prostrate form. "*Ple-ease*," he was singing.

"Come on," I said to Manfred.

Reluctantly, Manfred came.

We went up to the station to meet the spring on the two-fifty-eight. At the station we found Quinney, who had come to meet the spring on the two-fifty-eight. Shortly before three o'clock Waters arrived in a taxicab. He had come to meet the spring on the two-fifty-eight. He had spent most of the morning following in Christmas's footsteps, "backing him up", as a half-back supports a forward, duplicating all his telephone calls, confirming all his orders in case, in his dazed condition, he had got things wrong.

Oddly enough, the spring arrived on the two-fifty-eight. Oddly enough, it was the wrong spring, intended for the on side instead of the off. This meant that the other spring, which was an old and interchangeable model, would have to be transferred to the off, and the new one put in its place.

Manfred went to the garage, where I foresaw that he would spend a blissful three hours. I slept and, when dusk had fallen, went for a walk.

Enlarged, as landscape is, by the darkness, Dover's bay was as wide as the Bay of Naples. I turned into a Norman church which was sandwiched among the shops and the trams and the cinemas, as churches should be. So places of worship are in Catholic and Moslem countries; but with us, too often, they prefer to stand apart from the paraphernalia of daily life, cold and aloof, like the bourgeoisie, in their own grounds. A service was just finishing. Only a few old ladies, one young couple, and a clergyman or two on a busman's holiday formed the congregation. It was calm. The vicar, as he walked down the aisle after the service was over, turned to me and said good evening. I stayed behind a moment and thought of my journey. The past had been paid off for six months. Only the immediate future counted, and its prospect filled me with the keenest expectation. Who knew in what far-off countries I should contemplate the sea at night, remember this sea, and say, "How different!" I would think, "How peaceful!" or "How friendly!" and reflect by comparison on the rackety indifference of my own too civilized land. I should be wrong; for seas all the world over are substantially the same, peace is everywhere to be had for the asking, and mankind varies little at heart. But I should enjoy imagining that they were different.

I came out into the well-lighted street, where the trams jingled and the lighted shops looked warm in the fog and a couple who had followed me out of the church were crossing to the cinema opposite. (Miss Gumbleton assured me later that it contained sofas for two.) I seemed to discover the warmth and friendliness of England for the first time. For my journey had begun, and psychologically, in casting off the ties and responsibilities of my normal life, I was already abroad.

Back in the hotel, I found Mrs. Christmas in tweeds, revived by her day's sleep and declaring herself "ready for a party". Mrs. Mock came down in an elegant evening gown of black lace.

"How smart we are!" said Mrs. Christmas. "Trousseau for the desert?"

"Oh," said Mrs. Mock in deprecation, "it's the kind of dress that does for the opera or anything."

The Colonel arrived from the garage with the excellent news that we should be able to cross to-morrow. The Grey had gone to Folkestone, where there was an all-night Rolls-Royce service, and would be back early in the morning. The Dowager was ready. Heartened, we had a successful dinner, and afterwards repaired to a gay establishment on the front—*Tanz Bar* or *Bal Musette*, since we had discovered that Dover was a foreign town.

It closed all too early for Mrs. Christmas. "Come on," she said, "there'll be a piano in the hotel. We'll have some whoopee there."

But the hotel, despite her remonstrances, politely vetoed the piano, on the grounds that other guests required sleep.

"Well," said Mrs. Christmas, as we said good night, "it's a mixed collection, but you all seem all right. Some of you might have been awful."

. . . . .

Colonel Christmas, in collecting his passengers, had evolved a useful formula. The trip, he reiterated to applicants, must be embarked upon "in a spirit of adventure". And certainly, heterogeneous as we were, a certain harmony appeared to unite our various component parts. Perhaps this was the "spirit of adventure" : perhaps it was just a common element of eccentricity. But it seemed to work.

One day at Dover had given us leisure to distinguish and form some preliminary impressions of one another.

First, there was Mrs. Christmas. Mrs. Christmas was straightforward, outspoken, and partial to slang. Why she accompanied the expedition was never quite clear. She was not remaining with her husband in India, as she had children to look after at home. From the beginning her fear was that she should "miss the boat" (or, as she usually called it "the bateau"), not the boat from Brindisi to Haifa, but the boat from Bombay to London, which would get her home by Christmas-time. Mrs. Christmas imparted an atmosphere of jauntiness to the expedition.

Then there was Miss Gumbleton.

Miss Gumbleton, a spinster in the early thirties, was short, pink-cheeked, and well rounded. She knew exactly why she came : she liked to travel. As the daughter of the captain of an Atlantic liner, she had perhaps inherited the taste, which she preferred to indulge in a cheaper and less hackneyed manner than the normal. Miss Gumbleton, though you would hardly have diagnosed a "spirit of adventure" from her Tweedledum-like appearance, had travelled all over the world and seemed to possess an exhaustive knowledge of geography and cargo boats. An American had once said to her in Florence: "I always like to see *everything* when I visit a town, because it means I needn't come back." Such an attitude shocked and puzzled Miss Gumbleton profoundly, as the antithesis of her own. "People like that," she said, "have no hope in life."

Miss Gumbleton was a good traveller. She was neat in her person and punctual in her habits. I can see her plump little form seated firmly in the hall of any given hotel at the exact hour we were due to start, her handbag on her lap, her immaculate suitcase and haversack at her feet. Imperturbable as a tea-cosy amid the chaos of our evacuation, she would look patiently ahead of her at nothing, in nobody's way, waiting to be told when the cars were ready and where she was to sit for the day's journey.

The third woman in the party was Mrs. Mock. Mrs. Mock was going to India to join her husband, a prominent business man in Bombay. It was only three days before our departure that she decided to cancel her sea passage and accompany us. Poor Mrs. Mock! I do not think she fully realized what she was letting herself in for. This was, I believe, the first time she had ever travelled alone. A journey by Rolls-Royce car to India sounds so leisurely and luxurious. Our journey was neither of those things. The "spirit of adventure" is primarily another name for strenuousness and discomfort, and leaves little room for gallantry. Mrs. Mock, however, was courageous and good-humoured. She was pretty, but looked frail, and had stipulated in advance that she should, wherever possible, have the front seat in the car.

Of the remaining members of the party, Mr. Waters was the elder. Mr. Waters had a skeleton in his cupboard: it was his profession, from which he had recently and thankfully retired. Mr. Waters regarded his profession with the shame of an old lag or a regenerate gossip-writer. But Mr. Waters had known neither prison nor the interior of a newspaper office; he was not a private enquiry agent or a cloakroom attendant or a master in a girls' school; he had not misspent his life travelling in trusses, toilet-paper or toques. Mr. Waters was guiltless of all such ignoble pursuits. He was a doctor. Dr. Waters was his name; but if you gave him the title he would wince and beg you earnestly not to do so again. He had been a respected practitioner all his life, in various parts of the world. Now he had retired, to enjoy a life of leisure—if a motor trip to India could seriously be called leisure. It was odd that Mr. Waters, who seemed to have travelled in every country under the British Flag, should not now prefer to settle down at home. But though a quiet life was his goal, some itch still lured him to travel even further. He had been the first to answer Colonel Christmas's original advertisement, some months before, and was, I think, somewhat appalled by the proportions to which the party had grown at the eleventh hour; for he disliked a crowd. Another thing appalled Mr. Waters: it was the presence of women. Mr. Waters was the first to appreciate women in their place, but the first also to hold that their place was not a motor-car in the middle of Asia. And perhaps he was right. Mrs. Waters, in any case, had stayed at home.

Mr. Waters was tall and wiry, with rugged, regular features and close-cropped sandy hair. He wore puttees, as a rule, and khaki breeches. Clearly he had given the question of his luggage some thought, for his clothes were thoroughly practical, and he had a kitbag packed after the style of an old campaigner. But then Mr. Waters gave thought to everything. He was, by nature, intensely methodical. Each of his pockets was devoted to some particular purpose: fountain pen here, notebook here, watch here, knife here, maps here. On one sad occasion he resigned himself to the total loss of his penknife because, in the congestion of the car, he could not perform the acrobatics necessary to restore it to its proper pocket. Mr. Waters had formulae for everything. If asked to turn some knob a little to the left he would say:

"You mean to a quarter to three?"

"I don't know. I mean a little to the left."

"That is to say somewhere between twenty-five to one and twenty past ten?"

"Say twenty to seven."

"You mean ten past eight."

And Mr. Waters would turn the knob a little to the left.

If given some instructions, he would ask you to repeat them, repeat them after you, say was that what you meant, repeat them again, and note them down in his little book.

Mr. Waters had supplied himself with maps of every country we were going through, and as nobody else had thought of doing so they were much in demand. He had route-books, too, and for months before the start had been working out in his mind every detail of our expedition, forgetting nothing. Precise as he was, he was pained by the (to him) haphazard methods of the Colonel. He liked to have everything cut and dried, worked out carefully in advance. He must have longed, all the time, to take charge of the organization himself. Then we should have had time-tables and detailed marching orders (zero hour and eight ack emma) and everything would have been planned according to a written schedule. But whether it would have substantially affected the result is open to question. For vagueness is a form of efficiency, and the Colonel had that sort of temperament that is not easily ruffled by miscarriage of plans.

As it was, Mr. Waters had a pleasantly dry humour and never failed to appreciate the joke.

Lastly, there was Quinney. He was a lawyer, sick of the law, who had decided instead to become a gentleman of leisure. He was young and admirably suited to be a lawyer. This, his first venture on the career of leisure, had started with a book called *Brazilian Adventure*, where the author answered an advertisement in *The Times* and found himself in Brazil. Quinney had done likewise and found himself at Dover.

Quinney had been the object of some speculation on our part before he materialized. Christmas, endeavouring without success to find him at his flat, had sounded the porter as to what the gentleman was like—to which the porter's only reply was, "You should just see Mr. Quinney in his yachting kit. He looks fine." From this we had half expected a young man, if not in a yachting cap, at least in a solar topee or a suit of resplendent motoring tweeds, accompanied by several innovation trunks and smoking a cigar. But Quinney was not at all like that. He brought, it is true, a ciné-camera, his luggage was new, and his clothes were well cut. But he was unobtrusive, had perfect manners, and was always willing to perform prodigies of uncomfortable manual labour, prostrating himself, if necessary, in mud or dust at the wheels of the car. Hence he would emerge with filthy hands, a Savile Row suit irreparably stained, a face even pinker than usual, but never a word of complaint.

People had said to me, "You're mad to go off like this with a lot of perfect strangers. You'll be tearing at each other's throats before you get across the Channel. You're mad."

But there is a lot to be said for travelling with strangers. Though thrown together in circumstances which would normally spell intimacy, you have none of intimacy's demands. Your relationship is on limited, cut-and-dried lines. You expect nothing of one another beyond a certain politeness and consideration, so that there can be none of the recriminations which crop up so often between friends. If you are travelling with a friend and each wants to do something different it is difficult, unless your mutual relationship is perfectly attuned, to avoid certain searchings of heart. One will have a sense of guilt for not giving in to the other; the other will have a sense of grievance at having been forced to do so. If you are travelling with a stranger and each wants to do something different, each (within reason) does something different, and that is that. There can be no resentment on either side. If a stranger irritates you, you are under no obligation to dine at the same table; if a friend irritates you and you dine at a different table it is a rankling sore for the rest of the journey. You must know someone really well before you can quarrel with him really badly.

Selfishness, within the limits of good manners, is the golden rule of travel. Travel, then, with strangers. Or travel with Manfred. Manfred and I are both selfish. In all circumstances we each do what we want. Hence we rarely quarrel while travelling.

Chapter III

FRANCE

OUR departure from Dover was hectic. The hall of the hotel was blocked with a chaotic assortment of luggage: eight variegated suitcases, none exceeding the Colonel's statutory limit of 28 inches by 16 by 9; eight haversacks of diverse patterns and dimensions; eight bulging rolls of bedding; not to mention a hundred necessary (and unnecessary) etceteras in sacks, paper parcels, wooden boxes, tin boxes, cardboard boxes, or no wrappings at all. At one moment every member of the party, Miss Gumbleton included, could be seen on all fours in the lounge, picking up the spare parts which had been packed in a flimsy bandbox and swiftly reduced it to wastepaper. The Colonel kept on losing things. He lost an envelope containing his keys. He continually lost a battered attaché case, in which were large sums of money and all the papers of the expedition, and whose whereabouts was to be a perpetual source of panic throughout the journey. It was found forlorn and neglected on the cobbles of the quay, wide open in a tearing gale. The cars were hoisted on to the boat. The Grey took it well; but the Dowager regarded the process as a monstrous affront to her dignity, and creaked in impotent protest.

The sea was rough—very rough. They said it would be calmer half-way across. It was rougher half-way across. Frozen to immobility, like a man covered by a revolver, I let the waves break over me without retaliation, knowing that the slightest movement would be fatal; preferring, for some extraordinary reason, a soaking to the stigma of seasickness.

Brandy and a French luncheon restored us at Calais, and we were off by three o'clock across the cold plains of Picardy to Paris. No sooner had we started than the cantankerous Dowager began to go bump, bump, bump, on her lovely new off rear spring. The road seemed interminable, but we were in Paris by dinner-time, and our spirits rose. The traffic went to Manfred's head. He threaded his way in and out and over the crossings with spectacular deftness and speed, like an expert needlewoman. Motoring in Paris is a game without any rules, where each man is for himself, out to get through as best he can and at all costs before his neighbour. Neither resents the other barging in: it is all part of the fun. Two cars race from different angles for a crossing, like players for a ball. They meet with a screech of brakes. One proceeds in triumphant possession, the other retires; and the spectacle is as quick and expert and ballet-like as a game of Association football.

High-handedly (for the car, after all, was hers) we dropped Mrs. Christmas and Quinney in the Place de la Concorde and drove to Montparnasse. We dined with a Communist friend, off hors d'œuvres, larks, and vin rosé; dropped him a hundred yards down the street from a café where he had a rendezvous (lest his political associates should see him emerging from a Rolls-Royce); picked up Mrs. Christmas and Quinney, and were in Fontainebleau before midnight.

An aged hall-porter with a hook for an arm informed us that a party of four had arrived by car an hour earlier, and had gone to bed; so they were before us. We arranged about rooms. Madame would share a room with her husband, who was "déjà arrivé". He was on the point of showing her to the room, when we discovered that the whole party déjà arrivé was French. I went out to a café for some beer, and returned to find that the others had arrived. There was amiable confusion in the lounge. Mrs. Mock was protesting against an eight o'clock start next morning.

"I call it slave-driving."

"And what about the slaves that drive?" murmured Waters.

Miss Gumbleton was frozen stiff with neuralgia, and had been unable to leave the car for dinner, but remained good-humoured. Everybody wanted to be called at a different hour and to have something different for breakfast. The ancient understood none of this, so I made a laborious list of the various times and menus, and next morning we were all called at six with a cup of tea and an apple.

We ripped our way through France in insensitive style.

We gobbled towns and villages, but spat them out again on the road undigested, unmasticated. In the sedate days of travel a place was a place. With the arrival of motor-cars it became little more than a name. With their increased speed it is not even that, but at the most "the place we got petrol" or "that café where we stopped for a glass of beer". Places preeminently real to themselves have no more identity in the mind of the modern traveller than the people he jostles in the Tube, though for one short moment, as a scolding horn or a cloud of dust, he has entered into their daily lives. Speed is reducing, not increasing, the fortuitous contact of country places with the outside world.

We saw France impersonally and in the aggregate: as a countryside emptier and more antiquated than that of England. Motor-cars were relatively rare; the old-fashioned gig was common; bicycles abounded, and girls rode pillion on the handlebars—certainly a more appropriate position than the rear for a display of affection. There were no straggling country suburbs; towns began and ended with abruptness: syntheses of cobbled streets, wide market-places fringed with planes, old archways, children galore, tattered plaster, charcuteries, men drinking on narrow pavements, haberdashers' shops with unreal, flat-pressed shirts in lighted windows. Giant drums predominated among the traffic, filled not with petrol, but with wine: gallons and gallons of liquid for the Frenchman's pleasure; and everywhere, on hoardings, the message that "A meal without wine is like a day without sunshine".

It was a country of trees—but trees that looked as though someone had planted them, while English trees might have grown haphazard on their own. Autumn had begun, and the planes and poplars were turning to gorgeous burnished tints. Avenues of them made tunnels for the roads: sometimes a Gothic vault of shimmering leaves, sometimes a Roman arch, sometimes an Egyptian, and sometimes, where poplars sloped back from the road, an odd inverted arc. Sometimes one side of the tunnel was turned to autumn gold while the other stayed green. Sometimes all was gold but for a cluster of deep green around the capitals of the arch. Sitting in the back of the Dowager, with only an oblique and decapitated view of the countryside, I longed for Mr. Waters' penknife to slit a window in her blank Belgravian hood, and thought of a new form of hell: to be driven through an Elysian landscape in a prison van.

We reached Valence in the evening. The Grey, we had calculated, must be half an hour behind us; for the Dowager, despite her staid appearance, was easily the faster of the two. But at the hotel bad news awaited us. A monsieur, they told us, had telephoned from Lyon. He had had a "petit accident avec sa voiture", and would we call him up the moment we arrived? We waited with deep foreboding for our call to get through. I asked for Christmas. His voice was agitated. "I say, Balfour," he said, "a lorry loomed up from nowhere. Nobody hurt, but I'm afraid the car's pretty badly smashed. I hadn't time to do anything. It just appeared from nowhere. We were going very slowly up the main street, when suddenly ⸺" Mrs. Christmas seized the receiver from my hand. I left her to it and went to break the news to Manfred and Miss Gumbleton.

Mrs. Christmas was in despair. We must return to Lyon at once. We stipulated for dinner first, since Manfred had driven three hundred miles with hardly a stop. It was a gloomy meal in a small room upstairs. A wedding feast was proceeding in the dining-room proper, and little girls in clean white muslin frocks swarmed noisily everywhere, with a preference for the gentlemen's cloakroom. The feast had left our menu much depleted. Manfred, Miss Gumbleton and I were in forced good spirits, embarrassed by Mrs. Christmas's embarrassment at the débâcle, and reiterating with little conviction that it would "probably be all right in the end". But Mrs. Christmas was inconsolable.

"We've been right out of luck from the start. Everything's just died on us from the word 'go'. God knows what I'm to do: I've left my house, and I've got nowhere to go till the kids come back from school. There'll be an awful stink if my husband's late back from his leave, and he'll never get a passage now. We've let you all down good and proper, and I can't say I feel too good about it. Bad luck has dogged us: that's all there is to it."

"Never mind, my dear," said Manfred, "at least it's not been unfunny."

"Well, it's joke over as far as I'm concerned." And Mrs. Christmas, sickened at the sight of our food, went off to telephone again to her husband.

Miss Gumbleton saw the solution quite clearly. "One car will continue the trip, and the ladies will be asked to stand down. Mrs. Mock will probably be quite relieved. I shall hate it, but there it is. You'll have a man's four."

"Garsong," shouted Manfred, "oon autre bootay doo vang, if I've got to drive back over that bloody road again tonight."

On which we did the sixty miles in just over an hour. Miss Gumbleton grew almost lyrical with excitement as we tore through the breakneck leafy tunnels. "You, the road, and the car," she said to Manfred, "seem all to be one."

"That's the wine, my dear," said Manfred.

"I wouldn't mind dying, driving with you like this."

But Mrs. Christmas, in the back, felt and said otherwise. Misfortune had not yet conquered in her the desire to live.

It was one o'clock when we reached Lyon, and the others had all gone to bed in the hotel by the station. We followed their example, in rooms which gave direct on to platform two.

It was sad if the trip were at an end. We would look foolish returning from India by train a week after our triumphal departure. But at least we had discovered Dover.

It was a psychological accident, said Quinney. They had been lost in Lyon, crawling, stopping and turning amid that network of streets and bridges and watercourses. At last they had found the right road. Christmas breathed a sigh of relief and accelerated. At that moment the lorry appeared "from nowhere", or, rather, from a prominent street on the right. Mrs. Mock saw it coming and screamed; but too late. The heavy lorry struck the bonnet of the Grey broadside on, with a terrific impact. She bounced right across the road, missing trams by inches; there was a loud report as a tyre burst; she swerved back again and came to a standstill by the kerb. Christmas flung up his hands and said, "Well, that's the end of the expedition." A crowd collected even quicker than in Pall Mall. Quinney thought of Mrs. Mock, who had vanished from the car when it stopped. She was nowhere to be seen. He found her, deathly white, shaking, drooping, propped against a plane tree in the middle of the crowd, which disregarded her completely. He produced a flask of brandy.

"Drink this," he commanded.

"No, no, I never do that."

"You will now." And he poured it down her throat.

Meanwhile, in all that congestion of traffic, there was no sign of a gendarme. It is curious how gendarmes rarely materialize when they are needed, but always when they are not. It was twenty minutes before one appeared; but he was not interested. After all, we were English. No garage could be persuaded to remove the wreckage: it was a Saturday night. For the same reason the Lyon representative of the R.A.C. was nowhere to be found. The luggage was transhipped to a taxi. Mrs. Mock was put to bed. Christmas began to talk vaguely of wiring to London for another Rolls.

Several hours later someone was found to remove the car. It seemed, despite all appearances to the contrary, that she was not very badly damaged. The front axle was bent: otherwise her scars were surface wounds. She could be put right in a day or two. Meanwhile it was Saturday night, and nothing could be done before Monday. Christmas then employed all his powers of eloquence and persuasion to induce the mechanics to work over the week-end. He would pay them twice their normal charge. They were uninterested. He would pay them three times what they ought to get. They grew interested. For four times what they deserved they agreed to start work on the car next morning.

This was the situation when I appeared after breakfast. Vagueness reigned in the lounge. Members of the expedition were talking in low voices in pairs. Christmas was nowhere to be seen. Mr. Waters said he was too old for this sort of show; he had had enough of it all his career and had retired in search of a quiet life: he would proceed to Rome by train at his own expense.

Mrs. Mock (and small wonder) had been badly shattered by the accident. But that was not all. There were veiled references to the precarious state of her health. Mr. Waters, misogynist turned professional, had had a long talk with her the evening before, with regard to her symptoms, and felt very strongly that she should not undertake the strain of the trip any further. Mrs. Mock had not yet come down, and her emergence from the lift was awaited with some curiosity. Then Christmas arrived from the garage. The car, miraculous to relate, would be ready that evening. He proposed to engage a chauffeur, with whom he would drive through the night, in shifts, to Cannes, joining us there in the morning. Four of us could start off at once. Would Quinney care to wait and come with him? No, Quinney would travel to Cannes by train.

Meanwhile Mrs. Mock had appeared, unobserved except by Mr.—or, for once, Dr. ?—Waters, with whom she was now seen in earnest consultation over a table in the corner. Presently she rose and came towards us. "I've decided," she said wistfully to Christmas, "to go home." Waters looked satisfied. But the Colonel protested charmingly. Of course she must come with us. He knew it had been a bit of a rush and a strain hitherto, but that was only because we had a boat to catch. It would be very different when we got to Asia, and we were almost there.

Mrs. Mock was clearly in two minds, torn between the engaging smile of Colonel Christmas and the professional solemnity of Mr. Waters. We were tired of waiting. They must be left to fight out the Mock battle between them. We collected Mrs. Christmas and Miss Gumbleton and started for the third time along the Lyon-Valence highway.

It was curious to see in daylight this road which we only knew in the dark: like reading the right answer to a crossword puzzle which one has solved incorrectly. The leafy tunnels were sparser than they had seemed beneath the vault of darkness, the landscape was smaller and dustier, but the most startling revelation was the Rhone. It ran for many miles beside the road, where I had never guessed at any river at all.

At Montélimar we lunched off hors d'œuvres, brains, and thrushes, while before us, through an avenue of planes, the population took its Sunday walk: Zouaves in resplendent uniforms, rows of fuzzy women, thickly powdered and lipstuck, in absurdly high-heeled shoes. Chic as Frenchwomen's clothes may be, it would be idle to pretend that they are always appropriate to environment.

We travelled fast. The country changed its tones. Brick-red earth, magenta vines and a rose-coloured sky warmed us at evening. As his native Riviera approached, Manfred drove faster and faster, in an increasing intoxication of delight, oblivious of the Dowager's grinding bumps behind.

Cannes was empty. Manfred's friends said it was lousy, there was no one here at all. We were crazy, Manfred's friends said, not to stay in Cannes. Manfred's American friends saw the joke of our mad odyssey. In India, they said, it's two hundred in the shade and there's no shade, and what did we do when the Rolls broke down in the desert, strap it on a camel ? Manfred's French friends saw no joke at all. "Pourquoi ?" they said, with a mystified air. "N'est-ce pas qu'il y a des bateaux qui vont aux Indes ?"

Manfred and I dined with his friends and stayed in their hotel. Later we found Mrs. Christmas and Miss Gumbleton making whoopee rather gloomily together on stools in an empty bar. Still later, at one a.m., Quinney arrived after a hideous journey without a lunch or dining-car. Mrs. Christmas persuaded him to escort her to a night club. Mrs. Mock and Waters had come by the same train and were leaving together for Rome next day. Poor Mr. Waters ! The Colonel with his unprofessional ways had won.

The Colonel arrived with a chauffeur from Lyon at seven o'clock in the morning, having occupied thirteen hours over the journey. The chauffeur, apparently, proved incompetent to drive a motor-car, and Christmas had to drive all the way, stopping to sleep at intervals.

The immediate problem was to secure another chauffeur to accompany us to Brindisi. We all set to work, in the pouring rain, to find chauffeurs. The porter at our hotel thought he could find one. The man in the garage said he knew of one. Manfred's friends had a friend who was broke and would probably come for a consideration ; but he was not on the telephone and lived at La Bocca. Several chauffeurs were interviewed and said they would be pleased to come in a day or two, but in the meantime they had neither passports nor international driving licences. Besides, they must have time to say good-bye to their wives. Christmas reiterated pathetically that he *would* like to start at twelve, to get to Genoa that night. The rain became torrential. At twelve o'clock I returned in a small cloudburst from drawing a blank at La Bocca to find a chauffeur waiting in the lounge.

The hall-porter had found him. Yes, he knew all about Rolls-Royces and he had his licence and passport. He was ready to start at any moment. I had to keep him waiting while I telephoned to the garage to find out whether Christmas had in the meantime engaged their candidate. It took me ten minutes to get through. No, they had failed to find him. "All right," I said, "I'll engage this man." I returned to the lounge to find he had gone, in a fit of pique at being kept waiting. Quinney, arriving at that moment, said it didn't matter, he was just on to a chauffeur who was sure to be able to come. He turned out to be the same chauffeur, and his wife indicated that we could hardly expect him to drive a Rolls-Royce that was seven years old.

It was now one o'clock, and no chauffeur. The hall-porter in Mrs. Christmas's hotel said if only we had told him in the morning he could easily have found us a chauffeur; but now—he shrugged his shoulders. We lunched. Two o'clock, and no chauffeur. Christmas said he *would* have liked to start at twelve; now it was two o'clock, so we had better push on without a chauffeur.

But the Grey was locked in the garage of Mrs. Christmas's hotel, and the key could not be found. The man who had it had gone to his lunch. He would be back at four o'clock. We said really this was the last straw; whereupon the hall-porter completely lost his temper. He had been slaving for us all the morning, and now we complained about a little thing like the car being locked up for an hour or two. It was too much! Christmas went off to find the man at his lunch. We waited and waited in the lounge, surrounded by our luggage, and despaired of ever leaving Cannes at all. The porter continued to mutter with rage, but nobody heeded him. It was already Monday afternoon, and our boat left Brindisi on Thursday. Our chances of catching it receded with every moment we sat there.

Then Quinney appeared with the news that he had found a chauffeur through Cook's. He had told him to be ready in ten minutes. The chauffeur, unperturbed, had said could he make it a quarter of an hour, then he would have time to say good-bye to his wife. So Quinney made it a quarter of an hour. Christmas arrived with the garage key. The rain stopped. Things looked better. We started in the Dowager for San Remo. (Why or by whom San Remo, a comparatively close destination, had been substituted for Genoa was not explained.) Christmas, Mrs. Christmas and the chauffeur would follow later in the Grey, which now proved to have contracted some other ailment.

Monte Carlo's lights, in that short ten minutes which precede the dark, looked lovelier than I had ever seen them. We reached the frontier about six o'clock. Frontiers are apt to be drab, but this one is impressive. You suddenly meet it round a corner: a huge rock towering perpendicularly into the sky, then a bridge across an impassable gully into Italy. The French douaniers, shabby and shuffling, were a pleasant contrast to the Italians, with their martial demeanour, shining uniforms and tricorne hats. I had a sudden pang for France: it might be many months before I should experience again the exquisite sensation of speaking French.

We reached San Remo by six-thirty, but, as it was so early, decided to go on as far as Alassio, leaving a message for the others. Here we put up in the inevitable Italian pension filled with English ladies, and ate the inevitable and, in my opinion, eminently dislikeable Italian meal of spaghetti. Christmas rang up at eleven o'clock. He had left Cannes at six, but had only just reached San Remo. His batteries were run down and the lights would not work. So the Grey had made an ignominious entrance into Italy with an electric torch strapped on in front and a Japanese lantern swinging behind. When both these failed she proceeded in the dark.

Chapter IV

ITALY

IT was Tuesday morning. We had to reach Brindisi by Thursday, but the boat did not sail until the afternoon. That gave us two and a half days to cover the entire length of Italy. It could be done, provided we had no mishaps; but since mishaps had become part of our programme we were not too confident. In the circumstances it was less as cultured amateurs of the arts that we travelled through Italy, than as a business man in a hurry might travel through the English Midlands, blind to every consideration save that of reaching his destination by nightfall. Such romantic cities as Piacenza, Parma, Modena, Bologna were to us no more than muddy industrial towns like Preston, Wigan, Warrington, or Crewe. For, as if to deaden our aesthetic sensibilities still further, it rained in a deluge from the moment we left the Riviera.

It was curious to turn away from a silver, southern sea, breaking on warm sand in an environment of flowers and fruit trees, to green, rain-soaked country, where it was autumn again and where the fir trees gave a Norwegian air to the landscape. We were in the north once more. Every country has its north, which is less a question of latitude than of psychological atmosphere; so that even the north coast of Africa seems more northern than the south coast of France, and its inhabitants, swathed in the thickest of camel-hair, speak yearningly of the south, where it is warm. The points of the compass are but relative, and there is perhaps no land, however southern, but has this impulse towards the south. The Plain of Lombardy might have been the Great North Road around Darlington, and its cities to us were but a sordid conglomeration of shops and trams. Our main impression of Northern Italy was of the excellence of its roads, the dirtiness of its towns, and the noisiness of its hotels.

We lunched at Piacenza, where a delay was caused by the Colonel getting money from the bank. This used to happen almost every day, for Colonel Christmas, not without reason, was so afraid of mislaying his money that he would never cash more than five pounds at a time. At Piacenza we discovered that both Mrs. Mock's and Miss Gumbleton's bedding had been left behind. No one, except indeed Miss Gumbleton, appeared to take the disaster very seriously. Even she, after a moment of panic, bore the loss of her bedding-roll with philosophical reserve, and made an arch joke about sharing Mr. Quinney's. The bedding-rolls, presumably, were at Lyon or at Cannes; but since there could be no question of retrieving them in time, we could only bear Mrs. Mock's loss with cheerful resignation. Poor Mrs. Mock! The news was hardly likely to brighten her view of the immediate future. But I think we had all decided that we had seen the last of Mrs. Mock; that Mr. Waters, with three clear days to work in, would find little difficulty in getting her aboard the Paris express in a state of frenzied hypochondria.

Towards eight o'clock we reached Rimini, our night's destination. The Grey was a good way behind us. When we had passed her Christmas was crouching on the running-board in the rain, pumping feverishly at a recalcitrant pressure pump, while the chauffeur drove.

Miss Gumbleton this evening was in skittish mood. "Any room for little Muriel?" she enquired, and somebody hastened to find her a chair. During dinner she flapped her napkin playfully at the party and said, "Whoops! I've got another jumper to surprise you with to-morrow, boys." Then she told us how, while Christmas was getting petrol in Modena, a large Italian had circled round and round her in the piazza, smacking his lips.

Just before we retired to bed it occurred to someone to wire to Waters. He was expecting us in Rome that night, and now here we were, blazing down the opposite side of Italy with never a thought of Rome—or indeed of Waters.

Next morning Christmas left at half past six with Quinney in the Grey. We started about nine. At first there was a fog, but it lifted soon to disclose the Adriatic Sea and a rich, earthy country with low hills and olive groves stretching down to the beach. Ancona looked effective from a distance, with its citadel jutting out to sea, but at close quarters it was no more than a clanging industrial town. Entering Pescara we ran over a chianti-bottle and had our first puncture. A garageful of zip-fastened child mechanics, big, little and middle-sized, changed the wheel for us with alacrity. They diagnosed a slow puncture in another wheel too, and changed that. Uncovering the "brand new" spare tyres of which the Dowager's salesman had boasted, the children pointed out that they were both worn down to the canvas. It was a gloomy discovery, for there would be worse than chianti-bottles in the desert.

"I do call that a bit over the odds," said Mrs. Christmas. "You'd never think of looking at the tyres in a shop like that, would you?"

"Yes," said Manfred.

We drank golden wine for luncheon. Afterwards the hills grew steeper and our progress was tortuous and slow. At a village of indescribable filth called Termoli, where, equally, Mussolini was zipping 'em young, another slow puncture was mended by another regiment of small boys. A well-dressed individual flourished papers at us in menacing fashion and complained that we had almost swept him off the kerb. But the children assured us that he was a notorious imbecile. The roads grew better, and we caught up with the Grey at Foggia for dinner. We were now only eighty miles from Brindisi, and so refreshed by the nearness of our goal that we decided to drive on after dinner, making a half-way rendezvous at Bari.

But the moment we started we regretted our foolhardiness. The roads were so skiddy that, even on the straight, Manfred could not control the Dowager at all. She skated from side to side in the tipsiest manner, for once enjoying herself thoroughly and laughing at our discomfiture. Finally, in the main street of an exceptionally narrow village, she waltzed right round and faced the other way, as if to say: "There now, what do you think of *that* for an old girl?" It was enough for us. We crawled to Bari, where we spent the night, as usual, in an hotel which gave on a railway junction. My bedroom, this time, was right on the main line, where goods trains shunted all night, expresses roared through, and porters took pleasure in urging on the trains with cries even louder than their sirens. It was not a peaceful night.

In the morning there was no sign of Christmas and Quinney, and for the first time Manfred and I began to grow anxious. We had agreed to meet at this hotel in Bari. The hotel

Above: Dover   *Below:* Calais

Ostuni: Village in Apulia

on which, alternatively, we had fixed as a rendezvous in Brindisi proved not to exist; we telephoned to several others but failed to trace the Colonel. It was very possible that they had met with an accident on those skiddy roads : for the Grey was no steadier on her pins than the Dowager. They might be dead or dying; they might have run over somebody and be in gaol, unable to communicate with us. An eleventh-hour disaster was quite in the tradition of our journey. Had the last straw broken the camel's back ?

The Apulian landscape, however, was remarkable enough to make us forget our anxiety. Rain-clouds were still in the sky, but the sun shone vividly in a space of blue. A wide plain, dense with olive groves, lay between the mountains and the sea. The country was thickly populated, and the houses were whitewashed cubes which gleamed in the sunshine. Corbusier might have built them. Each, moreover, had a pair of curious white ovens, conical in shape, like solid stone tents, which enhanced the modern effect. Villages were perched on rocks : Ostuni was a pile of white solids against the indigo sky. Innumerable church towers of unwhitened sandstone stood out in ranks above each village like the spires of Oxford in miniature. Sometimes houses were washed pink : a pink which, in the deluge of the past two days, had looked flat and dead like sweets in a shop window, but came to life now with the sun and was light itself. The bullock- and mule-carts were painted with coloured peasant designs and jingled with silver harness. The Adriatic was a miraculous blue. Apulia is a county to dream of.

To our intense relief, the first object we saw in Brindisi was the Grey, and behind her Christmas, Quinney, Mr. Waters *and* Mrs. Mock at lunch on the pavement of a café. Christmas and Quinney had apparently forgotten our rendezvous in Bari and come straight on last night. They had combed all the hotels for us on arrival, to the diversion of the chauffeur who, at Christmas's umpteenth enquiry for the signora Inglese, would exclaim in undertones to Quinney, "Mais c'est une maison de rendezvous, quoi !"

Mrs. Mock looked flourishing and pronounced herself ready again for the fray. The loss of her bedding had not yet been broken to her. But after luncheon the rumpus started.

"Where's my bedding ?" rapped out Mrs. Mock, examining the Dowager with suspicion.

"Lost your bedding ?" said Mrs. Christmas. "Didn't you have it with you ? You must have left it at Lyon."

I thought that the time had come to do my shopping.

The *Martha Washington*, due at three o'clock, arrived at four. It was not without a certain sense of achievement that we saw her steaming into the harbour past the huge, impressive slice of brick which is Italy's naval memorial. She had loomed so large in our calculations of the last eight days that, like a word which is repeated so often as to become meaningless, she had assumed an almost mythical significance. Now here she was, as large as life and overflowing with German-Jewish refugees on their way to the Promised Land. Luck was with us ; we had performed the impossible ; we had caught the boat.

There was a good deal of difficulty about hoisting the cars on board. The contraption produced for the purpose was nothing more than a large string bag. It looked as though, with luck, it might bear the weight of a catch of codfish. Manfred and the captain had a heated altercation, Manfred insisting on boards and chains, the captain refusing to take responsibility except for the fish-net. With misgivings we gave in to the captain. It was a sickening moment when the huge grey Rolls rose in ungainly fashion into the air, swaying precariously, straining at the frayed rope. It seemed certain that she would fall, but all was well. The Dowager followed with hardly a protest ; she had little pride left.

We sailed for Asia at seven.

Chapter V

AT SEA

MR. WATERS is the sort of person who is very much at home on boats. He knows all the wiles. He lost no time in becoming intimate with the purser and was to be seen when we boarded the *Martha Washington* sitting side by side with him in his office, poring over a plan. Long before we sailed Mr. Waters had the cabin he wanted and everything fixed to his satisfaction. "Everything" was primarily that he should have a table to himself, apart from the rest of the party.

Mr. Waters, on boats, has a special technique, of which the motive principle is a rooted horror of conversation. When he is alone on boats the sort of thing that happens is this:

A lady approaches him as he paces the starboard deck.

"Looks like a change of weather," she says hopefully.

"What's that?" says Mr. Waters.

"*Looks like a change of weather.*"

"I beg your pardon. I didn't hear you. I'm rather deaf."

"LOOKS LIKE A CHANGE OF WEATHER."

"Yes," says Mr. Waters, "very crowded, isn't it?" and moves on.

On the port deck a lady approaches Mr. Waters.

"Looks like a change of weather," she says brightly.

"I beg your pardon. . . ."

That evening passengers are saying, "See that fellow who's always walking about alone? Stone deaf, you know. Awful affliction. Can't think why he doesn't use a trumpet."

And Mr. Waters is left in peace for the rest of the voyage.

"All my life as a doctor," he explained to me, "I have been accustomed to a duologue in which either the other person did the talking and I listened, or I did the talking and they listened. Now I find it very hard to talk to more than one person at a time. I can never concentrate on general conversation. That is why I prefer to eat by myself."

The moment we sailed Miss Gumbleton announced that she was giving a cocktail party in the bar. We were all invited. It was a great occasion. Miss Gumbleton appeared in a black evening dress with a green bow on the shoulder, and acted the hostess to perfection. We all felt very underdressed.

Miss Gumbleton had the cabin next to Manfred's and mine, and asked if she might use our bathroom. To this we readily assented. Thereafter, by the hour, at all times of day, we could hear Miss Gumbleton washing—herself, of course, but principally her clothes, and soon our clothes as well. She had a passion for washing and mending, and used to go about begging people to give her socks to darn or trousers to patch, much as a greedy child will beg for sweets.

Miss Gumbleton ate with us in the second-class saloon (the others were in the first) and regaled us throughout the voyage with the girls' gossip of the rest of the expedition. She told us all about her cabin companion, a gaunt American lady who lent her a book called *Sane Sex Living*. On the fly-leaf was an inscription from a gentleman: "Bon voyage on Life's Long Journey!" Miss Gumbleton said the worst inscription she ever saw in a book was, "A book is still the best frigate, n'est-ce pas?" We grew fond of Miss Gumbleton. She introduced us to Tishy, her fur coat. We even started to call her Muriel, since it was the name which she applied so frequently to herself.

Colonel Christmas, after he had recovered some arrears of much-needed sleep, became preoccupied with the tyre crisis. It was essential that we find new tyres for the Dowager before attempting to cross the desert. The difficulty was that our tyres were an awkward, obsolete size, and would not be easy to obtain. The Colonel spent pounds on telegrams. He cabled to Cairo and I do not know where else for tyres to be sent to him at Haifa. But the chances that we should ever get them seemed remote. When not in the wireless-room he would be tinkering with the cars, which the rest of us had all too thankfully forgotten. On one occasion he got underneath the Dowager, to grease her belly, and fell sound asleep, waking two hours later.

As we settled down on board and had, for the first time,

leisure for reflection, two things appeared : the uncertainty of our plans and the diversity of our motives.

Christmas's original idea was to go by Jerusalem. But he was perpetually subject to outside advice, and every man he talked to on board (all, of course, experts) advised something different. The first day a man with a pink face, who knew all about the roads, would say we were mad to go by Jerusalem because the first hundred miles was strewn with boulders and often impassable. So Christmas would decide to go by Damascus. Then a man with a yellow face, who knew all about the roads, would say that if we went by Damascus we would have to pay vast sums for a convoy. And Christmas would switch back to Jerusalem. Damascus and Jerusalem were like rouge and noir at roulette : now one would turn up, now the other. Sometimes we had a run of Jerusalems, sometimes a run of Damasci ; we never could tell which was up at the moment. Nor could we be sure that Christmas would not next meet a man with a white face who knew all about the roads and would suggest steering a course between the two of them. Zero.

With regard to motive there were, broadly, two schools of thought : (1) that of the Christmases, who wanted to get to India as quickly as they could with no loitering by the wayside, she to catch her boat to England, he in order not to overstay his leave ; (2) that, principally, of Waters, Quinney, Manfred and myself, who were in no particular hurry to get to India, were tired of rushing, and desired, moreover, to see something of the countries we went through. As far as the women were concerned, Miss Gumbleton had seen Syria and Palestine before, but was substantially on our side ; Mrs. Mock's views were altogether uncertain. Mr. Waters, most mornings (and evenings too) would call a "conference" in the smoking-room, at which the famous maps would be produced, alternative routes, with a great deal of a, b, c, and d, proposed, and pros and cons stated in tabular form (all by Mr. Waters).

But Mr. Waters' conferences were never altogether a success. Colonel Christmas would yawn, or go off to send another telegram about tyres, or catch sight of a man with a black face who looked as though he might know about the roads. Miss Gumbleton would be too busy over her washing (or too diplomatic) to come ; Quinney and Mrs. Mock would be called away to make up a bridge four; and Mrs. Christmas, at any mention of Palmyra, Baalbek, Petra or other wonders of the world, would simply reiterate a formula of her own which she found most useful. "You know," she would say, "we're not a Cook's tour."

Then there would be secret plottings in twos in other parts of the ship, at which each of us would repeat his views over and over again to the other. But we got no further. In the end I was inclined to sit back and take little part in the confabulations, for it is my experience that, in travelling, things are usually dictated by circumstance at the last moment, and that detailed plans made too far ahead are always liable to disruption and its consequent disappointment. I would wander off, instead, and watch the Jews.

The Jewish exodus provided a spectacle as fascinating as a zoo. Six hundred of them spawned in the third class and in the bowels of the ship: a swarm of sensuous, babbling humanity, a cauldron of life in the raw. They were awkward, large-limbed people: bulging females, shapeless males, stocky boys in bright jumpers, plus-fours or, pathetically, the Bavarian shorts of their adopted but now abandoned land. Small children, wrapped in rugs, lay as if dead wherever their mothers could find an inch to put them. Overcrowded as they were, the Jews seemed impervious to discomfort. They lay in heaps, clasped often in each other's arms. Contact was all they asked. One couple lay for days on end in the same spot, never stirring. Dressed alike in rough white linen—he in shorts, she in a tight, short skirt—they were a moving pair, curled side by side; foreshortened obliquely from above, they looked like figures in some modern picture.

I do not think these Jews were unhappy. They seemed to accept their lot with resignation, and their rude animalism was proof against highly sensitized emotion. They chattered incessantly. They sang in harmony and played musical instruments. In the evenings they danced: compressed humanity, jigging en masse to the ship's band, and the scene took me back to the Nachtlokaals of the Alexanderplatz. I grew to like the Jews. They had courage; and at least they were alive.

It was hard to believe that these creatures of the towns could ever change their urban habits for rural peasant life. Looking at them, I could not imagine a people less fitted for tilling the soil. But in fact they adapt themselves to it with amazing quickness, and show a real grip of the intricacies of afforestation and agriculture. Palestine is a booming country, whose enthusiasm and optimism are probably unequalled in the world to-day. These Jews, perhaps for the first time in their lives, had a future.

The women are as keen to work as the men. Recently a party of twenty-five Jewish women tried to get into Palestine from the Syrian frontier. They were refused admission ; their immigration papers were not in order. The news of their plight reached Tel Aviv. Instantly twenty-five Jewish bachelors rushed to the frontier, married the twenty-five Jewesses, and bore them in triumph into the Promised Land.

But it is odd, I thought, as I trod their decks, that though the Jews have wandered the earth for so many centuries, they should still be such very bad sailors.

Not that it worries them. I watched a Jewish boy being sick. He and his friends roared with laughter. He rushed to a tap to rinse out his mouth with water, found it was salt water, was sick again, and laughed till he nearly burst.

On Saturday the Jews had a good two hours' session of oratory on deck. Bearded rabbis harangued them on the joys of the Promised Land and painted the future in glowing colours. At the end there was a heated argument which almost developed into a riot. The trouble had started at luncheon, when a lot of the young Jews refused to go to the Kosher table, and the old ones took them to task. Youth argued that it must be nourished to build the New Jerusalem ; age held fast to the old forms of religious observance. The Jewishness of the young was racial, not religious, strangely like that very nationalism which had driven them from Germany.

That night, the eve of our arrival at Cyprus, there was a film. It was billed on the ship's notice-board as *The Desidered Woman*—a useful portmantologism of "desired", "deserted", and "dithering". It was an inane story of a bogus English earl, who looked like a butler in an eyeglass, paying blackmail money to the man who knew the real earl's identity. The desidered woman, who apparently had a corner in the title, married first the bogus earl and then, when he was bumped off, the real earl ; so she did not do too badly. (*Twice a Countess*, would have been a more appropriate name.) There was something peculiarly absurd about this American film of English high-life, rivalling the Mediterranean moon in an Italian ship for the entertainment of six hundred Jews from the ghettos of Berlin and Cracow. What, I wondered, could this polyglot crowd make of so nonsensical a farrago of hunt-ball programmes and parsons' collars and palms in the baronial hall and "I love you for yourself, not your title"?

But from the laborious unlocking of prone and supine forms, when the lights went up, I understood the measure of their reaction.

Chapter VI

CYPRUS

CYPRUS is a fraud.
I had imagined a fertile Mediterranean island, luxurious with eucalyptus and orange trees, gay with mimosa and bougainvillea, where one would laze in olive gardens and bathe in an aquamarine sea. I found a desert: a great biege island of barren rock and sand and gravel, like a chunk of the Sahara slapped down in the middle of the sea.

But Cyprus was not always like this. Nor, perhaps, will it be in the future. Alexander the Great built his fleet there, from the forests which were the pride of the Levant. From Cyprus, it is believed, came timber for the Roman galleys. From the days of the Phoenicians down to the Crusades, when Richard Cœur de Lion handed the island over to Guy de Lusignan, titular King of Jerusalem, Cyprus was (if decreasingly) rich and prosperous and fertile. Then in the sixteenth century the Turks came along, and the Turks have the same effect on a country as rickets on a healthy child. From the moment of the Ottoman conquest Cyprus went to pieces. Her land decayed, her forests became deserts, her fields fell out of cultivation. In three hundred years she had reached the lowest known stage of culture in any community: goats.

To-day, when the British Raj is striving to put Cyprus back on the agricultural map, the goats are a primary problem. They graze everywhere and eat everything that is planted. The goatherds brandish knobkerries, to intimidate the agricultural community, and the goats graze on. But knobkerries (together with knives above six inches long and other little lethal weapons) are now prohibited by law, and the British Raj is shutting up the goats. So Cyprus some day may again be the fertile paradise of which I had dreamed.

Her potentialities are immense. Almost anything can be

grown in her sandy soil, which lacks that proportion of silica fatal to cultivation. You can plant walnut trees, as the Persians do, and within a year they are nine foot high and bearing fruit. Cyprus can produce seventy-one varieties of fruits and nuts, and even the prejudiced Jaffa expert credits the Cyprian orange with a quality surpassing all the oranges of the world. So there is hope.

Meanwhile Larnaca, where we landed, looked like any parched colonial station on the Red Sea. We hired a car, with a jolly Greek chauffeur called Georg Nikolas. He said his name was George Nicholson, and proudly flourished a British passport. Few things are more incongruous than the British Raj in the Mediterranean. In darkest Africa Sandhurst gentlemen twiddling their moustaches, English signposts, tarmac roads and a left-hand rule of the road have come to be taken for granted. But on a Levantine island, populated by Europeans, they strike a note as fatuous as if the Isle of Wight were to be annexed by the Turks. It was Sunday, so the shops were shut : a British Sunday beneath Mediterranean skies.

We drove to Famagusta. On a barren bit of desert were the inevitable British goal-posts, and a polyglot collection of Greeks and Turks were taking part in a sports rally. In the blazing heat we watched a tug-o'-war, whose participants never stopped talking throughout, while a dense crowd of onlookers joined in the talking—and the tugging too.

From the roof of the Crusaders' Castle, its gateway decorated with the Venetian lion, we surveyed Famagusta, which once upon a time was Salamis. Bounded by desert, it has the look of an oasis without any palms. Its dwellings are mean and built of mud like the dwellings of Arabs. But from among them rises a Gothic cathedral : the presence of the British Raj is not the only incongruous feature of the place. The cathedral of St. Nicholas was built by the Lusignans in the fifteenth century, but is now adapted from its original Christian usage to be a Moslem mosque. Imagine the interior of, say, Salisbury Cathedral, swept, whitewashed and garnished, denuded of its monuments and tombs, Arabic inscriptions on its columns, windows blocked but for occasional openwork stone tracery where stained glass was, and, in place of empty chairs by the hundred, Turkish prayer mats stretched on the ground. The effect is pleasing, because of its emptiness and simplicity.

In the cathedral square men puffed at their hubble-bubbles in a café, while laden camels passed to and fro. Beyond, through an archway, was the market place, decorated with Venetian cannon-balls in pyramidal heaps, where prisoners, who otherwise wandered about quite freely, were submitting, in the highest spirits, to their weekly shave. Famagusta has the straggling charm of inconsequence.

Returning to Larnaca, we found a rare to-do. There was "trouble in Palestine". Arabs were besieging the police in Haifa and in Jaffa, and there had been a good many casualties. Since most of the trouble had been caused by the landing at Jaffa of the previous Lloyd-Triestino boatload of German refugees, our captain had orders to remain in Larnaca pending further bulletins. The Jews, who had heard a rumour that something was amiss, swarmed round us when we got on board, anxiously demanding news. But we knew as little as they.

After dinner they were assembled on the third-class deck, and addressed first in German and then in Yiddish. They were told that there had been trouble, but that the British authorities had the situation well in hand, that the British fleet was on the spot, and that they would all be allowed to land within a few days. The second speech was so impassioned that a cascade of saliva descended from the lips of the rabbi orator on to the heads of the people below.

They greeted the news with tremendous enthusiasm. They clapped and they cheered. They all began to sing, and presently the Polish community, arms tightly clasped about each other, whirled round and round in a great circle, dancing and chanting frenziedly to a rhythmical music like the Russian. It was a gala night in the ghetto. Hour after hour I watched the scene, strangely moved and fascinated. A British officer, returning to Palestine from leave, joined me. "That's what infuriates the Arabs," he said, "all this bloody row that doesn't mean a thing. It's a pity we haven't got a bomb to throw down on the vermin."

Next morning there was the usual mass of conflicting and misinformed rumour about our movements. We were sailing that morning for Port Said, that afternoon for Beyrouth, that evening for Haifa. The sane-sex-living woman in Miss Gumbleton's cabin knew for a fact that we were sailing at twelve—but was hazy about our destination. The man in somebody else's cabin knew, also for a fact, that we should be here at least a week. There was even a depressing report that we were returning to Brindisi. Not until we got ashore did we find an official notice to the effect that the boat would not leave before four p.m. So we hired George Nicholson again and set out for Nicosia.

The road was lined with attempted avenues; every few yards was a lonely palisade designed to surround a tree which had died at birth. We passed a leper colony and a lunatic asylum. Nicosia had a good many pretentious villas, but the cathedral close was pleasant, and the cathedral itself was incongruously surmounted by a minaret. We tried to do some shopping, but the shops were interested only in selling football boots. Even bathing-costumes were non-existent, and we had to make shift with ladies' pale-blue cotton drawers at a shilling the pair. We proceeded to Kyrenia, which is the great bathing resort of the island. Here we were promised luxuriant vegetation, and certainly, as we corkscrewed over a pass with a view of the northern coast, a bush or two was to be seen. We bathed in a warm sea from an agreeable, dusty, dead-alive village, and lunched at an establishment which boasted the incongruous name of the Seaview Hotel. It must certainly be the only Seaview Hotel in the world with a view also of the mountains of Asia Minor; but the mountains to-day were obscured by mist. We lunched, in the company of some retired English ladies, off roast beef and Yorkshire pudding, a dish called stewed kidneys with Spanish sauce (which, in the best English kidney tradition, was composed mainly of steak), blancmange, cheese (wrapped up in silver paper), and biscuits.

We returned to Larnaca to find that the boat was timed to sail at five for Beyrouth, so we drank some Turkish coffee on the quayside while Manfred played Greek backgammon with a Cypriote shopkeeper. The news from Haifa was worse. The railway station was hemmed in by barbed wire entanglements. Three British police officers had been seriously wounded. The police station was in a state of siege, with armed soldiers on the roofs. Arabs were holding up motor-cars and setting them on fire. This, of course, solved the question of our route. We could now only go by Damascus. What would happen to the Jews no one seemed to know. They could not, of course, be landed in Syria. It was suggested that they would either remain on board until the trouble had died or be disembarked at Jaffa under cover of night.

A charming and distinguished Iraqi, with whom we had made friends on board, came sadly ashore with his luggage. For political reasons, he was not allowed into Syria, and would have to wait a week in Cyprus for another boat to Palestine. Such a prospect, to us, seemed appalling, but we tempered our condolences with the trite reflection that "time means nothing to Orientals".

It was announced authoritatively that we would sail at six.

We sailed at ten.

Chapter VII

SYRIA

EARLY in the morning Manfred called me to the cabin window to take my first view of Asia. Plane upon plane, the compact silhouette of Beyrouth glowed through that pinkish haze which, in hot countires, is the legacy of the dawn. In the foreground, painted on the mist in tarnished silver, was a pair of sailing-boats, motionless and artificial. Soon the air began to clear, and as it cleared such beauty as Beyrouth possessed evaporated also. At nine o'clock the cruel sun exposed her ugliness as that of a middle-aged woman when the soft lights of her boudoir give place to the harshness of a two-hundred-candle-power glare. Beyrouth became a jangling, hideous port, without a trace of Eastern glamour. Importunate Syrian boatmen swarmed on board. Launches proclaimed on their canopies the comforts of the Beyrouth Palace and the Grand Hotel at Baalbek.

It is distressing that you should almost invariably have to enter a new Continent by one of its ports. For even where a port has charm it is a bastard, synthetic product, bearing little relationshp to the character of its country. For the sake of first impressions there is everything to be said for the aeroplane, which skips a country's ante-rooms to land you right in the centre of its stage. Approached by air, Asia would burst upon you in its integrity, instead of dawning gradually through the litter of discarded disillusion.

Confusion reigned on board. Asiatics in Homburg hats besieged the Colonel with exorbitant offers of advice and assistance. One of them struck lucky by happening to mention that he had plenty of tyres, at which Christmas at once took interest. He followed it up with the information that we might not proceed from Damascus to Baghdad without a convoy. For the small sum of ten pounds he would provide the requisite convoy and clear our cars through the Customs here—a proceeding which would otherwise cost us considerable money and time. The Colonel was not to be had by this, and the price at once dropped, suspiciously, to two pounds. This decided it. We would wait until we reached Damascus before bespeaking a convoy—if, indeed, a convoy was necessary at all—and, as we gathered from other sources, we could easily clear our cars through the Customs ourselves.

The French immigration officer asked my profession.

"Journaliste," I said.

"Correspondant ?"

"Non. Plutôt écrivain."

"Ah, homme de lettres."

The French Republic has a gratifying partiality for sonorous designations, which, unhappily, the United Kingdom of Great Britain and Northern Ireland no longer shares.

When the Colonel's turn came he was grandly, if inaccurately, described as *"Gouverneur de la ville de Peshawar aux Indes"*.

Released, we proceeded to the town, which was hot and ugly. The bazaars sold principally zip pullovers, smart felt hats, umbrellas, cheap perfumery, spats and patent leather shoes. We spent an hour assisting Mrs. Mock to send a telegram, and returned to the ship for luncheon.

They did not disembark the cars until the afternoon, rudely interrupting a number of Jewish couples who had found, in, on and under them, an admirable refuge throughout the voyage. The Dowager and the Grey were put into string bags once more and lowered into a barge. In driving off the barge on to the quay they had to leap a two-foot parapet, a manœuvre which drove Manfred almost demented.

Our luggage entirely filled the Customs shed, where we were assured that the official would deal with it in five minutes. But a Syrian minute is equal to ten European minutes. When finally the stuff was cleared we found that we had been annexed by a young man, who had sprung up from nowhere as people do in Customs sheds, and now took possession of our luggage. He assured us that he would charge us nothing, told us that he was called Nagib Traboulsi, asked us to call him by his Christian name, and gave us Turkish coffee to revive us. For two hours the party sat huddled in Nagib's office, which appeared to be that of a minor tourist agency, while the Customs made endless palaver about clearing the cars. By the time all this was over it was too late to think of starting for Damascus, so we decided to spend the night in Beyrouth and improve the shining hour by looking for tyres. Nagib conducted us to the hotel where he lived himself. The tyres proved difficult to find. The individual on the boat who said that he had some was lying. The Michelin garage had none to fit us, but said that in two days they could make us new wheel-rims to take tyres of a different size. But this seemed altogether too fantastic a proposition.

We dined on the terrace of a vast and empty restaurant overlooking the sea, and later Manfred and I fell in with Nagib's suggestion that he show us the night-life of the town.

Though from experience I know very well that night-life is a fiction, an egregious, boring fraud whose glamour exists only in the imagination of the more lubricious French weeklies, for some unaccountable reason its rumours still deceive me. When someone tells me that the night-life of such and such a place is the best in the world I believe them; I go there; I find it altogether dreary; but I do not learn my lesson. I had somehow expected much of Beyrouth's night-life, chiefly because it was my first taste of Asia and I visualized Asia in terms of Arabian Nights, as a haunt of seductive houris, dope-orgies and weird, intoxicating music. Beyrouth would have all this, grafted on to the more prosaic debaucheries of a big port.

But Beyrouth proved no exception to my rule. We visited one or two cafés and saw an occasional French sailor drink beer with a Jewish harlot to the tinkle of a mechanical piano. We passed down deserted streets where women of unnatural proportions and unhealthy complexions peered through bars. We entered a house and joked for half an hour with two huge Damascene strumpets in an over-furnished room reminiscent of a German pension—save that the enormous coloured photograph of the maîtresse de maison depicted her clad only in a pink chemise. We went to a big café like Lyons' where a slightly smaller woman rotated a phlegmatic tummy for the benefit of a few French soldiers.

Such is the modern Arabian Night. I might have known it. Night-life, if indeed there is such a thing, could never flourish in a land so lethargic as the East. Vice and its trimmings belong exclusively to the West.

That night, beneath a mosquito net, I slept naked in a bath of perspiration and revelled in the feeling that we were in a hot country at last. At five a.m. a tram started outside one of my bedroom windows, a train started outside another, and a ship started outside the third. We were in a noisy country as well.

Cannoning sharply off a tram, we left Beyrouth in conspicuous style. Mr. Waters leapt nimbly from the back of the Grey to inspect the damage, but the Colonel decided there was none, and shot ahead, forgetting all about Mr. Waters. We could see his lean figure pursuing the car as if it were an omnibus, catching it up, taking a violent blow in the stomach from the open door, and disappearing inside. This was a familiar bit of pantomime. At the slightest suspicion of trouble Mr. Waters would climb helpfully out of the car, would be left behind, would have to run, until, despite his game leg, he became as proficient at boarding the Grey at speed as a guard boarding a moving train.

Colonel Christmas, who had a miraculous independence of sleep, had been up since five a.m. on the tyre hunt. As we were strapping the luggage on to the Grey he arrived beaming with triumph : he had found some tyres in a garage outside the town. Manfred (who had been up since nine) drove up in the Dowager.

"I got some tyres from the garage the cars were in," he said casually. "I had them put on the wheels."

The Colonel looked crestfallen. His efforts had been wasted. But he was not to be done out of his find, so we set off with enough spare tyres to take us to China.

The road into Asia from the Mediterranean seaboard at Beyrouth could hardly be more dramatic. In a series of long zigzags we climbed a sheer five thousand feet to the top of the Lebanon, where there are no cedars (any more than there are cypresses in Cyprus, Persian cats in Persia, or hanging gardens in Babylon), but, by way of compensation, a landscape of surpassing loveliness. Up and up the Dowager went, steaming and spluttering with the exertion.

The mountain around us was grey where it had weathered, russet brown where the plough had scraped the surface. Dark green pine-trees clung doggedly to its flank, and below the curved, terraced vineyards looked like the contour lines of flotsam and jetsam traced on a beach by varying tides. Beneath us, Beyrouth, as from an aeroplane climbing in spirals, dwindled in size until it was a miniature design on a carpet of ocean blue. At each fresh turn we would think we had shaken it off, but it would reappear persistent as the tail of a kite, like an unwinding bobbin of white wool to which the road still attached us. But with a last sharp jerk the painter snapped, Beyrouth had gone, the ridge ahead of us parted, and we looked with amazement upon a new world.

I had not believed that the contrast between Europe and Asia could be so vivid. Below us was the great plain of Rayak; and it *was* a plain : flat and wide like the plains in the geography books, a gigantic rectangle of brilliant patchwork spread at the feet of the mountains. It was its colour which proclaimed the Lebanon to be the scenery of another continent. In Europe we are accustomed to a landscape whose basic colour is green. It may dissolve into an infinite variety of greys and blues, but these are but permutations of the predominating green, without which a European countryside seems to us barren and ungrateful, and browns are but incidents in the general scheme. But the *motif* of the landscape before us was red. Green had no place there, and when it occurred looked neutral and irrelevant. The colour of Europe is in the things we grow in the soil. The colour of Asia is in the soil itself. As we wound down the mountainside the tumbling earth in the foreground was a rich ochre. Farther away it turned to rose-colour against pale grey rock. Villages were built of a whitish grey stone, and autumn vines flared yellow on the bright-pink soil in an intoxicating vividness of colour

We were soon in the plain, where the road branches to Baalbek. After an acrimonious discussion it had been decided to pay it a visit, so we stopped at a café to buy a picnic lunch. The others—the Christmases, Mr. Waters, and Mrs. Mock—decided to lunch on the spot and follow. We started up the plain. In a curious way the earth's hue seemed to change at regular intervals : so many yards of ochre, then an abrupt change of gear, when a certa'n limit of the eye's vision was reached, to red, and so on through an infinite variety of deep shades until, in the middle distance, a strip of whitish green was introduced like a sorbet into a rich meal. Stripes of brown, apricot, coral pink, brick red, purple, magenta, and dark wine succeeded one another until it looked as though a sunset had been spread upon the ground. On our left the grey Lebanon rock was striped like a skeleton with ribs of white whalebone. On our right the mountains of the Ante-Lebanon, with serrated vertebrae, sprawled skywards over one another like vast, huddled mammals. In between, the plain was slashed with colour.

Presently we came to the great Roman temple encircled by the mountains, towering above a grove of tall and gently waving poplars.

I should doubt if there were another place on earth where natural and man-made beauty coincide as at Baalbek. Too often beautiful scenery is barren of beautiful architecture, while the great creations of man languish in negligble surroundings. But in this one spot nature and man have simultaneously achieved the infinite.

Baalbek was the Greek Heliopolis, or City of the Sun, and, though the Roman temples are dedicated to Jupiter and. Bacchus, it still belongs, in spirit, to the sun. You walk through its entrance to sunlight. From the foot of a long staircase you see the great walls part—walls which, next to the Inca temples in Peru, have the biggest stones of any building in the world. Their monolith flanks are slashed with sunshine, their monolith roof is gone, so that they make a gateway open to the sky and to the six soaring columns of the temple of Jupiter beyond. Sand-coloured, washed by the sun, these look like pillars of sunlight solidified : sunlight harnessed and brought to earth in tangible form, captured from the solar system to stand as a lasting monument to man's love of warmth and light.

Such is the ruined Baalbek. But of course the temple was not always like this. As we sat by the Temple of Bacchus, eating our lunch, and an old man brought us, not what Bacchus would have recommended, but a pitcher of ice-cold water to drink, I reflected upon the psychology of ruins. I am not what you might describe as a "ruin-fan". The remains of a Gothic abbey leave me relatively cold ; but give me the undamaged whole and I will admire where admiration is due. Nothing moves me less than the battered relics of a medieval fortress ; but show me its bastions intact, and I am profoundly stirred. On the other hand it occurred to me, as I looked across at those five immaculate columns of the temple of Jupiter, that the classical (like so many of one's friends) is often improved by ruin. How was Baalbek when there were thirty-nine columns, not six, surmounted by pediment and roof, and hidden, moreoever, from this angle which we had chosen as the perfect view ? Perhaps it was sublime ; perhaps, in its mammoth conception, it was just one degree too much of a good thing. The German restorers of Baalbek, with a characteristic reluctance to leave things to the imagination, have reconstructed the place as it was, in the form of a model. The result, suggestive of municipal offices erected regardless of expense, gives a jar to the illusions.

Moreover, I have an uneasy feeling that the interior decoration of the Romans tended to vulgarity. The purplish pillars of polished Assouan granite, of which some remain, seemed to me ugly in colour and grain. The Early Christians, who were digesting the Gospel of their neighbour St. Paul at the time the Temple of Jupiter was built, must have seen it as some of us to-day see a monster luxury hotel or super-cinema : as a monument of ostentation and materialism, prompting a reaction to simplicity and purity of spirit.

In religious architecture the merit of the Gothic arch lies in its spiritual quality : it points to heaven. The classical gateway, on the other hand, completes a square and is brought back to earth. Thus the Temple of Jupiter may be finer now that its six proud pillars hold uninterrupted commune with the skies than when they and their thirty-three brethren were denied access to the heavens by a flattening roof. Where a classical building is but human, a classical ruin may be divine.

It was one of the tantalizing features of our journey that we were always in a hurry. I could have remained in Baalbek for days, exploring in detail the beauties of its architecture and carving. But we must be in Damascus before nightfall. As we drove back across the Plain of Rayak the sun was setting and a pale moon appeared above the rose and yellow and grey of the Lebanon. The road to Damascus did not take us high, but over a gentle, narrow pass. The soil was rich, russet brown on either side, and in the half-light might have been autumn bracken in a Scottish glen, with patches of purplelike heather. Nearing Damascus, we came into a grove of trees with the sound of rushing water at their feet, and a sudden rush of cold air struck us with an aromatic smell as of Corsican maquis. So we entered the oldest inhabited city in the world.

The rest of the party had not followed us to Baalbek. A subaltern on the boat had said that there was "nothing to see" there. (Whenever any of their chaps wanted a bit of fun they went to Beyrouth, which was a wizard spot.) Mindful of this oracular advice Mrs. Christmas decided after lunch that they proceed directly to Damascus.

I did not like Damascus. Manfred insisted that this was due to the condition of my liver. Be that as it may, Damascus seemed to me all trams. Its position, cradled among the hills, is fine; but it is a bastard city, born of an irregular union between East and West. The mosque with its frescoes is beautiful, but we were not permitted to see it; otherwise Damascus has been so often ravaged by fire that it has few old buildings left. The bazaars had more of the true Oriental flavour than those at Beyrouth, but I was still unable to dissociate the huge iron-girded vault of their central aisle from that of the railway station at Leeds. The Biblical river of Abana is a scum-ridden canal, blossoming into a series of noxious drains which trip you up at every turn. In the jangling modern Street Called Straight, where only professional letter-writers in their booths testify to an earlier civilization, an Arab in rags knelt upon the pavement and cried incessantly upon Allah. I was inclined to sympathize with his call. Manfred, still intent on converting me, took me up to the roof of an uncompleted luxury hotel to look upon the beauties of Damascus from a height; and here, indeed, we had an admirable view of the railway station on our right and a dump for derelict American motor-cars on our left, suffused by an exquisite pink sunset.

In my opinion, it was the chemist's shop which so disposed Manfred in favour of Damascus. Manfred has a peculiar peccadillo. "Oo," he will ask, the moment he arrives in any town, village, hamlet, encampment or conglomeration of wigwams, regardless of their nationality—"Oo ay la pharmasee?" for Manfred, who lives all his life in France, speaks the language with remarkable fluency in an accent of remarkable originality. Unless in the meantime I have succeeded in bribing the inhabitants to tell him that there is no pharmacie,* he will spend the greater part of the morning in the beatific contemplation

---

* N.B.—Pharmacie: French for pharmacy.

of lotions, salts, pills, tonics, herbs, soaps, brilliantines and every sort of medical gadget, emerging with a huge and fragile parcel. In Damascus Manfred spent no less than three-quarters of an hour in the pharmacie, which he declared to be a particularly good specimen of its breed. It was perhaps as I awaited him with angry impatience in the square, with its trams and its tawdry French cafés, that I formed my first evil impression of the city.

We all did some shopping in Damascus. We bought tunny-fish, chocolate, sausage and biscuits in case of starvation in the desert. Mrs. Mock sent some more telegrams and bought herself a topee. Mrs. Mock was in the best of health and good spirits and became more like her Indian self the further East we got. Hopefully, but without response, she tried out her Hindustani in each new country, talked about nullahs instead of wadis, shouted "Boy !" with a practised air, and remarked upon features of the country which were "so like India". Mrs. Christmas bought eiderdown quilts for Mrs. Mock and Miss Gumbleton, to replace their bedding. Beggars pestered us as we walked about the streets—tiny beggars of a few years old, in traditional rags : clever little beggars, with an ear for music, since in their plaintive whine they achieved just that cadence in just that key which was appealing and impudent and wistful without being too obsequious. One found oneself imitating it and then all was lost. Mrs. Christmas announced that she would scream if they touched her, and called them "dirty little ticks". And so, of course, they were.

We soon found that the desert journey was not as straight-forward as we had imagined. To begin with, the French authorities insisted that we attach ourselves to a convoy. Convoys leave for Baghdad on Tuesdays and Fridays. It would in fact be perfectly safe to do the journey without an escort on either of those days, because of the volume of traffic, but the authorities must safeguard themselves in the unlikely eventuality of some foolish driver straying from the track and necessitating an expensive search. Besides, there was the possibility of bandits. Though to-day this risk is negligible on the Damascus-Baghdad highway, news had come through that very day that a French carload had been held up on a neighbouring track between Palmyra and Homs, robbed and "dévalisé", of which the English translation, presumably, is "debaggaged". So, at some expense, we secured a convoy from Nagib's firm.

SYRIA

Then another difficulty arose. The five hundred miles from Damascus to Baghdad are covered in two days. But the convoys, as a rule, do not stop for more than an hour or two at the half-way house at Rutba Wells. They change drivers and proceed through the night, reaching Baghdad in the morning. Moreover they travel at a good speed throughout. It was obvious that, even if we succeeded in keeping up with our convoy, we could not continue through the night, as we had no spare drivers. Therefore we must hire a guide, with whom we could take our own time, and be independent of a convoy. This privilege cost us eight pounds.

We had timed to start at seven a.m., and did so an hour and a half later. The packing of the cars was an even more intricate affair than usual, since each had to carry ten large tins of petrol in addition to its normal load. This was to save buying petrol at an exorbitant price at Rutba. Our loading was a Heath Robinsonian affair, with singularly little method. Whenever one saw a vacant space one would seize a bit of luggage and attach it, haphazard, with a bit of string. Then it would be found that none of the Dowager's doors would open because they were blocked with luggage, and everything would have to come off the running-board. There were the usual miscellaneous articles—a nondescript tin of something, a basket of grapes—which, like an odd guest at a dinner-party, seemed to fit nowhere. One would try in vain, and then leave them, hoping that in the meantime someone else might notice and cope with them. But there they always were when next one looked, forlorn, unwanted, on the pavement. What with spades to dig us out of bunkers in the desert (whose heads came off at the first jolt), odd bits of rubber which might come in useful, objects at whose identity it was impossible to guess, objects (of equally questionable identity) which people had bought in the bazaars, baskets, each of a shape more inconvenient than the last, containing the party's various luncheons, a disintegrating suitcase full of cooking utensils which would never be required, the guide's luggage, pumps, spare tyres, biscuit-tins, and the Colonel's famous ever-open attaché case, it was a heterogeneous collection, and as we drove out of the city we must have looked like a sort of jumble sale on wheels.

Quinney, Manfred and I were packed closely in the front of the Dowager, while Miss Gumbleton bounced about like a ball behind and struggled to stem the cascade of luggage which fell upon her at every bump. Mr. Waters, Mrs. Christmas and Mrs. Mock, topee and all, lay in the back of the Grey, their feet, which alone were visible, propped up on petrol-tins some inches higher than their heads. Beside the Colonel, in the most ample and comfortable seat of all, sat the guide : no one else would sit next him on the supposition that "he smelt". Since it was convoy day there was a busy atmosphere about the town, and the quantities of motors coming and going shamed us by the scientific methods of their packing ; for their luggage was confined to the running-board, where a stout network of rope held it in.

I am a snob about deserts. Earlier in the year I had crossed the Sahara, and the Syrian Desert, by comparison, was poor fry. It was a boring desert, lacking in majesty. It was endlessly flat, without so much as a dried watercourse, a sandhill or a hummock to break the monotony. The stream of traffic deprived it even of the illusion of loneliness ; the continuous mirage, suggesting a lake which hemmed us in at close quarters, destroyed the impression of space and induced an irritation amounting almost to claustrophobia. A pillar of cloud guided us by day, as it guided the Israelites in this region, but it was a cloud of dust from the car in front, clouds of dust in echelon from the many cars in front, which settled on everything, penetrated into the farthest crannies of our suitcases, and caked our faces with ochre. Even in the evening, when deserts usually soften into a cool haze of gentle lights, this desert stayed odious and hard.

We were fifty minutes at the French Customs post, where a hoarding stood up to mock us in French and Arabic :

> AIR ORIENT
> DAMAS–BAGDAD
> PAR AVION
> EN 4 HEURES

We stopped for lunch at the lonely fort of Descarpentries ; otherwise no human habitation broke the emptiness. At the fort, among a handful of French native troops and armoured cars, we found an English wireless operator of the Foreign Legion. His name was Portman, he came from Birmingham, and he never stopped talking.

"The Legion's a grand life," he said, "if you know a

language and go in for specialized jobs. Take me. I can rub along in French and I've studied wireless. I get three hundred and sixty francs (that's three pounds) each fortnight, and it costs me two francs a day to live. So I don't do badly. But take the ordinary legionnaire, who hasn't got the sense to learn a job. Why, he sweats away with pick and shovel and doesn't get more than one shilling and fourpence a day for all his slaving. I've been in the Legion nine years and here for two and a half; and I don't feel like going home yet, neither."

He showed us his quarters: a room large enough for two beds, with photographs of girls pasted on the mud walls and a coloured postcard of the gardens on Eastbourne front. By contrast, the more sophisticated French assistant who shared his room favoured modern nude photographs in the German style, and a postcard of the Croisette at Cannes.

Portman posed for his photograph, and Quinney filmed him.

"My word," he said naïvely, "at this rate I'll be becoming a millionaire."

The track was very rough in parts, worse than is usual in the Sahara, though intended to carry a far greater volume of traffic. After dark we were continually blinded by the dust of the car in front: a trail extending for nearly a mile. We would drop back out of its radius; the car in front not seeing our lights would stop, thinking it had lost us, and we would be enveloped again in its dust. The guide lost us the way, but an armed Bedouin, looming through the darkness like a white column, directed us, and twelve hours after our departure from Damascus we were at the fort of Rutba, eating a very English dinner, at English prices, and drinking Allsopp's beer, while a number of young men who had something to do with petroleum shouted at the Iraqi servants in the approved jargon of the British Raj.

CHAPTER VIII

IRAQ

NERVES were frayed, the second day in the desert. Even the Colonel's singularly equable humour was affected. We heard him pursuing us in the Grey, with frantic blowings of horns. "Look here," he said to Manfred, "I've got to get these cars to India. You can't go blazing along at that speed on desert roads." On the rare occasions when the Colonel became rattled, he invariably explained, more in sorrow than in anger : "Look here, you know, I've got to get these cars to India."

The Colonel and Manfred had very different styles of driving. Manfred would lean back in a casual manner, one hand on the wheel, the other draped lackadaisically out of the window ; he would talk (or cackle or sing) incessantly, and he would drive very fast.

The Colonel would lean furiously forward, with a set expression, both hands gripping the wheel, every ounce of energy concentrated on the business in hand as though he were driving a fiery chariot, and he would drive very slowly.

After luncheon we came into bad dust-storms, our mouths were filled with grit, we averted our eyes in pain and visibility was bad. We lost sight of the Dowager (we had all changed places), and Christmas again remarked that he had to get these cars to India. But tempers were saved by his hat blowing off and scurrying away into the desert, performing hilarious parabolae as it was caught in an eddy of wind and dust. The guide was sent to chase it. Like a true Oriental, he had clearly never run in his life and looked like a ludicrous penguin in a city suit, as he flapped away in an ambling, effeminate canter. Occasionally he would dip, and only his large behind appeared behind a sand-dune. The hat mocked and tantalized and eluded him, soaring away with a "catch-me-if-you-can" expression, and on he waddled. Finally he fell bodily upon the hat, in a cloud of sand, bottom upwards, legs in the air like a clown in a circus turn, and returned with a sheepish expression, brushing the sand off his suit.

Apart from its entertainment value this was the first useful or energetic thing the guide had done. Throughout the journey he slept soundly in the only comfortable seat. In his rare wakeful moments he would make a vague pass to left or right where there were alternative tracks (invariably selecting the worse of the two), or exclaim "Kamerad!" to indicate that the other car was out of sight. Then he would go to sleep again.

It was a relief to reach Ramadi, where for an exorbitant sum the police gave us strong Indian tea and Huntley and Palmer's biscuits. But we were not allowed to proceed to Baghdad without a police escort. The only part of this country where there is any real danger from bandits is the immediate neighbourhood of the city after dark, and no car is allowed to leave or enter it unprotected. Our two policemen in grey uniforms, bristling with weapons, were delighted with the prospect of a joy-ride to Baghdad. One of them said it was very providential, as he had wanted to attend a wedding there on the morrow. The guide, who had hardly opened his mouth since we left Damascus, poured out a flood of conversation now that he had a fellow-countryman to talk to: we had not thought him capable of such animation. We pointed out that a guide and a police escort who did nothing but tell each other stories in Arabic were of very little use to us in either capacity, and the flood was temporarily stayed.

The policemen, however, earned their passages, if not in the intended manner. The Dowager contracted a puncture involving, since it was the third that day, a change of tyre. With ferocious energy they set to work to lever off the old tyre and pump air into the new with a pump which did not work. But this took over an hour, thus destroying our chances of reaching Baghdad till late.

The roads were bad, and even the Grey began to buck. "My one fear," exclaimed Quinney, "is that I shall enter Baghdad a eunuch."

The Euphrates was suddenly before us: black reeds etched on a blade of white metal, which shone dull and inimical against a portentous red moon. The moon had risen small and white when we reached the Baghdad aerodrome. Our luggage was passed through the Customs. We cluttered on to the pontoon bridge across the Tigris and drew up at the Tigris Palace Hotel. Colonel and Mrs. Christmas went off to stay with friends. Half an hour later the Colonel rang up in a frenzy to ask if anyone had seen his attaché case. Someone had, on the pavement. We dined, principally off caviare, at half past ten.

At a neighbouring table was a party which had driven from England on charcoal, had got as far as Fontainebleau, had returned to England, had set out again, and had taken five days over the journey from Damascus. They found the charcoal useful in the desert, they said, for boiling tea, which they sold at night to the drivers of passing lorries.

Our rooms gave on to a wide terrace, which in turn gave on to the Tigris. Here the view, as Mrs. Mock remarked, was "ripping in the early morning". We sat at breakfast and looked down on the sluggish, colourless river, mud flats sloping down to low water, with the pontoon bridge on our right and a band of dusty palm-trees opposite.

I had expected little of Baghdad. My friends had warned me that it was a hot, featureless town of little glamour. And indeed, in substance, it is hardly more than an endless street running behind, but parallel with, an endless river. But, expecting little, I found more, and Baghdad did not disappoint me as Damascus had. The difference was the difference between a French and an English mandate. Each indents a native town with its own impression; but whereas the Frenchman likes to mix with his natives, the Englishman does not. The Frenchman spreads everywhere: the Englishman keeps himself to himself. Damascus is turned into a French provincial town, with cafés frequented by Arabs and Europeans alike. Baghdad, apart from its commercial quarter, is left to the Arabs, while the Englishman lives in the seclusion of an elegant suburb outside the city, in an ample villa with a garden, tennis court, and all that he holds most dear. This English aloofness from the Arab may (or may not) be bad policy from the point of view of colonization; but at least it preserves native life relatively free from European influence.

In Baghdad there are few trams or indeed means of popular

transport at all. To see a European in the bazaar is rare (they send their servants), and the cafés are purely Arab. In a saloon hung with carpets, open to the street, the Arabs squat in their robes on long wooden benches, drinking their Turkish coffee or sucking at their hubble-bubbles, a blank, incurious look on their faces. And outside, in the beaten mud street, an endless procession of victorias clops up and down. The noise of Baghdad is the jingle of harness, not the jangle of trams.

But it is a busy city. As you wander through the bazaars, you conclude that Oriental languor is a myth. When it comes to making money for himself the Arab and his children will work from dawn until dusk, weaving, sawing, joining, beating, forging in a frenzy of industry. Among the leather-workers you watch tiny children sewing saddles and belts with astonishing deftness. Among the metal-workers they are swinging newly-forged chains about in a skin, to blacken and polish them, and three or four men with enormous sledge-hammers are attacking an anvil with the numbered regularity of bell-ringers. The copper bazaar is a deafening chorus of percussion, as the workers beat the inanimate metal into shape. It might be the forge music of Siegfried in the original; and to walk from its blare into the muffled quiet of stuffs, streets of silks and of cottons, is to modulate into a slow movement of soothing calm, like the peace of death after a hammering fever.

The fascination to the European of an Oriental bazaar is that it gives us a glimpse behind the scenes. Machinery has not destroyed in us the appreciation of craftsmanship: its tradition is too deeply ingrained, and we still recognize in the "hand-made" a nobler quality than the machine can create. In the East, despite the importation of manufactured goods, things are still, for the most part, hand-made. It is true that the ancient traditions of craftsmanship are dying, that the Baghdad brass-worker is copying by hand the hideous machine-products of Birmingham, that the Arab carpenter is drawing on the Tottenham Court Road for his designs, and that, in short, the aesthetic value of the hand-made is now nil. But this does not affect the fascination of "seeing how it is done". In the East you will find yourself buying horrid little bits of marquetry because they have taken shape before your eyes from fragments of mussel shell inserted in the wood, useless canvas saddle-girths because children have woven them in your presence, worthless articles of silver which you have seen moulded and engraved by the silversmiths in that street beside the Tigris.

In London I always stop in front of those shops where women are invisibly darning in the window, tailors, cross-legged, Dickens-like, are sewing away in public, tobacconists are rolling their cigarettes for passers-by to see. I infinitely prefer the cobbler who will mend my shoe in the shop, while I wait, to the superior shoemaker who sends it away to be done discreetly in the background. How different is the cake "straight from the oven" or the apple "straight from the tree" to the apparently synthetic article in baker's and greengrocer's shop; just so a lettuce plucked from the garden, a real egg wrested from beneath the hen, genuine milk from a bowl in the dairy, a grouse that comes in a box from Scotland and not in a bag from the poulterer; and a flower from the florist is never quite as real as a flower from the nursery garden. In a newspaper office there is a similar quality about the paper hot from the press; and it is fun to be shown over a factory and to be presented at the end with some object one has seen in the making.

I believe that it would be an immense stimulus to trade were the methods of the Oriental bazaar to be adapted to Piccadilly, were it possible in the absence of the hand-made for shops and factories to be combined. Shopping in the West lacks the personal element: this would be a way of bringing it back. How much more likely would you be to waste your money if you could watch your diamonds being set in Monsieur Cartier's window, your cigarette-case being turned on Mr. Dunhill's lathe, your porcelain being baked in the ovens of Mr. Goode, your perfume simmering in the distilleries of Mr. Yardley, your jumper being woven on the loom of Messrs. Hawes and Curtis. But of course it would cut both ways, for you would also see the worm-holes being injected into your genuine Chippendale furniture, the unaccountable absence of another kind of worm from the premises of your dealer in silks, the suspicious quantity of water-taps in the cellars of your wine-merchant—and, come to that, your cow being slaughtered in the windows of Messrs. Fortnum and Mason.

In Baghdad we were "taken in tow" by a prominent

English resident, whose name, if I remember rightly, was Mrs. Catarrh. Mrs. Catarrh seemed to have bought us over our heads before we arrived, and no one else had so much as an option. She was the kind of woman who does what some people describe as "killing you with kindness". In other words she made it clear from the start that we were exclusively her property. If only Mrs. Catarrh had known how many of us there were she would have got hold of a special bungalow to put us all up in. But it was too late now. Never mind, we would be very comfortable at the Tigris Palace Hotel.

Her mission, as she now conceived it, was to show us th sights of Baghdad. No, no, it was no trouble at all; besides which there were a great many sights that only she, Mrs. Catarrh, could show us, and it would never do to miss them. (One of these, presumably, was Mrs. Catarrh herself.) Now then, let her see, it was eleven-fifteen. At twelve o'clock we were to be at the British Club, where she was entertaining some friends. Meanwhile, there was just time, if we would get into Mrs. Catarrh's car (another of the sights of Baghdad), to take a look at the Customs House, and the old Turkish barracks which were now the new Government offices, and then she would rush us round the bazaars: one could get quite a lot done in three-quarters of an hour. So Mrs. Catarrh showed us the Customs House, and the old Turkish barracks which were now the new Government offices, and there was hardly time to see anything of the bazaars, but she pointed out to us a singularly ugly building across the river, which was "of course" the Residency. (I was reminded of a woman whom I once encountered on a ship, and who startled me by announcing, "My greatest friend, Lady Chalmers-Mitchell, lives, of course, in the Zoo.")

Then we were hurried to the British Club. Here Mrs. Catarrh was entertaining a number of Englishmen who, oblivious of the climate, wore thick tweed suits and were consequently somewhat pink in the face. We drank John Collinses, and, as Mrs. Catarrh's eager, harassed eyes raked the room in search of more gentlemen in tweed suits, she told us a thing or two about Persia. I had heard of the beauties of Hamadan, but Mrs. Catarrh put me right on this. No, she said, there was nothing at all to see at Hamadan except the Residency, which had an attractive swimming-pool, and ("of course") the British Consul's house. But beyond Teheran we would go through a magnificent bit of mountain scenery which was one of the Seven Wonders of the World (the tenth, so far, of which we had heard since landing in Asia), and which, though we would hardly believe it, was even more beautiful than Switzerland.

After Quinney, at her request, had filmed Mrs. Catarrh and her guests on the terrace of the Club, we were given an hour off for lunch. But we must be at Mrs. Catarrh's house by two-thirty. She dealt out visiting-cards, so that we might remember the address. She had arranged for Mr. Catarrh to take the afternoon off from his office (which used to be the old Turkish barracks) and drive us out to Ctesiphon. But we could not spend very long there, as she had fourteen people to tea, and we must be back in time.

Punctual to the minute we arrived at Mrs. Catarrh's house. But Mr. Catarrh had not yet come back from the old Turkish barracks. So we were shown over Mrs. Catarrh's house. Mrs. Catarrh said the natives were always so amused because she used their plates (big round bronze ones) as tables and their garments as curtains—and indeed it would be startling, in an Oriental house, to find a Worcester soup-plate on legs serving as an occasional table and suit-lengths for curtains.

Mr. Catarrh (who was charming) arrived at three o'clock, without having lunched, and was hustled off to do so. Mrs. Catarrh said she hoped we would excuse her from coming to Ctesiphon but she had got up an impromptu dinner for the Christmases that night (she reeled off a list of parenthetic names), it was very short notice, and her cook was "a treasure" but she must stay behind and see to the arrangements.

The country we drove through was dead flat, populated by kites and clouds of sand grouse. In the days of Babylon it was a marsh. But the marsh was a danger, through floods and disease, so it was recently drained, and now the British population of Baghdad hunts the jackal over it with a tidy little pack of hounds.

We crossed a bridge at "Lancashire Landing", where the Lancashires were mown down in the war, and were on the road to Kut. The name of Kut stirred me more than that of Babylon; for events in one's own time, which have become history, are surely more exciting to the imagination than the events of hundreds of years ago. Similarly the most moving of all ruins, qua ruin, is a derelict railway station or a gutted Irish country house. The ruins of Ctesiphon are surrounded with earthworks; but they are not the excavations of Alexander the Great; they are the trenches and dug-outs of the Mesopotamian campaign, and as such incomparably poignant.

Ctesiphon, in the second century B.C., was the Parthian capital, and its ruins represent the architecture of the Persian dynasty of the Sasanians, which perished in the eighth century A.D. Little now remains but the arch of an enormous hall, like an ancient airship hangar in sand-coloured brick. It is a superb example of the brickwork in which the Persians always excelled. It is impossible to say how many millions of bricks have been used in its construction; where it is ruined you can see that the walls of the arch are ten feet thick with solid brick, and at the top must have been a good deal thicker. Small boys ran up the walls, now fallen away to an easy slope of steps, and, hardly visible at such a height, called for baksheesh.

Here again, as at Baalbek, I thought that the height of the arch must be more impressive now that it is half in ruins. For its whole span shows against the sky, where formerly it was covered; and the jagged edge of the vault only emphasizes its immensity. In the evenings the bricks were bathed to the colour of amber and the desert beyond glowed purple. Just so may it have done a millennium ago.

We returned to Mrs. Catarrh's tea-party for fourteen, where the guests consisted of our six selves and a Major Gudgeon. Our orders for the following day were given us: at nine-thirty Mrs. Catarrh would conduct us to Kadhimain, where she could show us the golden domes from the roof of the Chief Priest's house (a unique privilege to which no one in Baghdad but Mrs. Catarrh was entitled); she would arrange for the police escort without which we would not be permitted to visit the Kadhimain bazaars; then in the afternoon she would try to organize a river-party. We bade her good night, with profuse expressions of thanks.

But Mrs. Catarrh must have grown tired of us—and small blame to her if she had. Perhaps she had decided that we were a "bad buy". In any case, a message arrived in the morning to the effect that she was sorry, but her car would not be available to take us to Khadimain. So a jovial and rubicund friend of Mrs. Christmas, whom we happened to meet in the street just as we were starting, accompanied us to Khadimain without a police escort, and took us up on the roof of the Chief Priest's house to see the golden domes.

Though the domes are striking enough, their gold softening beneath the brilliant sunshine, the mosque is debased in style and its tiling is poor. But in the bazaars of Kadhimain, centring round the mosque as the market centred round a medieval cathedral, was the smell of the East; a smell of which Europeans normally complain, but which I found to be agreeably musty, with a faintly chemical flavour. There was the silence of the East, none of the constant rumble of wheels which underlies all noise in the West, but human noise alone: the busy sound of voices and the muffled tread of robed Arabs as they walk softly about their business. Sometimes the streets are covered alleys, sometimes narrow lanes; but nowhere is any regularity of shape. The roofs make a jagged conflict of projecting planes against the sky, and sometimes one stretches so far as to meet its opposite neighbour. Windows jut so that one trembles for their equilibrium, each venturing farther than the last until it would be possible, by leaning out, to embrace the lady on the other side of the street were it not that (for this very reason) they are shuttered and barred.

But the true beauty of the bazaar is in its sharp contrasts of black, black shadow and brilliant white light: not a gentle light, like ours, which filters with an air of apology into dark places, but a bold light which storms its way like a torpedo through every unsuspected cranny: stilettos, darts, and assegais of light, rays from every angle making a criss-cross pattern like a crazy prison cage, a strong beam pouring across your path, simmering in the air, so thick in texture that you involuntarily check your stride for fear of collision, and indeed half expect to see Alice's Cheshire cat come skidding down it to your feet.

Only Rembrandt could have painted light as you see it here. But while Rembrandt's light and shade are yellows and browns, these are blacks and whites. And here and there is a spot of vivid colour where the shaft strikes some piece of merchandise, or illuminates some ordinary scene to which the natural grace of the people, in their Rembrandt-esque robes, can never fail to give the quality of art.

Miss Gumbleton enjoyed Baghdad. She had lived there in

the past, and was met by an old admirer, so on the rare occasions we saw her she was bubbling with frolic, and gave rise to much facetious speculation.

Mrs. Christmas enjoyed Baghdad. The cocktails with which her English friends entertained us could not have been improved upon. There is something rather wistful about Englishmen in an outpost like this. They have few of the amenities which a full-dress British colony provides. There, where they rule the roost, they can swagger with plenty of their kind and organize their sports as if they were still at school. Here, since they are not the governing but merely a mandatory race, they are a lonely, circumscribed community, neither fish nor fowl. Pathetically, they would tell us how their office hours, under the Iraq Government, coincide with the only time at which it is feasible to play games, and how difficult it is, in the circumstances, to "keep fit". They were isolated, chastened, naïf, of enquiring minds, consulting us as though we, from the great world, must be a species of oracle. What, in London, was the general view of the Assyrian situation? What did people at home think of the Army as a profession, nowadays?

But Baghdad is less of a backwater than might appear. Aerially speaking it is the Clapham Junction of the Near East. All the great aviators must pass through it at some time or another, not to mention the minor fry, among whom a good few comic and eccentric types provide a diversion. It is curious to be in a country which is at once so primitive and so advanced, which has, so to speak, skipped one era of transport altogether, so that in many parts you travel either by aeroplane or by camel, and ever since the early days of aviation the native has been almost more familiar with flying-machines than with motor-cars.

One of the first aeroplanes to be seen in Iraq was in 1912. An American oil man at Basra, of go-ahead stamp, read about this new invention and wrote to de Havillands to send him one out, complete with book of instructions how to fly it— much as one might order a new kind of patent kettle from an advertisement. It came. He put it together as best he could, studied the directions carefully, and took it up into the air. For forty-five glorious minutes he remained aloft, to the admiring astonishment of a huge crowd. Then he crashed. He was not killed, but the toy was irreparably broken. Its remains decorate the Club at Basra to this day.

For myself, I appreciated Baghdad, if only in my Scots capacity. For I took my camera to a Jewish shop to be mended, and when I told the proprietor my name he fell on my neck and refused to charge me a penny.

Colonel Christmas enjoyed Baghdad, because he found some Kurdish cronies with whom he discussed old times. It was, I imagine, due to an excursion with these Kurds that our start, on the third morning, was delayed. We were timed to be off by eight a.m. so that we should be well into Persia by nightfall. But at seven came a telephone message from the Colonel to the effect that he had been out with the Grey last night and had slightly bent her grid while backing into the garage. It must be seen to before we could leave. We went to the garage to find the grid buckled and twisted to an unrecognizable extent. The Colonel looked a trifle shamefaced when he saw the damage in daylight. Its origin was tactfully not alluded to and was never, in fact, cleared up. But it meant that we sat in the lounge of the hotel from nine a.m. until four-thirty p.m. eating our sandwich lunch where we sat, unable to move, because the grid was always going to be "ready in an hour", but never was.

As usual, we were treated to a spate of expert misinformation about Persia from people who "knew", who had arrived only that morning from Teheran, who had motored thousands of miles in Persia, who knew fellows in the A.P.O.C. who said— and so forth. The road to Teheran, we were advised, was very bad. Alternatively it was very good. Alternatively there was, to all intents and purposes, no road to Teheran. The passes would—or alternatively would not—be blocked with snow. There was nowhere to stay en route. There were plenty of places to stay en route. We would not be allowed into the country without vaccination certificates (alternatively paratyphoid injections, Pasteur treatment, I forget what all). They would never let us take all that luggage in without duty. It was not safe to drive anywhere in Persia after sundown, because of bandits. Alternatively Persia was the only country in the East where there were no bandits at all. Finally nobody in their senses (and on this most were agreed) would think of motoring across Persia in Rolls-Royces anyhow.

Accordingly we set off for Teheran in two Rolls-Royces, after dark, with no vaccination certificates and no precaution against snow and a fantastic quantity of luggage. And we got there.

We lost ourselves in the darkness on the way to Khaniqin, which is the frontier town, and were not too confident of our safety; for while every motor-road in Persia is, thanks to the Shah, now free from bandits, the same cannot be claimed for the environs of Baghdad. Once or twice we lost the road altogether, and strayed among low, sandy foothills. Men rose up before us in the moonlight, but gave amiable directions in answer to the Colonel's fluent Persian, on which he now began to draw for the first time; and in fact they nearly always proved to be policemen, for the road was well patrolled. In the station at Khaniqin a white, Russian-looking train, with third-class passengers sleeping in heaps, was on the point of leaving for Baghdad: it would take all night to cover the seventy-five miles. We slept in the waiting-rooms, unpacking our own bedding for the first time. The women had one room, with three beds; the men had another, with two. But so smitten were we with the novelty of trying out our bedding on the ground that only one of the beds was used—by Manfred. Christmas and Quinney nearly burst themselves blowing up their mattresses, for they had omitted to bring a bicycle pump. Miss Gumbleton slept on six jazz cushions of casement cloth, bought in Baghdad. I slept well, on an ordinary beach mattress from the South of France. The rest complained of the howling of jackals, which kept them awake. But it was a quieter railway-station than any we had slept in in Italy.

Chapter IX

PERSIA

JUST outside Khaniqin there is a signpost: an ordinary English signpost, such as you might encounter on the Great North Road. But I do not believe there is a more romantic signpost in the world. It contains the one word, PERSIA. The name of Persia conveys a very subtle enchantment, and I think we all had a feeling of suppressed excitement as we passed that signpost.

In Khaniqin Christmas had to pay a deposit of sixty pounds on the cars and obtain a guarantee for the balance of their full value from a Persian. By ten o'clock we had passed the Iraq frontier post and were at Qasr-i-Shirin. A gate, as of a level-crossing, barred the road: on the other side of the gate was Persia. Persian travellers squatted with bundles of luggage in a cool Customs house, where they were evidently resigned to spending the day. We had a more Occidental sense of time. An official was persuaded to deal with our papers at once, we unstrapped the luggage from the cars, he passed it without a look, we strapped it on again, the gate opened, we slid into Persia.

To us Persia was a new country, and as such sent our spirits soaring. But its psychological effect on the Colonel, for whom it is a second home, was astonishing. From being detached, silent, absent, morose, insensitive to his environment, weighed down by the responsibilities of the expedition, he became gay, impish, light-headed, talkative; he laughed and joked with the Persians; he exulted in his surroundings, and the cares of the expedition fell from his shoulders as at the unveiling of a statue. A more literal unveiling followed, for at the first Persian stream he tore off his clothes and plunged into the cool, clear water. Henceforward the Colonel was an enchanting and irresponsible schoolboy. Time tables, marching orders (to the

Ctesiphon

In the Bazaars of Khadimain

The Great Persian Plateau

distress of Mr. Waters) went to the winds. This was Persia. What else mattered ?

My first reaction was relief at finding myself in a country which was itself, instead of a bastard adoption of Europe. Persia throughout the centuries has kept her frontiers and her individuality, and in her inhabitants I sensed at once a certain independent spirit, contrasting with the underdog demeanour of the countries we had traversed. Moreover, as I began to absorb some of the atmosphere of the country, I seemed to detect a European rather than an Asiatic flavour. Here was another Europe, very different from the one I knew, and in no way deriving from its culture ; but indefinably another, and as it were parallel, Europe. There was an urbanity in the demeanour of the people. With their fairish complexions and little dark moustaches, they might easily have been Frenchmen; even their language sounded like German.

The moment we left the frontier of Iraq the landscape changed. It began to spread itself on a noble scale, to prepare itself with gentle undulations for the great wall of mountains which appeared ahead. In the spring this country is a carpet of corn and flowers, but now it was a desert. It cannot go under the plough until the coming of the winter rains, and the margin of time, before it is too late for sowing, is often no more than two or three weeks. During this space the peasants work like slaves, from dawn till dusk, to get the land cultivated in time. They work on a communal system, each man receiving a share of the crops in proportion to his labour. Then they sit back and wait for the seed to grow.

We stopped in a mud village and bought grapes. They had no pips. The land of the pipless grape must surely be the epitome of civilization.

Beyond, we were still in parched, sandy country. Then all of a sudden, folded between two naked hills, there burst upon us the heavenly greenness as of an English glade. Willows and poplars fringed a tumbling stream, where silvered trout darted swiftly through the shallows and wagtails flitted from stone to stone. It might have been the Itchen, removed to the middle of an Asian desert. Here we ate our lunch, and contemplated the whole sum of Persian loveliness. For the beauty of this country lies in contrast, in the greenness suddenly encountered amid eternal brown, in the coolness of water amid a land which burns and tortures. I have been grateful for the shade of an oasis amid the glare of the Sahara. But the dead evergreen of its palms can never compare with the fresh, living green of a Persian valley.

Till a few years ago it was possible to fly by German 'plane to Teheran, over the three great passes which we were now to traverse by car. It was one of the loveliest air routes in the world, since it afforded a unique prospect of Persia's dramatic geographical configuration. Range after range, plateau after plateau, unfolded itself beneath you in an immense landscape. But the Shah allowed a concession to the company only on condition that a certain proportion of the pilots should be Persians; and Persians have a long way to go before they can provide a service of reliable pilots. Hence the company failed, and I believe that one of their Junker machines is still in Teheran, going for a song to anyone who cares to pay the heavy export duty. So since Persia (except on the Gulf) has no railways, the only regular route to the capital from the Mediterranean is the road used by ourselves and Alexander the Great!

After lunch we climbed the first of the three passes. The road corkscrewed steeply up through a scrub of holly-oak, but its surface was good. Originally it was built by the British, during the war, and the Persians have kept it up well, as befits an arterial link with the outside world. Though later on the passes are blocked with snow, the road itself is always kept clear. A stream of traffic accompanied us, chiefly motor-lorries of formidable size. On the steepest part of the slope we passed a team of eight mules harnessed abreast to a loaded cart, straining every muscle, slipping at every step, belaboured fiercely by their drivers; a more primitive but possibly also a more reliable form of transport, since the load they pulled was the disintegrated remains of a motor-lorry.

At five thousand eight hundred feet we topped the slope; but there was relatively no descent on the further side. From now on we remained aloft on the great Persian plateau, with the tops of the mountains for company. It is its height rather than its breadth which gives the country a unique atmosphere. Throughout our Persian journey we were travelling on a rarefied plane, higher than all but the topmost peaks of Great Britain, where the light and the air had a quality all their own.

The landscape was thickly populated, chiefly by nomad

Kurds on their way down to winter quarters in the plain. Their tents were of matting, roofed with black goat-hair; their flocks were black against the yellow ground. But they had an oddly urban look in their frockcoats and Pahlevi hats —the pill-box cap with a peak, suggesting the headgear of a French postman, which is now enforced by law. The uniform of the road police—a glorious blue to match the sky—was more picturesque.

Outside Kermanshah we were held up at the police post for about half an hour. This ceremony delays you at the entrance and exit of every Persian town, for the price of safety is bureaucracy. A policeman, with a stub of pencil on an odd scrap of paper, would record at random particulars concerning us. He would note the numbers of our cars, the numbers of our passports, the numbers of our various licences and permits and any odd number he could find, add them up, take away the number he first thought of, and stand in puzzled contemplation for some minutes before the double R of the Rolls-Royce trade mark. The Colonel, on these occasions, would invariably be roused to his most impish mood, so that the formalities became a diversion rather than a nuisance. Asked our professions, he now replied:

"We are all philosophers."

And the fact was recorded with due solemnity. Then the policeman scrutinized the document which gave our names and professions in Arabic lettering.

"But," he said, "you have other professions. You are not philosophers at all."

"It is the ladies of our party who are philosophers."

"Ah, I understand."

But still he seemed suspicious.

"Where," he demanded, "is your chauffeur?"

"I have no chauffeur."

"What, you are by profession a colonel in the British Army and you are travelling without a chauffeur?"

"I am a philosopher," said the Colonel, "and I have no chauffeur."

"But one of these gentlemen in the back, surely he is your chauffeur?"

"No. They are both philosophers. I have no chauffeur."

Here was evidently an unprecedented situation. The policeman, thoroughly suspicious of this foreigner who called himself a colonel yet drove his own car, went to fetch another policeman. A similar dialogue ensued. The second policeman stood in sceptical silence. Suddenly he dissolved into smiles. You couldn't deceive *him*.

"Ah," he laughed, "I see you are joking with me. The gentleman in the spectacles, he, of course, is your chauffeur." And thenceforward, to save argument, Quinney and Manfred were described to the police as professional chauffeurs.

Those Persian police stations must contain an immense variety of curious and undecipherable archives. An Englishman in Teheran told me that on one occasion, bored by these continual questionings in every town, he replied that his name was Methuselah, and that by profession he was the heir apparent of China. The information was noted in all seriousness.

Kermanshah was in the throes of modernization, and new bazaars of glazed brick were taking the place of the old. There were traffic lights, and even a traffic policeman mounted on an imposing dais at the junction of four streets. But there was no traffic. The Bristol Hotel, though the ladies found it hard to resign themselves to its complete lack of sanitation, was comfortable enough. There was a cosy dining-room with garish pictures of Swiss peasant scenes on the walls. Two naked, painted Atlases held on their shoulders golden globes with the faces of clocks, and a table was stacked, not with cheap magazines and handbooks, but with copies of the *National Geographic Magazine*. We had an excellent dinner of soup, meat and spinach, rice as light as only Persian rice can be, with a sharp sauce, chicken, fresh fruit cup, amber Persian wine to drink and a fizzy Russian mineral water. Christmas commented politely to the proprietor on the superiority of his establishment to many we had encountered on the journey out from England.

"Yes," he said, quite as a matter of course, "you are now in a civilized country."

The Colonel's daily visit to the bank delayed us in starting, but we had time to stop at Taq-i-Bustan, some few miles outside the town. Here water trickled from a steep cliff into a square and spacious tank. Amid groves of poplars peasants watered their donkeys at the stream, and strapped fat, shining water-skins on to their backs. Two tall grottoes are hewn out of the rock, and here are rock-carvings of the sixth or seventh century. They portray principally hunting scenes, reminiscent of a medieval tapestry, carved in bas-relief with little trace of the primitive in their technique.

Farther on, at Bisitun are the Cuneiform rock inscriptions deciphered by Sir Henry Rawlinson in the nineteenth century. More than two thousand years ago these inscriptions were carved three hundred feet above the ground in the face of a mountain which rises a sheer two thousand feet. The manner of their carving, at such a height, seems miraculous. The quality of the rock is so little subject to the ravages of the weather that they remain in perfect condition. But soon, in Persia, one ceases to be astonished by periods of time, and the reign of Darius I, whose history these carvings record, seems hardly more remote than yesterday, so little has the country changed in the interval.

Beyond Bisitun, miles from anywhere, we passed another car. In it was an Englishman whom I knew; nor had either of us the remotest idea that the other was in Persia. We bowed, smiled at each other, and passed on without stopping, much as if we were in a couple of taxicabs in Piccadilly. Thus do Englishmen conform to type even in the wilds of Asia.

We were travelling towards the winter. At this height the trees were in autumn leaf, while only yesterday, in the plains, they were green. Their magnificent reds and yellows and golds outrivalled England's November foliage because in place of a green background they shone against neutral grey. It was curious to see autumn tints in this new setting, much as a familiar pair of drawing-room curtains will change its personality to appear in a new and perhaps more vivid light when the colour of the walls is changed. Alternatively, each valley looked like a bright-coloured tie worn, out of its context, with a grey flannel suit. Among the autumn golds was sometimes a dash of neutral green, while grey villages grew from the grey earth and fixed us with square, black eyes.

We lunched by a stream which sparkled by the dusty road. An importunate beggar in rags, with a miserable child which balanced a swollen belly on pins of legs, pestered us throughout our meal, though we showered him with food. He wanted clothes for the winter months and took a particular fancy to Tishy, Miss Gumbleton's fur coat.

As we climbed the second pass the mountains tumbled

away in sculptural folds beneath us and looked as though they were sprinkled with gold-dust. Then we remained on an even higher plateau all the way to Hamadan, where we arrived in daylight. Except for Brindisi, it was the first destination we had reached in daylight since leaving England four weeks ago.

Hamadan is a centre of the carpet industry, and there was time to visit the principal factory before it grew dark. In a rickety, unlit barn, with a haphazard network of branches for rafters, four hundred and fifty children sat cross-legged on shelves, working away with tiny fingers at looms which towered above them. None was over twelve or under seven years of age. Their faces were pinched and wan, and the older girls covered them modestly with their veils as we passed. There were nudgings and gigglings and weak, falsetto nursery sounds. While in nurseries thousands of miles away other children work kettle-holders for their aunts, Persian children work carpets for the hostesses of Park Avenue. The scene was straight out of Dickens. Not a hundred years ago in our own country such conditions stirred the reforming zeal of Lord Shaftesbury. Persia has no Lord Shaftesburys.

The children work in these factories from an hour after sunrise until dusk. They are paid by the stitch. Some can do as many as eight thousand stitches per day, which represents about a shilling. Others do a good deal less. But in Persia five shillings a week is a princely wage.

The carpets were for the most part of debased design. This is dictated entirely by the New York decorators, who decree the fashionable pattern of the moment. The carpets cost the manufacturers five shillings per square foot and are sold in New York at five times that amount. The Customs duty takes a lot, but the decorator pockets a good ten shillings per square foot, so that the manufacturers' profit is hardly more than 15 per cent.

In the hotel at Hamadan, a pleasant place in a secluded garden, I had my first taste of opium. The Colonel, Quinney, Manfred and I squatted round a charcoal brazier in a dimly-lit room, while a Persian servant prepared the pipe. It resembled in appearance the pipe you play rather than the pipe you smoke. He handed it to us each in turn. When my turn came I was nervous of disgracing myself, like a schoolboy with his first cigarette. The Persian prepared the black paste, handed me the pipe and held a burning coal to it. I let my breath right out, for the longer the pull the better the smoke. I inhaled the opium, which spluttered and melted at the end of the pipe, drew it right into my lungs and tried to keep it there, so that as little as possible of the smoke escaped when I let out my breath again. At first, to our humiliation, we let out great clouds of smoke, and very little of it got into our lungs. But slowly we became more proficient. We swallowed the smoke, as it were, with draughts of tea in between each puff, and got the full benefit of the drug. I felt a delicious languor permeating my limbs. I was conscious of my arms and legs, but of a vivid feeling of ease in them. I began to feel tranquil and lethargic. There was peace but for the quiet sound of intaking breath, a damp smouldering sound of the opium as it liquefied, the tinkle of spoons in the teaglasses, the slow burning of charcoal embers. I felt all the mellowness with none of the restless excitement induced by alcohol. It was perfect contentment to lie by the dying embers and talk softly by the hour. Christmas recited Persian poetry, which the servant at one identified, continuing the verse. They went on reciting to each other in musical Persian accents.

Then the Colonel began to talk of Persia and of his experiences. He told us tales which have been told elsewhere: how he was imprisoned by the Jungalis during the war, how he escaped through the impenetrable, fever-ridden Caspian Forest, how he was recaptured and kept hobbled in chains for months in a peasant's house with only a child to guard him, how he was finally set free because the Jungalis had a bumper crop of rice and knew they could get better prices from their enemies than their friends in return for a release of prisoners. He spoke of Luristan, whose mountains we had seen on our right that day, and which only a handful of Europeans have visited. He had travelled through a great part of the country under cover of darkness, hiding during the day. He had stayed with a tribe in an atmosphere of diplomacy and intrigue which seemed too fantastic to credit. It would take days to organize a journey of five miles, for talk of ambushes and so forth. The chief was surrounded by an army of jabbering intriguers, who never stopped talking from morning till night. On shooting expeditions the Colonel was accompanied by a guard of some four hundred men, and at night they would sing poetry to one another from hill to hill, across the valleys. Once he organized a mountain race, to bring back goats from a certain fixed point, but it nearly ended in bloodshed, for the losing tribe tried to shoot up the winners.

He wandered from the subject of Persia to recount other reminiscences of travel. Once he travelled with a friend in France who had a weakness for creating ridiculous situations and carrying them off with a perfectly straight face. They ran out of petrol and had to push the car to the top of a hill. A passing Frenchman enquired "Pourquoi ?" "We understand," he was told, "that it is illegal to travel without a rear light in this country. Our rear light has given out, so, as law-abiding foreigners, we are pushing the car to our destination. Bon soir." Thenceforward the Frenchman knew that all Englishmen were insane.

The Colonel proceeded to the discussion of locusts, of which he had once made an intensive study. All the locusts in the world, he said, breed in a certain spot in Central Arabia, where they never die out. At certain periods conditions are favourable to bring them East—or West, as the case may be. They set out in armies. They have children, which begin to eat. In one year four eating generations are born, but the last is killed by autumn cold, so there are none left. The next year, and for so many years, another expeditionary force is sent out from Arabia. Then the visitation may cease for as much as twenty years and the East (or West) will be free of locusts.

Far into the night we talked until the opium made us drowsy and Quinney fell asleep where he sat. But for once we made an early start next morning. I had no hangover from the opium, except a strong propensity to sleep.

The higher we got, the more beautiful did the landscape become, for in the rarefied atmosphere the light played a symphony of colour on the earth. The spectrum on the plateau was in browns and greens with stripes of burnt sienna toning to amethyst at the foot of the mountains. As we climbed to eight thousand feet over the Pass of Aveh, round foothills of many-coloured earths piled themselves up into mountains of a thousand creases. They looked like heaps of powdered precious stones: amethyst, ruby, topaz, cornelian, agate, coral, with here and there an olive green like the dust of jade, against the purple background of mountains.

A Persian Bridge

Tiling in the Tomb of Khoja Rabi, Meshed

By a Persian Stream

The turquoise domes of Qasvin rose above hovels of mud, and its poplars were hung with golden coins. Towards evening we reached the foot of the Elburz range, topped with snow, which separates Teheran from the Caspian Sea. Here we were in the backwash of a big city : the roads grew proportionately worse from the greater density of traffic, and the streams coming down from the mountains ; the people had a busier look, the police were more efficient. At the last village, twenty-five miles from the capital, we waited for the Grey, expecting to reach Teheran by six o'clock. Crowds of people thronged the streets, like a Saturday night crowd in an English provincial town. It was dusk, and from the police post where we waited we could see their heads and bodies bobbing up and down at the top of a slight incline. Every few minutes there would be hooting, a lorry would appear. It looked, in the half-light, as though the crowds were mobbing it, but they parted, and on it came to the police post where the road, by now, was blocked with stationary lorries pointing in either direction. A caravan of camels sloped its way in between the lorries, with doleful bells ; discontented beasts, regarding us inimically, kicking out at each other in exasperation at life in general. A thicket of golden poplars fringed the road, and the stench within it was overpowering.

The Grey arrived, but her pressure pump was being obstinate, and she had a puncture into the bargain. So we drove the cars into the garden of a café where a thin orchestra played Russian music with very little abandon and the crowds paced predatory without. The damage was repaired. At eight o'clock we saw the Qasvin Gate of Teheran gleam silver in the night. We passed through it into endless streets reminiscent, in the darkness, of the suburbs of Paris.

CHAPTER X

PERSIA (*continued*)

NOTHING is pleasanter, after several days' intensive motoring, than the moment you awake to the prospect of a respite. A leisurely toilet, no haggling over hotel bills, no hurried packings, no luggage to be strapped on the cars, nothing to do but lie in bed a bit longer and perhaps wander out later in the morning, to visit a mosque (or a pharmacie); a comfortable lunch, an afternoon siesta, an evening walk followed by a drink—no agonizing hurry and bustle to reach a destination by nightfall. Our journey worked out as a rule in the ratio of four days' travelling to two days' standstill. The Colonel would remark that he had to "get these cars to India", and talk ominously of "pushing on"; Mrs. Christmas would refer again to her bateau and urge that we "step on the gas". But fortunately there was always something to be done to the cars, and we would get our two days.

Of course it was never enough. It took two days for the numbness of travel to thaw. Only by the third morning would we have mustered the energy to sit up and take intelligent notice of our whereabouts. And on the third morning we would have to set off for the next destination. But in Teheran we were comforted by the thought that we could laze with impunity. For it is not Persia's most interesting city.

I found Christopher and Robert on the evening of our arrival, staying at a pension called the *Coq d'Or*. They had left England two months before us, and Robert was still awaiting the other charcoal-burners whom we had met in Baghdad. Despairing of their arrival, he left the next morning in a second-hand Morris for Afghanistan. The proprietress of the *Coq d'Or* was a Frenchwoman. Our unexpected arrival and clamour for rooms so dazed her that she fled to Christopher.

"Mon dieu," she exclaimed, "on demande un lit pour huit personnes!" The *Coq d'Or* boasted the best food in Teheran. Madame's husband was a chef by profession and had won a gold medal in Paris for his chaudfroid of chicken. There was plenty of trout, and caviare from the Caspian, and vodka, and a passable Russian hock. There was heaps of hot water, but very little cold, in a bathroom which locked only from the outside. There was a garden with a goldfish pond behind. In a hole in an outhouse, Madame kept a pig "pour le réveillon de Noël". The hole was so deep that you could hardly see the pig, but you could hear its grunts. "Down in a deep dark hole", I remembered, "sat an old cow munching a beanstalk." In another dungeon was a fox. There had been a boar as well, but it had a habit of getting into the guests' beds, to which the guests objected. This, said Madame, was unreasonable. It only wanted its stomach scratched.

Teheran, like so much of Persia, was in the process of being pulled down and rebuilt. The Shah is everywhere intent on Europeanization, not from any particular devotion to Europe, but through shame lest Persia be dubbed old-fashioned. An imposing modern mosque turned out to be the offices of the Imperial Bank of Persia. The streets were full of trenches, as if a war were raging. Half-finished modern buildings in the Doulton manner stuck up gawkily into the sky. Waste ground predominated where nothing had yet replaced the demolished mud dwellings. The bazaars were still intact. There were carpets to buy, and ornate filigree silver, yellow leathern jackets lined with sheepskin and crocheted silken shoes. I lost myself in their ramifications and ran hither and thither in a claustrophobic frenzy, like a country cousin new to the London tubes. My leg disappeared down a drain, spattering me with evil-smelling mud, and I was fortunate not to do it an injury. (Afterwards I learnt that this was not a drain at all, but the town's supply of drinking water.)

The streets were dusty and there was little shade. In the evenings Christopher and I would take a droushky outside the city, which comes abruptly to an end in a desert, spotted with hundreds of black crows. We would walk towards the Elburz, which was starting to glow like an electric fire, to a deserted garden called Yusufabad. It is a pleasant, haphazard place, with pine-trees and a wide pool of water. (Water, in

Persia, constitutes a garden as flowers do in England.) In the spring, Yusufabad is a mass of rivulets, but now it was November, with autumnal sounds in the air. The crows lamented, and the sound of the muezzin summoning the city to prayer came to us across the evening stillness. A fox broke through the undergrowth. We chased and lost him. We turned to look at the city. From here it is a mass of trees, for every house has its garden, imprisoned behind high walls, unsuspected as you walk through the streets. The situation is as imposing as it could be: a spacious city of the plain, open to the western horizon, surrounded north, south and east by a wall of mountains which culminate in the giant snow peak of Demavend.

In such a setting you should be looking upon a fairy-tale Oriental city of domes and palaces and minarets; but you are not. Teheran does not do justice to its surroundings. The fairy-tale city of the East exists nowhere but in imagination. There is no such thing as complete perfection. Perhaps that is why we travel, always seeking, never quite finding it, tantalized and lured to continue by flashes of it here and there. If we found the perfect place we would travel no more. It may be better that it should elude us.

It is not only that man is limited, falling short of perfection in what he creates. Nature is notoriously imperfect. She sees to it that you do not have everything. England's pastoral scene is drowned by rain, Mediterranean brilliance is swept by mistrals, tropical luxuriance is tempered by vermin, Persia, with all her glorious landscapes, chokes you with dust. Nature holds a scrupulous balance. She exerts a discipline through which we must fight to realize beauty.

Teheran itself might fall short of expectations, but here in the Garden of Yusufabad I was in the centre of a mighty land. Beyond the mountains vast expanses of continent stretched to far-off seas: to the north eight hundred miles across the Caspian to Astrakhan, fifteen hundred miles more across Russian steppes and the Ural mountains to the Arctic Ocean; to the south five hundred miles to the Persian Gulf, eight hundred more across the great Arabian desert towards the African continent; to the east four thousand miles across unbroken land—Turkestan, Tibet, Mongolia, the Gobi Desert—to China and the Pacific. Our thousand miles from the Mediterranean seemed paltry by comparison.

Above: Village in Khorasan

Below: In the Shah's Palace of Gulistan

Above: Caravanserai in Khorasan   *Below:* Ruined Mosque at Tus

Teheran's position is surely one of the most dramatic in the world.

The white cone of Demavend shoots far above the Elburz range, which he appears to disown, aloof and angry. Sometimes his ill-temper is such that he will not show himself for days at a time, but sits enveloped in cloud. Now, as the sun began to set, Demavend slowly took shape like a spidery ghost through the mist. His snowcap sat loosely on his peak as if indeed it were no part of himself but a garment. In a few moments he shone white with heat. Presently the white began to fade into a red glow which grew paler as we watched. The sun had long since gone. Even the topmost ridge of the Elburz was now in shadow; it was as if Demavend were setting, and Demavend were mightier than the sun. The glow vanished, the mist returned. Demavend had set.

Our droushky-driver too watched Demavend's performance. He was a lively, stubbled creature.

"Thanks be to God," he said, "I am happy."

He laughed and talked with his horse as he drove us back, exhorting it with falsetto, childish shrieks. Christopher seized the whip from his hand and started to belabour him as if he were a beast of burden. Doubled up on the box, he whinneyed with laughter. It was an admirable Persian joke. We told him that our evening had provided us with the utmost felicity.

"That," he said, "puts joy in my heart."

But he still had presence of mind enough to dispute the fare.

As usual, a hitch prevented our leaving at the time arranged. The garage, suspecting a leak, had removed the Dowager's petrol tank, without telling us. This gave us time to visit Gulistan, the Shah's official palace. Its decoration consisted principally of a thousand representations of ourselves, since cut looking-glass provides the principal motif: baroque transformation scenes of mirrors, a fantastic, pantomime forest of shining facets, enclosed in richly varnished woodwork. Stalactites and stalagmites of crystal hang in festoons from the ceiling; pom-poms, tufts and tassels of glass adorn each cornice, scrolls and stars and spirals of it decorate the panels. In the midst of all the glitter, at the end of the great throne room, is inlaid in silver looking-glass a huge, enlarged photograph of the Shah. Below it is the famous Peacock Throne, said to have been looted from Delhi by Nadir Shah in the eighteenth century. Inlaid with hundreds of jewels, it is yet not ostentatious but soft and mist-like in colour and delicate in design. The Garden of Gulistan is pleasing, with tall cypresses and pools : the water, as often in Persian gardens, on a level with the paving, draining into a narrow channel round the edge.

We left Teheran by the Meshed Gate, and after ten miles of dust found ourselves proceeding up a narrow valley of astonishing loveliness. Little hills crowded curiously around, so close that one was tempted to pat them. They were rounded and smooth with occasionally a dent which had shivered the surface with a hundred creases, like glass when it is cracked. The autumn colourings exceeded in beauty anything we had yet encountered : plane-trees of burnished copper, with ivory trunks, poplars of gold, willows of green bronze, by a stream which ran now deep blue, now deep olive green. Crimson bushes splashed the opposite hillside with blood.

We wound up the narrow glen until we began to grow suspicious. This was much too intimate, too deserted a track for the great pilgrims' way to Meshed. It was. We had taken a wrong turning.

Ten miles back we joined the dusty highroad again and the mountains swept away from us incuriously. It was a frequented route. Long caravans of camels and mules and donkeys supplemented the stream of lorries. In England the donkey is a pet, a joke : in the East he is neither domestic nor funny, but a patient, pattering beast of burden, bearing his heavy loads with no suggestion of a smile. We lunched in a valley of poplars by a bridge of grey stone, like a medieval bridge in England. Then we rose again to the plateau. The mountains on either side were curiously smooth in form, like sand-dunes, yet rougher in surface, more masculine than sand-dunes. Their texture and colour could have been copied in tweed : heather-mixture, buff and fawn shades, sometimes a lovat green, browns and pinks and greys, arranged so that the material fell in ample folds. In the evening we passed camels at rest, their loads of charcoal standing upright in sacks on the ground. The sunset was indescribable, and to the east the mountain ranges were outlined one upon the other, dark upon light, light upon dark.

After nightfall we were lashed by a rainstorm which for a moment turned to snow. The pressure pump of the Grey was again recalcitrant, and every ten minutes or so we had to stop and adjust it. It was cold, and we were glad to reach the rest-house at Amiriyeh. The place was crowded, but they gave us a small room with wooden beds, whose mattresses and blankets we discarded in favour of our own. In a rough eating-room we fell upon a meal of hot chicken broth, rice, vegetables, and a wine which tasted of camphor. On a carpeted wooden settee in the corner a man was puffing at his opium pipe. Besides a long table the only other furniture was a varnished washstand of the type common in ships, let into the wall. The mirror was cracked and the basin was inlaid with hideous posies of flowers. Now and then a lorry driver would spit into it, or make a show of cleaning his teeth with a finger dipped in water. It was a bitter night, and huddled circles of men warmed themselves at charcoal braziers. A pinched Rumanian woman was there, muffled and cold, an Italian who had a contract in connection with the unfinished Caspian-Teheran railway, and with him an English-speaking chauffeur, late of the British Legation at Teheran, who put our pressure pump right.

The next morning was cold and frosty. Through the trees I looked on to a plain whitened with frost. Beyond, the mountains were black against the early yellow sun. Christmas looked dubiously towards the north. It had been his intention to make a detour and show us the Caspian. But a pall of grey cloud sat upon the ridge above it, and to one who knows the country that cloud portended a mist which may shroud the Caspian landscape for weeks at a time. Sure enough, we soon climbed out of the sunlight into thick damp fog. The country became suddenly a Scottish moorland, and the settlement of shacks, where the railway is under construction, was forlorn as a Northern mining-camp. We topped the crest, where unaccustomed mosses grew by the roadside, but the vapour rolled up at us, cold as a wet blanket, from the cauldron of sea-fog below. If we continued we should come, within a few miles, to rain-soaked woodland of a European character and ultimately to tropical jungle infested by malarial swamps; for the transition in height is sharp, and the Caspian ridge is one of the geographical curiosities of the world. But it was useless to proceed, for the landscape would be obliterated by the mist. It was curious to emerge again from the cloud into a sunlit plain of golden grass, where we immediately began to peel off our superfluous clothes.

We should leave Persia without seeing the Caspian. We should leave it, too, without seeing Isfahan. Our journey was thus punctuated with regrets for cities we had not time to see: Jerusalem, Petra, Palmyra, Babylon. But perhaps it is part of the essence of travel to leave places unseen, curiosities ungratified, so that always at the back of the traveller's mind is the feeling that one day he will return. Every such place is a treasure in store for the future, an illusion still to be tested. "Some day," I think to myself, "I shall see Isfahan," not "I have seen Isfahan, and maybe I shall never see it again." It does not occur to me to think, "I have not seen Isfahan, and may never see it."

The day's driving was like many others: a plain, a high pass, another plain, another pass. But trees were fewer and colours richer. We forded shallow streams, passed through a narrow sword-cleft with perpendicular walls two hundred feet high, and climbed round the edge of a vast punch-bowl, carpeted thinly with green. At the top we came suddenly upon a stretch of vivid, brick-red rock, before mountains of purple velvet shot with gold. There was green vegetation on the red soil, chiefly juniper—or gin bushes. (Gin is the only drink with a mean and ugly name. How much more attractive to drink a juniper and tonic, a juniper and vermouth, even a juniper sling!) This time the plain below us was an empty, circular stage, with a purple Persian carpet. Little pink, pointed crags formed the wings, and there was a gap in the centre, awaiting the entrance of the actors. But the scene remained empty and solitary. Then the mountains changed into curious strata, so that they looked like Chinese pagodas or the frilled skirts of a Spanish dancer. Their forms grew less soft, more naked and jagged, while the clouds made piebald patterns on their rocky surface.

Mountains are good travelling companions. When we stood at their feet they were menacing and aloof. But when we had travelled for several days amid the tops their manner began to thaw. It seemed that their intentions, after all, were friendly. They respected us as equals now that we were on their level. Sometimes they would follow along beside us, sometimes crowd round and invite us up their slopes, then they would make a sweeping detour· and wave to us from a distance, but we knew it would not be long before they joined us again.

Over the next pass the mountains turned so far aside that we could hardly see them and were alone in a wide, light plain, like the sea. In the centre, like an island, was the village of Semnan. As we approached it, Semnan appeared to be no more than a conglomeration of deserted gardens : an uninhabited village within mud walls, with here and there a stream or a pool banked up with earth, and in the centre, like a jewel, a tiny turquoise dome. Then we came into a shady square, where men sat on carpeted benches and offered us melons to buy.

We were now in Khorasan, and the villages looked very different from any we had encountered on the road to Teheran. Built of mud, they were an attractive trigonometrical composition of solids : cones, cubes and domes ; but always they had this tumbledown air. The inhabitants were simpler, country people, whereas before they had the appearance of town-dwellers.

From the plain of Semnan we passed into another wide amphitheatre, which the clouds had commandeered for a gala afternoon, to stage a masque. It was a deliciously rococo entertainment, where billowy ladies reclined and cupids pirouetted in arabesques and eddies of dance. Ranks of white dancers, light as balloons, advanced and retired as in "Nuts in May". They played pranks with the mountains, flecked their sides with swirling shadows, caught them up into a rondo, disguised them as clouds so that you could not tell earth from sky. On a carpet stained with wine was a coral-coloured reflection of cloud. All through the afternoon the revels continued, culminating at sunset with a dazzling set-piece. Transformation scene merged into transformation scene in an orgy of colour. Slowly the party broke up ; you could see the guests go straggling homewards, jaded and frayed, while some settled down to sleep where they sat, on the mountain-tops ; the lamps and the fires burnt slowly out, and all was dark.

We slept that night at Shahrud, in a garage. These garages are built on the pattern of the old caravanserais, but for cars in place of camels. There is a large courtyard with lock-ups on two sides, rooms for travellers on another, kitchens, etcetera, on the fourth. Sometimes the rooms have wooden beds, sometimes no more than a bare floor. Primitive as they were, I grew to like the atmosphere of these modern caravanserais. Towards dark the lorries would begin to arrive (lorries in which, incidentally, it is possible to travel all over Persia as a passenger for a negligible sum) : two Diesel-engined German monsters from Beyrouth, ordinary, more plebeian vehicles in varying stages of disrepair, overloaded with merchandise; then the buses, conveying pilgrims to Meshed. These would disgorge a human cargo which scattered in every direction, like carrion, chattering loudly, in search of rooms.

From the dishes steaming on the kitchen hob we would help ourselves to rice and soup and vegetables, and squat on carpeted benches to eat and drink. We would fill our mugs with tea from the samovar. There would be mint, which we put in the tea, and chupattis. (When first I saw someone tearing at these strips of felt which pass for bread I thought he was eating his hat.) The kitchen was ill-lit and pleasantly stuffy after the cold night air. It was noisy, and indistinguishable, muffled forms moved in and out. Pilgrims prayed on mats; a group of women crouched like black crows on the ground; a servant noisily distributed food; chauffeurs, who might from their appearance have been Europeans, squatted over their pipes of opium; a policeman wrote things down at a table in the corner; children flirted; a man of incredible age played on a balalaika and sang a mournful song.

The noise would continue all night through; we would be too tired to hear it; but, redoubling, it would wake us early; a man singing a monotonous prayer for hours on end, the hideous racket of lorries starting up, the pandemonium of Persian voices. The pilgrims always sounded as though they were engaged in a violent dispute, even if it were only gossip; but as a rule they were engaged in a violent dispute, about seats, or prices, or whatnot. Later we would overtake them on the road, packed like hens in a crate, with often an insensible and apparently unclaimed pair of legs protruding behind. They might have been loads of corpses.

We would dress quickly, because of the cold, make shift with a minimum toilet, roll up our bedding, and hurry across to the kitchen to warm ourselves at a brazier. We would breakfast off tea and mounds of caviare from the Caspian, and be off an hour or so later than we had arranged.

We were held up at the police post as we left Shahrud.

"By the grace of Allah and the mercy of the Shah, with great felicity and bliss, we have come a long distance from lands across the sea," said Christmas to the policeman. "Surely you will not delay us in a place so insignificant as this?"

Nor did they.

We hoped to reach Meshed by nightfall, but the chief man of a village insisted on entertaining us to tea at eleven o'clock in the morning, and later we lingered over luncheon in a deserted garden, drinking the nectar of water-melons in the shade of a beautiful but derelict brick caravanserai. Surfeited with melon we flung the remains to a calf. The creature buried her face in it and sucked it up in such an ecstasy of greed that she even forgot to be afraid of us. Melon-fed veal would surely surpass even peach-fed ham as a delicacy for the sophisticated.

The Persians take melons seriously. They have a theory that there is just one psychological five minutes at which a melon is in its prime. The rich Persian employs a melon-diviner, to watch the fruit day and night when it is on the verge of maturity. When the moment comes, no matter at what outlandish hour, he will take it to his master; and no true Persian will object to being wakened in the middle of the night to eat the perfect melon.

It is a race of epicures. I know of one Persian who keeps a douche bag and tube for a peculiar purpose. Every morning, while he still sleeps, his servant gently inserts the tube between his teeth, and into his mouth is poured a mixture of warm milk, whisky and honey. Thus his first conscious sensation each day is the taste of nectar.

The further we penetrated into Khorasan the more attractive grew the architecture. The Persians were always masters of brickwork, and here are many perfect examples of bridges, caravanserais, mosques, minarets and towers where peasants took refuge from the perennial Turcoman hordes which scourged the plain. At Sabzavar is a brick minaret a hundred feet high, with an intricate embossed pattern of Kufic writing, in brick, at the top. Though built in the twelfth century, it might equally belong, in some more commercial capacity, to modern Germany. Many examples of this brickwork are even older, particularly in towers surmounting the shafts of underground watercourses. These tunnels, four feet high, were dug on a slope, sometimes at a depth of three hundred feet, and emerge where the plain becomes level. Polybius refers to them: "There is no sign of water on the surface; but there are many underground channels, and these supply tanks in the desert, that are known only to the initiated." They form a network for hundreds of miles, all over Persia, and are among the earliest and most remarkable feats of engineering in the world.

The chances of our reaching Meshed that night grew remoter when the off headlight of the Grey went suddenly mad. For no apparent reason its beam shot crazily off at a right angle, to rake the surrounding country and leave the road in almost total darkness. We drove along in this skew-eyed fashion for a bit, much to the astonishment of the traffic which passed us. Finally we stopped. But it was a good half-hour before the light could be induced to see reason—and the road. Then it began to rain. That settled it. We stopped at Nishapur. This despite violent protests from the women, who were prepared to undergo any amount of discomfort—hours' driving in rain and cold and darkness, with a probable loss of the way and at the best a frozen arrival in the small hours of the morning—all for the prospect of a water-closet at the other end.

Next morning Mr. Waters, fully-dressed, banged on all our doors. "Half past five!" he announced in sepulchral tones. It was a self-imposed task, for Christmas had remembered that the following day was Friday, the Mohammedan Sunday, and that we must at all costs reach the bank by midday if we wanted to get off from Meshed before Saturday. We were away by seven-thirty (what poor Mr. Waters did with himself in the intervening two hours I cannot think). For the same reason we had no time to visit the Tomb of Omar Khayyám, which is at Nishapur. All we saw of it was a large black onion on the horizon. But the Colonel's inconsistency was one of his principal charms, and further on, to Mr. Waters' astonished indignation, we stopped for a good three-quarters of an hour at the Shrine of Kadamgah.

It is an enchanting spot, with three walled gardens in tiers and a waterfall, as at Tivoli, harnessed to run through each in square tiled pools and channels. There are some fine, thick plane-trees and towering pines. Through a square doorway you look into the innermost garden to the vivid tiles of the mosque above a herring-boned brick wall. The dome is tiled, as well as the walls, in green and blue and yellow. A man was washing a plucked chicken in the pool behind the shrine; hens and sheep wandered about at will, and the cloisters—once intended to house pilgrims—had been converted into rough stables. There was that tattered, untidy air about the place which gives every Persian garden its charm, and reminds you of decaying gardens in Ireland. We had a view over a wide plain towards distant ranges of mountains. Marco Polo referred to its luxuriance, which is represented to critical European eyes by meagre though welcome strips of green. As we left, a bus-load of pilgrims was conducting a wake in one of the stables, with much wailing and beating of breasts.

We came into really wet weather over the last pass, and the winding roads were alarmingly skiddy. However, the rain cleared in time for us to look down on the holy city of Meshed with its turquoise and its golden dome burning against a dull grey sky. But no pilgrims plodded their way into Meshed. They were all in buses. Nor is it permitted, any longer, to carry corpses there for burial, since it was computed that the entire soil of the city, to a depth of seven feet, is composed of human remains.

As far as we were concerned it was composed of mud. We floundered through a morass to the bank, which we reached at one minute to twelve—only to find that the clock, for some reason, had advanced and it was one minute to one. The bank, in any case, had not opened at all that morning, since it was a Persian holiday; so we should be here for forty-eight hours before we could get money to proceed.

At the hotel we found Robert, seeking means of transport to Afghanistan, since his car had died under him on the road from Teheran. Together we visited the bazaars, which encircle the two great mosques and which, like the rest of Meshed, were in the throes of modernization. We ferreted about among Bokhara embroideries, Turcoman rugs, velvets, bronzes, turquoises and pale-coloured emeralds of Khorasan mixed up with the usual junk. In the tray of one dealer, reposing among jewels and ivories and various treasures, was the top of an old bicycle bell, which had long since forgotten its identity.

Decorating the hovel of an indigent Persian tailor, I found snapshots of the Mayfair élite on Derby Day, cut from the *Tatler*. Four thousand miles across a continent and a half, the fame of English morning dress had travelled. There was no sign, however, that the grey top-hat had caught on in Meshed.

Meshed is Persia's back of beyond, her most easterly city. Within a few miles are the respective frontiers of Afghanistan and Russian Turkestan, whence traders and pilgrims come, and in the bazaars is a Central Asian mob of many races, the tall fur hats of the Turcomans protruding like chimneys above the crowd. The amenities of the place are meagre, but there are Russian confectioners' shops which put the pâtisseries of Paris to shame, there are stalls which sell an infinite variety of delicious almonds and pistachio nuts, and on the evening of our arrival an Armenian musical comedy was being presented in the hotel.

No unbeliever may approach the shrine of Imam Reza, which is among the holiest in the world. It is tantalizing to walk round and round it, with only an occasional glimpse of its gilded dome through the alleys of the bazaars. Not since an American consul was murdered in Teheran a few years ago, for photographing a sacred place, are you allowed to take photographs of any building in Persia without a permit from the police. But just outside the city is the lovely tomb of Khojah Rabi, which the visitor may enter, but of whose whereabouts our droushky driver had only the haziest idea. The building stands in a spacious orchard of trees. Octagonal, it is built of brick, but every part is tiled with a variety of geometrical patterns in blue and green and yellow. Each of the four main sides has a central bay with a pointed arch; this is recessed to contain a similar arch of half the size, which in turn frames a small, rectangular door. The lower part of the dome, in which turquoise predominates, has broad bands of Arabic writing, making a coloured pattern of tiles. Scaffolding enveloped half the building as, curiously enough, it did when Lord Curzon saw it fifty years ago. In a Western landscape these tiled mosques would look garish; but in the bright Persian light their colours soften so that they compare in hue with the wild flowers of an English wood, harebell and celandine, rather than the gaudier delphinium and sunflower of an English garden.

In the morning we hired a car to take us to Tus, some fifteen miles to the north of Meshed. The driver brought a friend with him, as Persian drivers invariably do, and Ali, the hall porter from the hotel, insisted on coming as well, so we were somewhat congested. Ali had spent some years in London, trading the famous turquoises of Nishapur with the jewellers of Hatton Garden, and spoke passable English. Tus was the native town of Firdaussi, the great Persian historian. Firdaussi wrote a Persian epic for which the Sultan Mahmud of the eleventh century promised to pay him one gold piece per verse. But when it was completed Mahmud broke his contract, and paid in silver instead of gold (much as if Mr. John Long were to substitute shillings for guineas in remunerating me for this work). Firdaussi left the Sultan's court in a rage and returned to his native Tus, publishing a bitter satire on the subject of Mahmud's meanness. At this the Sultan repented, and sent messengers post-haste to Tus to pay Firdaussi the full amount and more. But he was too late. The great poet was dead. To-day, exactly a thousand years after, the Persians are building a pyramidal tomb for him at Tus, which was nearing completion when we saw it.*

There is little left of the ancient Tus but a partially ruined mosque: a dignified monument of brick, with vertical brick ornament, like narrow buttresses, such as you see on modern buildings in Hamburg. It stands alone, in fields of dry grass, amid ruined earthworks which were the walls of the ancient city of Meshed, and which hide to-day a small mud village.

Here it was winter. In ten days we had passed through the gamut of three seasons; the trees, which had been green in Baghdad and golden in Teheran, were naked now. A long thread of snow gleamed on the distant mountains above the plain. The sound of camel-bells fell upon the air, shepherds cried to their black flocks, muleteers watered their caravans beneath the arches of an old brick viaduct. The wintry stillness gave me a feeling of homeliness and comfort. It

---

* The millennium of Firdaussi is being celebrated at Tus as this book goes to press, with the unveiling of the tomb in question.

was the first morning for many weeks that we had been at peace.

Our load of passengers on the return journey was increased by a hen, which the chauffeur's friend had bought (or stolen) from the villagers.

A mood of exhaustion fell upon us in Meshed. We were tired of travelling. From now on the journey offered us little, for the country to the south, between Meshed and the Baluchistan frontier, is dreary and the roads are bad. We would have liked a magic carpet to deposit us straight away in Quetta.

And then, with dramatic suddenness, something happened.

The night before our scheduled departure, Christmas dined with Major Daly, the British Consul.

"Why," asked Major Daly, "aren't you going through Afghanistan?"

"Because we'd never get visas."

"I don't see why not. They say the country is perfectly quiet. If you like I'll send round to the Afghan Consulate and sound them."

"By all means," said Christmas. "There's no harm in trying."

Afghanistan had indeed been mentioned as a remote possibility in the early stages of the tour. But enquiry in London elicited the information that visas would never be granted, and we banished the idea from our minds. Afghanistan, after all, is to all intents and purposes a closed country. Robert had pulled strings for months to obtain his visa, and was even now uncertain of being allowed across the frontier; for in Teheran we had heard that Nadir Khan, the Afghan King, had been murdered, and it was assumed that the country would be in a state of upheaval.

But the Afghan Consulate seemed amenable. Here indeed was a change of horizon.

Though the permission was not yet official we decided to make plans as though it were. First there was the problem of currency. We were told that we must have Persian silver, since notes, in Afghanistan, were invalid. So, after an hour or two in the bank, we emerged with enormous quantities of silver money, which the Persian cashier counted out into bags with the fascinating dexterity of a conjurer. On returning to the hotel we were informed:

(*a*) That Persian silver was not valid in Afghanistan, but that we must have rupees;
(*b*) That the bank had no rupees;
(*c*) That the Persian Government would not permit the export of silver.

There was another difficulty. Our Persian exit visas were valid only for the Indian frontier. We must get them changed over to the Afghan frontier before we could get our visas for Afghanistan. Then if we failed to get Afghan visas we should have to get them changed back again. We could not get our new exit visas before three o'clock. This meant that we would not get our Afghan visas—if we got them at all—till four. This meant that we must give up all idea of starting before to-morrow.

At six o'clock Christmas returned from the Afghan Consulate to say that it was all right about the visas but that photographs were required. Four of the party had none. The photographer's shop was closed. They must be photographed the moment it opened, at seven a.m. Mrs. Mock said she couldn't possibly be photographed before breakfast.

"It's your face they want to photograph," said the Colonel, "not your stomach."

The photographs were taken. Some of the money was converted into rupee drafts, which we were informed could be changed in the Afghan bazaars. Robert decided to cancel the seat he had reserved in a pilgrims' lorry and accompany us. The cars were packed. But at the last minute there was a hitch.

It appeared that the visas had been promised by an underling at the Afghan Consulate, without reference to his superior. The Consul now refused to grant them unless the British Consul made him a special request in writing—i.e. shared the responsibility. This Major Daly very kindly agreed to do, but with one proviso: that we should not proceed beyond Kandahar without permission from the Legation at Kabul. He would wire to Kabul to warn them that we were on our way. The visas were signed. We were off.

But we still had another hundred and twenty miles of Persian roads to cover, and they were very different from the highroads we knew. This is an unfrequented route, and only a rough track covers it. We took the wrong road, because it was the best, and found ourselves in the middle of the Shah's private property. Having led us across country to the right track, the peasants informed us that we were "twelve farsakhs" from Turbat-i-Sheikh-Jam. After an hour's further driving we learnt that we were "fourteen farsakhs" from Turbat-i-Sheikh-Jam. Ten minutes later we were "four farsakhs" from it. The farsakh is a strangely elastic Persian measure, which may be anything between two miles and ten, according to particular local fancy. Directions become even more obscure when you are told that a place is distant a Horse's Gallop or a Sheep's Bleat.

The road was in transverse waves, and often an enormous ditch stretched right across it. Having lost the Dowager for half an hour we turned back to find her stuck fast across a small bridge, and looking most ungainly. The centre of the bridge had caught the under part of her chassis, her rear wheels were embedded, and her front wheels waved foolishly in the air.

"Look here," said Christmas, "I've got to get these cars to India. We'll have to turn back to Meshed if this sort of thing's going to happen."

And it seemed as though we might still be baulked of Afghanistan.

But we jacked up the rear wheels, put boards under them, scraped the ground away from beneath the chassis, and after an hour and a quarter's strenuous work in the darkness dislodged the car. Thereafter we stopped at every bridge, in trepidation, to guide the Dowager across. We made slow progress and, relying only on the wheel-marks of other cars to guide us, continually lost the way. We found ourselves in total darkness in a village of blank mud walls. There was no sign of life, no wheel-tracks ahead, no room to turn round. Somewhere in front were the lights of an encampment, but dogs were barking ferociously and to approach it on foot would have been tantamount to suicide. After half an hour's impasse Christmas managed to wake up two inhabitants, who said we were quite off the road. But we could continue, and by bearing right, should strike it again. This, by the mercy of Providence, we did. The Colonel was by now so exhausted that Mrs. Christmas had to prod him to keep him awake at the wheel. We got to Turbat at one a.m., eleven hours after leaving Meshed, and in as many minutes were asleep on our mattresses.

Curiously enough it was not the first time that a Rolls-Royce had covered this appalling stretch of road. King Amanullah, after his fantastic and triumphant tour of Europe, returned by road from Teheran to Kabul. Outdistancing his guard like a naughty child eluding its governess, he and his Rolls were lost for several hours. The guard finally overtook him in a small Persian village, where he was haranguing the inhabitants, telling them that they were not Persians at all, but Afghans, and urging them to enrol beneath his banner. The inhabitants, it may be said, were not best pleased.

Next morning we saw the last of Persia at Kariz. A French-speaking Customs official regarded our cars with admiration and assumed that we were all English lords. We did not disillusion him. Robert's lorry trundled in after us and unpacked itself as if for a whole day's stay. He did not regret having spurned it in our favour. We proceeded across twelve miles of No Man's Land to the Afghan frontier at Kuhsan.

Chapter XI

AFGHANISTAN

WE were not in Afghanistan yet, and all of us, I think, had an uneasy feeling that we might still be turned back. The frontier, doubtless, would bristle with guns, as befitted a bellicose country. Interminable questions would be asked; we should be under suspicion—possibly even under arrest. We should be detained while it was decided what to do with us.

In point of fact the Afghan frontier was so sleepy and unobtrusive that we whisked past it into Afghanistan without so much as observing its existence, and were only recalled by a shout. It was no more than a tumbledown farmyard, where peasants eyed us with amusement, donkeys wandered around, hens pecked amid the refuse of mud styes. There was no sign of officialdom, no one in uniform. But as we were sighted an awkward youth had evidently been sent off in a hurry to dress himself up as a soldier, that the place might wear a more martial aspect ("Go on. It's your turn. You're the youngest."); for he appeared in khaki a few minutes later, buttoning his leggings, while the others tugged at his tunic to get it straight, like nannies dressing a child for a fancy-dress party. Thereafter he stood firmly at attention, attempting to twirl an adolescent moustache and regarding his rifle with suspicious curiosity.

Presently we were invited to take tea with the chief in his sanctum. We were ushered into a clean, whitewashed room, with Persian carpets on the floor and a table laid with bonbons and Russian cigarettes. We shook hands ceremoniously with our host, who was in white robes. He motioned to us to sit down while a noiseless servant poured out sweet green tea in little glasses. For half an hour he and the Colonel exchanged civilities. He welcomed us to Afghanistan. He

Above: Minarets of the Musalla, Herat *Below:* An Afghan dawn at Farah

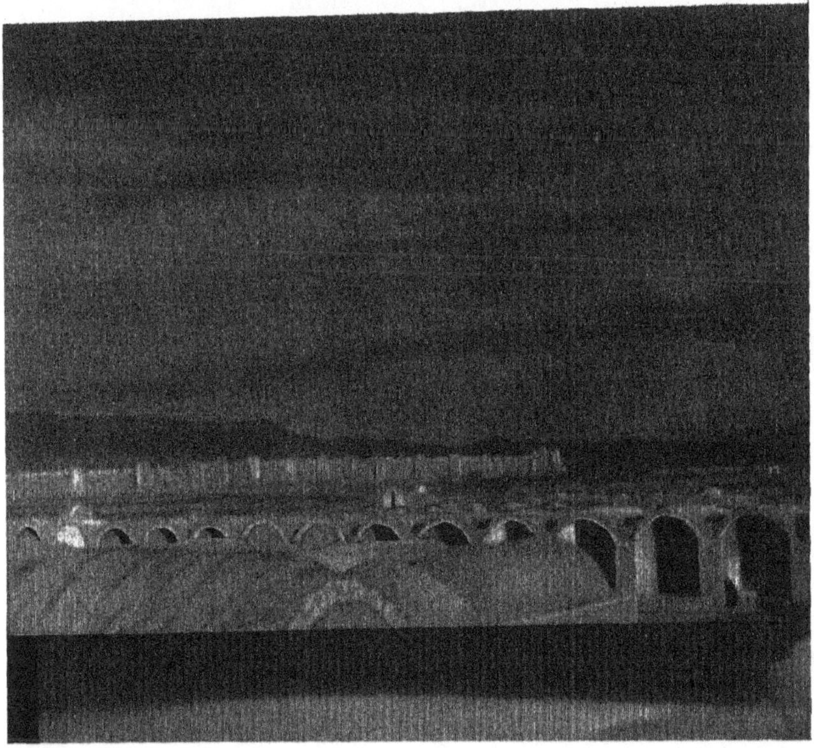

In the Afghan Desert
Above: Ourselves   *Below:* Soldiery

would telephone, he said, to the Governor of Herat to warn him of our arrival, so that every comfort might await us. He was interested to hear that we had come from London. We were the first people ever to motor from England to Afghanistan.

In Afghanistan, evidently, a visitor was an honoured guest, where in more civilized countries he is an interloper admitted only on sufferance. There were no tiresome questions, no examination of our luggage, hardly a mention of passports, which were unobtrusively collected, stamped off stage, politely returned, and the Customs chief wished us bon voyage. Frontiers must have had some of this courtesy in the eighteenth century, before the days of passports, when the world was a freer, though admittedly not a safer place than it is to-day.

The Customs staff posed delightedly for their photographs and the toy soldier came proudly to attention. We waved them good-bye, and set off into the unknown.

Somehow I had expected great ranges of mountains and a suspicious, hostile race. But here was gentle yellow prairie, inhabited by herons and wild-geese and a jolly, pastoral people. They turned to look at us and smiled and waved as we passed. The children ran down to the cars, shouting, and scampered back again. The dogs, big creatures like St. Bernards, raced us. The villages, for the most part, stood a mile or two off the road, but we passed large encampments of black tents, and the men in white, and women often in crimson, showed up attractively against the black. The men wore fine big turbans, long, kilted, white tunics, wide baggy trousers, sandals which curled at the toes, coats of quilted cotton or silk. Many had yellow pushtins or coats lined with sheepskin, such as we had seen in Persia, and cloaks of thick woven camel hair so stiff that they could have stood up by themselves. The sleeves of these garments have been so long disused that they are now a mere convention, too narrow to take an arm, flapping absurdly behind or sticking out at right angles like the horns of an animal. But in addition there were a good many European jackets, overcoats and waistcoats of dark cloth.

The Afghan is exceedingly handsome: dark, usually bearded, rarely clean-shaven, often long-haired, with clean white teeth when he smiles. But when he does not smile he looks fierce and proud, with his high cheekbones and concentrated, narrow eyes. He has none of the urbanity of the Persian, nor his intelligence: it is a race of rustics with an agreeable humour but a noble demeanour and a ruthless fighting spirit when roused.

Among them were a number of Chinese types, for a large Mongolian tribe has made its home in the northern part of Afghanistan.

We came into the valley of the Hari Rud and suddenly seven gigantic columns like factory chimneys shot up before us into the darkness. They were the minarets of Herat.

A myrmidon of the Governor received us.

"Did they not tell you at Kuhsan not to come?" he asked cryptically.

"No. Why?"

But his answer was evasive. He escorted us to a guest-house, whose proprietor was in a state of great embarrassment. The place, he said, was not yet built. But we assured him that we had no objection to sleeping among bricks and mortar; the absence of doors and yawning gaps for windows did not worry us.

In a sort of restaurant below we dined to the strains of a His Master's Voice gramophone playing English records of Indian music. Afghans sat mute, regarding us curiously. One draped a black veil across his face like a stage villain trying to look sinister. The dinner was delicious: two kinds of rice with a variety of meats and a sweet cranberry jam. Mrs. Christmas refused to eat anything.

"You're lucky," she said. "You've no imagination. I have."

Mrs. Mock came into her own in Herat. At last the natives understood her Hindustani. Incidentally, a remarkable metamorphosis was occurring in Mrs. Mock. From being supposedly delicate and helpless she now worked like a Trojan, her strength was untiring, she remained invariably cheerful and of the female members of the expedition she alone never complained of discomfort. At the beginning of the trip Mrs. Mock had had various fads. She could never, for instance, eat eggs. To-day at lunch, Mrs. Mock was heard to exclaim: "What? I can't have more than three eggs? But I'm ravenous."

I strolled into the street after dinner, but it was picketed at either end. Perhaps we were under arrest. The attitude of the Governor's myrmidon had been curious. We had a guilty feeling that we had no business to be here; that we were somehow in disgrace, like truant schoolboys, and would be sent back in the morning. It occurred to the Colonel that the Legation at Kabul might have wired to stop us. It would be galling if we had to return to Persia like stowaways, our tails between our legs.

But at least we should have spent one night on Afghan soil.

Our fears were unfounded: the Governor put no obstacles in our way: we could proceed.

We had time to see something of Herat. The city was the Aria of the ancients, a cradle of the Aryan race in Asia. But none of its monuments are pre-Moslem. First and foremost there is the Musalla, whose minarets we had passed in the night. The Musalla contained a great college of the fifteenth century, and must have been one of the most prodigious groups of buildings in the world until, to our shame be it spoken, it was destroyed by the British in 1886. But the seven minarets of sand-coloured brick, each over a hundred feet high, are still visible for miles around, their tiles gleaming blue and green in the sunshine. In the centre are the remains of a small tomb, with a perfect, fluted dome of turquoise. But that is all. In between, where buildings of a size proportionate to the pillars must once have stood, peasants now cultivate the earth.

In the centre of Herat the impregnable bastions of the ark or citadel rise from a stagnant moat, while the outside walls of the city are immense in proportion, as befits a fortified place. Around the citadel are shops, full of grapes and pomegranates and melons, and the covered bazaars lead out of a square by its entrance. They run for miles and far exceed in beauty any I saw. The old brickwork, still intact, provides specimens of lovely vaulting and decoration. Here and there, down a few steps, you come upon deep green pools beneath vaulted brick archways, like flooded crypts. The light is even more astonishing than at Khadimain, for instead of shooting transversally across the shadow it pours through the roof, straight as rain: thin perpendicular shafts of white falling on a procession of white-robed figures. There is little colour, since the Afghan rarely introduces it into his costume, and this, together with an effect of muffled stillness, as in a cathedral, creates the impression of a beautiful silent film—but with subtler and more varied tones of black and grey and white and silver than the camera could ever produce. There is so little trace of Europeanism in costume, traffic or merchandise that you get an impression of what all Asia must have been like before the West began to penetrate its barriers. It is true that modern streets are building in Herat, but through the wisdom of the late King these stand quite apart from the old, which they supplement but do not replace.

There was an absence of antiques in the bazaars, which do no more than administer to the needs of a peasant people. At the most there were stalls of cheap white silver jewellery, large and triangular, and in a central square rows of bright-coloured embroidered waistcoats not unlike those of Spanish bullfighters, which Afghans wear on special occasions, together with little round hats, large enough only to cover the crown, serving as a base on which to wind their enormous turbans. Beyond was a quarter where, in place of various herbs and nuts, were various kinds of shot, slugs, bullets and cartridges, set out in trays. The stalls bristled with guns and rifles. It was not a place to linger in. The Persian has been disarmed by law, but in Afghanistan almost every peasant in the remoter districts, and even in the bazaars, carries a rifle slung over his shoulder for protection. It would be curious to see the British peasantry similarly armed on market day.

In Herat, remote as it is, we found a garage-mechanic who knew all about the insides of Rolls-Royces. Oriental monarchs have a preference for the Rolls, and discarded chauffeurs of King Feisal and the Shah throng the garages of Persia and Iraq. Now it was an ex-chauffeur of Amanullah's who ministered to our needs. He warned us that between Herat and Kandahar we would be unable to get petrol, so we must carry enough for three hundred miles. This made us again as congested as we had been on the stretch from Damascus to Baghdad; so in the circumstances it was impossible to take Robert on with us. We left him to the mercies of three Indians who were bicycling round the world. They were taking ten years over the trip, had left Bombay six months ago, and expected to be in London the year after next. But they were looking well ahead, and

Afghans

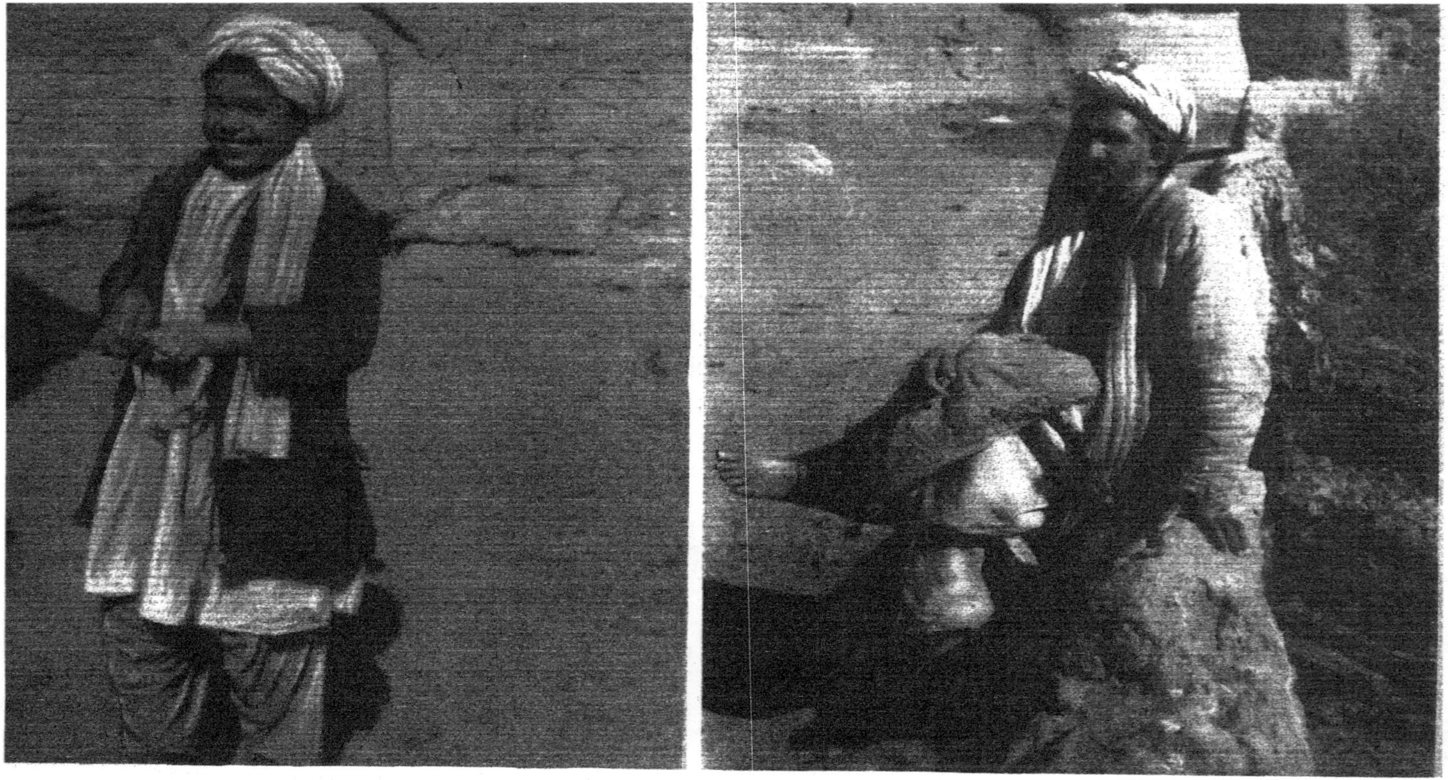

Afghans

asked us if we could give them English money in exchange for Afghan. In the Welsh accents typical of the educated Indian they pestered us, not with questions, but with information. They brought out notebooks, made us do the same, dictated to us tables of money values, "useful phrases", and details of roads and distances from everywhere to everywhere between Herat and Bombay.

It was a feature of the expedition that we never learnt our lesson. Whenever we drove at night we invariably either lost the way or encountered some other disaster, we invariably vowed that we would never again drive at night, and we invariably continued to do so. It would now have been more sensible to wait where we were until morning and start with the dawn (just as on our journey from Meshed two days earlier). But somehow we never seemed able to get off within two hours of the time arranged, and dawn, for us, was in the neighbourhood of nine o'clock. So off we set from Herat with an hour of daylight to go and eighty miles of unknown and, to all intents and purposes, non-existent roads to cover, to say nothing of possible danger from the inhabitants in the dark. The tracks were bad and the jolts terrible. No one can imagine what a jolt can mean until he has travelled through Afghanistan in a car with a dicky spring. I was dozing, relaxed, in the back of the Dowager when there was a tremendous jerk, accompanied by a sound of breaking glass, and I was flung two or three times with a crack against the roof. The sensation of impotence was terrifying: I was hurled up and down as in a cocktail-shaker, and subsided with a bump upon my elbow, which must surely be dislocated. I felt sick and faint and presently I began to shiver, as though I had caught a chill. With chattering teeth I lay enveloped in rugs and coats for the rest of the journey, exhausted, but afraid to sleep for fear of being caught unawares by another bump. Remembering the reports of motor accidents in the newspapers, I supposed, vaguely, that I was what is called "suffering from shock". It was certainly an unpleasant sensation.

We were all thankful to reach Adraskand, the village fort where we were to spend the night. The villagers took us in the darkness to two small upper rooms with walls of mud. Despite the constricted space, the entire population crowded in after us, discharging what they took to be the obligations of hospitality by watching us eat. In the middle sat the head man, portly as a stage eunuch. The rest stood or squatted round the walls, the whites of their eyes shining in the sinister half-light, as we ate the pilau and partridges provided. We were guests, and were not permitted to pay a penny for our night's food and lodging.

Next morning we had not been going an hour when one of the Dowager's rear wheels went straight through a bridge, leaving her with a perilous list to starboard and the other wheel splayed on its side. It was the end. Here we would be all day; perhaps several days. We hooted furiously at the Grey, in front, but she did not hear us. Finally she stopped, but did not return. It seemed that she too had met with a mishap. It was grotesque.

We examined the damage. It was the same sort of bridge as had entrapped the Dowager three nights ago: a humped affair of mud and branches, over a ditch. But since so much of it had fallen right away beneath her weight there was no support for the jack. Mr. Waters, Quinney, Manfred and Miss Gumbleton produced various suggestions, but the problem of extrication seemed insoluble without planks and crowbars to lever up the car, an army of men, and horses or camels to drag her out. We had none of these things, and the nearest village was some miles away.

I walked ahead to tell the Colonel what had happened and found that the Grey had indeed stuck, in a ditch, but not seriously. Christmas went back to cope with the Dowager, leaving me to guard the women and the money-bags from a handful of peasants whose intentions might be hostile—but clearly were not. For an hour we sat there. The Afghans stood round, surveying us with amiable curiosity.

"Niffy, aren't they?" said Mrs. Mock.

But I did not think that they were.

They were keen to be photographed and posed, smiling. But as I lifted the camera to my eye one of them rose abruptly and motioned it away: a sudden loss of nerve, due, perhaps, to fear of the Evil Eye.

It was a pleasant spot to be wrecked in: a wide, irrigated plain, smeared with tamarisks, bounded by distant hills. I felt that I would not mind remaining here for a day or two: it would be a chance to see something of the country. But Mrs. Christmas hoped otherwise and referred again to the urgency of "stepping on the gas".

Her hopes were realized. Christmas returned with the astonishing news that the Dowager was already out. The Afghans had made light of the accident. A dozen of them, who had sprung up from nowhere as peasants do, seized the heavy Rolls by every projecting portion of her anatomy, and with a single heave lifted her back on to the road as if she were a perambulator. The Dowager, in fact, was so taken aback by her sudden release that she bolted crazily down the opposite slope of the bridge and careered along by herself for a distance of some thirty yards until Mr. Waters overtook her and applied the brake. We were lost in admiration of Afghan strength.

Nevertheless we approached bridges in future with the greatest circumspection, and since these bridges occurred every few miles our progress was necessarily slow. Invariably the Dowager struck the hump with a sickening scrape of her undercarriage, and sometimes she again stuck fast. Once we encountered a bridge which was palpably inadequate to our weight, so we spent an hour building it up with tombstones from a neighbouring Mohammedan cemetery, looking guiltily around us for fear of caravans to detect our sacrilege. But as it was we left a trail of broken bridges sufficient to embarrass any motor traffic which might wish to follow us.

Though we could see a bridge in good time it was not so easy with the bumps and clefts in the track, which would come upon us suddenly, before Manfred had time to slow down. In this respect I had lost my nerve completely since last night's shaking. All day long I clung to the side of the car, straining every nerve on the road, tautening every muscle in preparation for a jolt, hardly aware of the mountain scenery around us. We had heard that Afghanistan was a dangerous country. In my experience it affords the traveller a perpetual risk of being knocked insensible, not by hostile natives, but against the roof of his own car.

We reached the Farah River at sunset : a red Turneresque sunset above a gleaming strand of magnesium and opal, with a stylized mountain outlined in the background. Just ahead were the walls of Farah, great grey battlements like Carcassonne, which looked to be built of solid stone, but when we came near dissolved themselves into mud. Every Afghan town has these forts and ramparts, more or less intact, for the country is kept permanently fortified. But they are most impressive from a distance: at close quarters they look less like medieval fortresses than the giant sand-castles of a child.

An inviting room, with a colonnade giving on to a huge farmyard, had been prepared for us at Farah, where they had been warned by telephone of our arrival. Special carpets were being spread on the ground and curtains nailed to the windows. The commanding officer of the district, with another official, paid a ceremonious call and sat with us, bored and silent, for an hour. We had a meal of rice and pomegranates, and lay down to sleep on the carpets.

Next day was a bad day. We had continual punctures, and, besides trouble with bridges, started running into soft sand. The Dowager stuck hopelessly, with the Grey a mile ahead. We slaved away for three-quarters of an hour with a spade whose handle came off at every attempt to dig. We lay flat on our faces and burrowed sand from under the wheels like rabbits. Ahead was a worse morass of soft sand, so the only thing to do was to get the car out backwards. Just as we had got her ready to come out the Grey arrived back, and we waited a moment for some felt to put under the wheels.

Christmas said, "Felt? You don't want felt! Where's the jack? We'll get her out forwards."

After some discussion we put felt under the wheels and got the Dowager out, backwards, with little difficulty.

"What you want to do on these occasions," said Christmas, "is to dig out and then put felt under the wheels."

The cars were beginning to look very battered by this time. One door of the Dowager refused to open at all, since her encounter with the bridge, so that we had to climb in and out by the window.

To our relief the sand gave place to gravel. The mountain ridges on the skyline were serrated like a Yale key. Long caravans straggled across the plain, jingling with harness: camels, donkeys, mules and pack-horses, sometimes with huge packing-cases slung across their backs. Mounted soldiers passed us from time to time, indicating that the country was well patrolled. We lunched by a river, among tamarisk bushes, and enjoyed our first decent wash since leaving Meshed. These rivers are a feature of Afghan scenery. There are five of them to cross between Herat and Kandahar. In the winter they are often impassable through floods for weeks at a time, and traffic is at a standstill, for none of them is bridged. But except for the Helmand, which we would have to cross by ferry on the following day, we forded them all without difficulty. Persia has no rivers of any size, and it was a new joy, in this barren land, to stop at midday by a wide, flowing stream, bathe, and sleep for an hour after luncheon. But the surrounding country is hardly irrigated at all. There are no wide cultivated valleys, such as you might expect from streams of this size : just the river, encountered suddenly in the middle of desert, with perhaps a thread of rough trees ; no more.

That night we reached Girishk. A castle towered above the rest-house, water rippled, trees were motionless in the moonlight, colonnades shone white. By night these places were noble and calm and spacious. But in the light of morning they dwindled to half their size, the castle was built of mud, streams became stagnant ditches covered with scum, dust enveloped the landscape.

Each night a procession of sick creatures heard of the foreigners' arrival and came to us for medicines. So Mr. Waters was forced to remember his profession. It was perhaps fortunate that we had him. A friend of mine was travelling once in a remote part of Persia when two villagers asked him for medicine for their sick children. He had nothing with him but some Dover's Powders, and gave one to each. In the night he heard wailings and gnashings of teeth, and next day his guide told him that the two children had died. Some time later he told the story to a doctor.

"What did you say you gave them ?"

"Dover's Powders."

"Then you killed them. Dover's Powders in that quantity contain enough opium to kill any young child."

Next morning we had the Helmand to cross. All that was provided in the way of a ferry-boat was a sort of rickety Viking coracle, an enlarged canoe which tapered to a point at either end, its deck composed of a few loose branches. Because of the elegant points it was impossible to drive the car on endwise. Equally it could not go across the boat because it was too narrow. The cars had therefore to make a diagonal approach, and an abrupt turn when half-way on. There was no such thing as a plank to assist this operation : simply a couple of inadequate stretchers, made of branches.

Confronted in Europe with such a problem one would have seen at once that the thing was impossible and gone some other way round. But in Afghanistan there are no other ways round, and besides our standards of what was and was not possible had undergone a change since our arrival in Asia. Provided we were not in a hurry, the manœuvre presented no sort of difficulty to the Afghans, who treated our arrival as a welcome and comic diversion. They produced some odd bits of firewood with which to supplement the stretchers, hurriedly forcing them under the wheels when they threatened to be suspended above a void. They heaved, they pushed, they lifted, they levered. The deck collapsed and had to be reconstructed with branches. They chattered without ceasing, fought, argued, cackled with laughter, bandied a hundred pieces of conflicting advice from one side of the river to the other. The obstinate Dowager wedged herself half on the boat and half on land and for half an hour would move neither forward nor back. But with a last gigantic heave she was lifted on to the branches, amid cheers. To get each car off at the other side took just as long and, one way and another, the whole proceedings occupied exactly four hours.

Without the co-operation of a mass of volunteers we would never have got across the Helmand at all. But we were accustomed, by now, to geniality and a helping hand among these people of hostile reputation. The truth is that the Afghan is becoming slowly civilized. He no longer mistrusts nor will ever molest the individual foreigner who, for the first time since the Afghan Wars, can now travel securely through the country. You can motor through Afghanistan as you might through Scotland, and this is a great step forward. Of any sign of organized foreign influence, on the other hand, he is still suspicious. This is natural. The Afghan is race-proud. On every hand he sees his neighbours in foreign bondage, and determines to avoid their fate. With the aid of foreign capital the land could be irrigated and its great mineral resources developed to his profit. But this, for the present, is not to be. It is hard for foreigners to obtain concessions of any kind. Afghanistan remains, substantially, a desert.

Meanwhile development on other lines proceeds. Nadir Khan was a great man, and his assassination was a tragedy. (His murderer was being tortured with boiling oil as we passed through the country, and was finally bayoneted to death; but not before he had implicated all his associates.) Nadir Khan began to do gradually what Amanullah had attempted to do in too much of a hurry. Education is making strides with the aid of Indian or German, but preferably native teachers educated in India. Roads and bridges are slowly taking shape. Outside Kandahar a bridge across the Arghandab was already half completed by means of native labour, and its engineer is an Indian-trained Afghan. There is no reason why, if development continues on the same lines, this road should not in a few years' time be the main overland route to India; for the present route, by Birjand, Duzdab and Baluchistan, is circuitous and bad. In any case, whatever the shifting conditions on the North-West Frontier we found the interior of Afghanistan to be entirely peaceable. At such a time a certain element of unrest would have caused no surprise. But deputations from all the tribes were proceeding to Kabul to swear allegiance to the new King. Nadir Khan won the loyalty of his people to the monarchy and no breath of sympathetic revolt followed his assassination. The traditional conception of Afghanistan as a lawless and bloodthirsty land is to-day a myth.

We crossed the battlefield of Maiwand, where General Burrows met his crushing defeat against enormous odds in the second Afghan War. We forded the Arghandab River and came into the orchards of Kandahar, which provide India with fruit. The sunset washed the trees with gold, and dark cypresses stood sentinel. There were prosperous villages and in the brighter costumes of the native women signs of India. Ahead a stylized pink mountain of striking shape stood up lonely and irrelevant from the sandy plain. It was the Baba Wali Kotal Ridge, whence Lord Roberts drove the armies of Ayub Khan at the culmination of his famous march from Kabul. Presently we passed through the magnificent fortified walls of Kandahar, thirty feet high, through bazaars which were open avenues of plane-trees, into a square with a formal pond, cypresses and whitewashed, colonnaded buildings.

The British Vice-Consul, an Indian, courteously offered to put us up. We admired his chrysanthemums, drank his Lipton's tea, and revelled in our first hot bath since Teheran. He was surprised at our arriving so soon, and indeed three hundred miles in three days represented good going over Afghan roads.

Between us we occupied most of the Consulate. Quinney, Manfred, Waters and I slept amid files and bottles of Stephens' Inks and O.H.M.S. stationery. The Consular official whose office it was found us there in the morning. He was a tall, lugubrious Indian with a grey moustache, enveloped in a greatcoat. He had just had a bad attack of malaria.

"Kandahar is a terrible place for malaria," he said. "This is the worst building for malaria in Kandahar. This room is the most malarial room I have ever known."

We hastened to dress. The man continued his litany. His pessimism was Russian in its intensity

"Afghanistan is a terrible country. I have been in many countries, but this is the most terrible country I ever was in. There is no social life, no culture, nothing. I yearn for culture. My room is no better than a stable. When my servant cooks my food I choke with the smoke. Fifty or sixty sparrows they have their nests in my ceiling. The ceiling it drops on me while I sleep. It is a terrible country. You are cultured men. I hope you may not go away from here at once, so that you give us the joys of social intercourse."

Whether or not this boon would be granted him rested, for the moment, in doubt. The Vice-Consul had been instructed by telegram from Kabul that we were to communicate with the British Minister on arrival and that probably we would be allowed to proceed by that route. But to get an answer from Kabul would take time; Mrs. Christmas was anxious about her boat; Christmas was very much tempted by the proximity of the Indian frontier, seventy-five miles away at Chaman, in the direction of Quetta, and was inclined to cut out Kabul.

The Consul thought it probable that we should be instructed to take a guard if we went by Kabul. This would be a nuisance. The guard would be slower than we were, and we should be continually delayed. His own experience of guards was that he invariably reached his destination many hours ahead of them. The Colonel's experience of guards was no more reassuring. Once he had been ordered to take an escort for a journey from Bushire to Bander Abbas, in Persia, because of bandit hordes in the mountains. They

Above: Afghan Village   *Below:* Fort at Girishk

Half-way through an Afghan bridge

met the bandits, who said they would be delighted to let the Colonel pass, but in no circumstances could they permit his guard to do so. He had to return ; otherwise it would be said that the British Government was in league with the bandits.

I discovered a Polish diplomat who was on the point of leaving in his car for Kabul and suggested accompanying him. But since Christmas was responsible for me as a member of his expedition he could not let me go without permission from the British Minister.

The Pole was a comic young man in horn-rimmed spectacles and a city suit who said he was an Orientalist and made a great many polite speeches in French. We had heard of him in Meshed, for he had left twenty-four hours before Robert's arrival, much to the latter's mortification, as he had been looking for a companion. His chauffeur had deserted him and he had had appalling adventures with his car, beside which our own mishaps were trifles, taking a week to get from Herat to Kandahar. Apropos our expedition he expressed admiration for the courage and hardihood of Englishwomen.

"I have observed it already with your compatriotes," he said. "I meet an Australian young girl at party in Paris. I invite her accompany me on excursion to Rambouillet le lendemain, and French friends also. She go to bed very late, you understand, ayant fait la bombe. She have no more than six hours' sleep. But at nine o'clock in the morning la voilà at the rendezvous, though it is bitter cold autumn. But my French friends they do not come. They still sleep. The Englishwoman is strong and courageous."

It was the weather which finally decided our plans. The atmosphere was charged with grey clouds and a feeling of thunder, and Christmas feared that the rains were coming before their time. In this case, within thirty-six hours the rivers on the road to Kabul would be impassable and we might be held up for days, even weeks, either in Kandahar or at some small village. On the other hand the road to Chaman, bad enough at the best of times, would be a morass of liquid mud if it rained. Our only chance, since we could not afford the time to wait, was to try to make Chaman that night, before the rain broke.

It was asking for trouble to start as late as four-thirty,

when it was already dusk, over one of the worst bits of road in Asia. But there seemed to be no reasonable alternative. At first our luck held. The thunderclouds menaced but did not break. But after an hour the trouble began. Simultaneously the lights of the Dowager gave out and the Colonel ditched the Grey. Our mad start had gained us nothing. We might just as well have spent the night in Kandahar and possibly received our permission to go by Kabul next-morning. It was the more enraging since the rain seemed to be a false alarm and we could have reached Kabul after all. The Grey took over an hour to extricate. There happened to be a heap of stones, for building the new road, just by the wayside, or it would have taken a great deal longer. The Dowager's lights were irreparable, since the batteries were smashed. But the moon rose, to facilitate our driving without lamps, and we decided to go on. By eleven o'clock the lights of Chaman were in sight. Things were not so bad after all; we should be in India by midnight; the journey was almost over.

But in reality it had only just begun. Those lights must have been fifteen miles away. We took five hours to reach them. Our first inkling of what was in store came to us when the Dowager stuck firm in soft sand. Then we realized that a battlefield of deep, sandy ruts stretched unbroken between us and India. It took us two hours to get out of our first rut. To make matters more difficult there was water in it. First we had to drain the water off. Then dry earth had to be put under the wheels to give them a grip. Quinney, kneeling in mud, slaved away at the recalcitrant jack which had become his special preserve. Waters and Manfred took turns. The Colonel prostrated himself beneath the car, clearing away with his hands. Mrs. Mock dug. Mrs. Christmas dug. Miss Gumbleton sat patiently in the car, more like a tea-cosy than ever. I stood about, endeavouring to look efficient, and collected earth; but, through incompetence rather than laziness, I am singularly useless on such occasions. I cannot make the jack work. My spade comes to pieces in my hand. I put felt in the wrong place. Three times the Dowager was jacked up; three times dry earth was put under her wheels; three times we strained every muscle to push; three times she moved an inch, and the operation had to start all over again. But the fourth time we got her out.

Thenceforward we moved no more than a few yards at a time, sometimes lurching across the ruts in the vain hope of finding a smoother track to left or right, sometimes swaying through them at an alarming angle and feverish speed lest we should stick. We would come upon a bit of hard ground and would sigh with relief, believing the worst over. But back came the ruts, relentless. The moon had disappeared, so we proceeded in almost total darkness, with only the rear-light of the car in front to guide us. Mr. Waters led the way, dancing in front of the Grey's headlights, directing us now left, now right, a wiry, agile silhouette executing the strangest ballet with lightning side-steps to avoid being run over, frequently finding himself left behind because we did not dare to stop. Each time one of us did stop there was a sickening moment of apprehension. Had we stuck ? There would be fearful difficulties in starting again because the Dowager's self-starter had gone with the batteries, and the handle would have to be swung for perhaps twenty minutes before the engine responded. She had other trouble : the battery-box must be seen to ; the exhaust pipe started trailing on the ground, had to be tied up and finally wrenched off altogether. All the time the lights of India twinkled just ahead, to tantalize us.

There comes a psychological moment in all such adventures when a tiresome bore turns suddenly to sheer nightmare. I had been contemplating the lights with exasperation. I looked at them again ; the moment had come ; something snapped, exasperation became despair. The nuisance of getting to bed rather late became the probability of never getting to bed at all. It was like a scene from Dante's *Purgatorio*. The ruts in our outer darkness yawned like horrible canyons, in face of which we were infinitely cumbersome and helpless. The lights of India mocked us like fiends. Derelict fruit lorries which had given up the unequal struggle and succumbed to the sand loomed like solitary ghosts in the night to haunt us. If they, practised hands, had failed to get across why should we, mere amateurs with wholly unsuitable craft, succeed ?

But somehow or other—I shall never know how—we did. A crazy yokel of a sentry, dazed by our headlamps, barred the way. Terrified out of his wits, he jabbered loudly. Other men appeared. Then came the culminating blow. No one might pass the frontier after midnight and it was now after four. For half an hour Christmas wrangled, while most of us dropped off asleep in the final stages of exhaustion. The soldiers were loud and adamant. Nothing would move them : it was the law. Nor was there any place for us to sleep ; we must stay where we were, in our cars, till the dawn ; or go back. Finally they agreed to haul the chief out of bed, and the chief, after some wheedling, gave in. He invited us to drink tea with him : our Afghan adventure was to end, as it had begun, with a tea-party. Those of us who were still awake slouched into his bedroom and subsided on the bed or the floor. The chief sat on a mat, shock-headed, bloodshot, polite in a mauve-striped flannel nightshirt. He sent for his hubble-bubble and seemed to feel better. Tea came. Half dazed with sleep, we drank it.

Suddenly there dawned on me the full realization that we were about to enter India. Unthinkingly we had pursued this goal through a nightmare of ruts : thankfully we had reached it. But, gracious heavens, what had we done ? As I contemplated the ludicrous figure of the nightshirted Customs chief squatting on his mat, rubbing his bloodshot eyes, sucking at his hubble-bubble, I was overwhelmed with a desire to remain in this crazy land. In a few minutes we would be in a dull, British country where things were neat and ordered and respectable. There would be roads and bungalows and Colonels and newspapers, and tea-parties of a very different nature. An awful home-coming yawned ahead of us : a home-coming with none of the compensating warmth of welcome, without even the comforts of home. That shock-headed figure epitomized Central Asia in all its mad haphazardness. I was stung with nostalgia for Afghanistan, Persia, the wild, romantic countries which were now on the point of escaping from our grasp. For two pins I would have gone straight back again over the inferno of ruts, straight back to the rains which must by now have broken over Kandahar.

But it was not to be. Our passports were handed back. To India we must go. The lights of Chaman had gone now, for it was morning. Two very English ladies in red fox furs, stumping off to early service (for it was an English Sunday), stopped to regard our battered Rolls-Royces with astonished disapproval. From the Khojak Pass we took a last look back on Afghanistan. It can never have looked more romantic or unreal. Its crags, planted on the flat desert like scenery on a stage, were taking an early-morning douche of mist. The clouds dappled the pink sand with their shadows. We topped the pass and looked ahead upon a new and beige-coloured hemisphere.

We had got these cars to India.

PART TWO
Further East

Chapter I

INDIA

QUETTA is the Aldershot of Asia, but a relatively inoffensive town. It is spacious, with long, wide boulevards of trees. There is not too military an atmosphere about the streets, for the Army is housed in ample barracks and bungalows of its own.

All the way across Asia Mrs. Mock and Mrs. Christmas had been preparing us for the superior comfort of India. "Just wait till you get to India," they had said. "You've no idea how comfortable it is: bathroom to every bedroom, real English food again, servants to do everything for you. It'll be nice to get to India." So it was with relief, after four weeks of what is known as "roughing it" (roughing what ?) that I anticipated the luxuries of Quetta. There is something to be said for the British Raj, I thought, when it comes to the amenities of civilized life.

We drove to a single-storeyed building labelled *Dak Bungalow*.

"Why Dak ?" I asked.

"Dawk," they corrected.

"Why Dawk ?"

"Because in India you always stay in Dawk Bungalows."

It was, I gathered, the apology for a hotel in all but the larger Indian towns.

In my bedroom was a fireplace and an armchair covered in faded cretonne. There was a bed, with spring mattress complete; but it appeared that I must still desecrate it with my moth-eaten sleeping-bag and Army blanket: bedclothes are not provided in India. Behind an inner door was a circular tin tub on a strip of duckboarding, a washstand and basin, a commode, and another door into a kind of yard.

"Marvellous having one's own bathroom," they said.

"Marvellous."

"Shout 'Qua-haie', if you want anything, and the boy will bring it you."

I shouted "Qua-haie"! Nothing happened. I shouted it again. A brown, bony old gentleman, clad in a loincloth, hobbled in. Evidently the boy.

"Bath," I said to the boy.

"Sahib ?"

"*Bath.*"

The boy cringed, salaamed, disappeared.

Presently he brought me a cup of tea.

I took him into the bathroom, indicated the tin tub, my sponge, myself, and made a motion as of throwing water over my shoulder.

"Bath," I said.

He went away.

Twenty minutes later another boy (quite a young boy, this time, not a day over forty) covered the bottom of the tub with a small bucket of boiling water, cringed, salaamed, disappeared. From another bucket I poured in cold. Too much cold. I splashed about in three inches of tepid water.

A whisky-and-soda was welcome. Dinner was announced. In a room decorated with a great many brass and silver ornaments, with Victorian engravings of Indian scenes in enormous frames on the walls, we ate soup (from a tin), fish (from goodness knows where, since we were six hundred miles from the sea), two courses of meat (one tinned, one frozen), tipsy cake, cheese and dessert (from a tin).

"Marvellous," they said, "to have real English food again, after that Persian muck."

The Anglo-Indians, despite the complete absence of plumbing, bedclothes, fresh food and electric bells, staunchly maintain the fiction of India's comfort. "After all," they will say (and believe), "it's really much more comfortable to travel with your own sheets and blankets, and you don't need running water when you've got masses of servants to fetch and carry." And India, I suppose, *is* comfortable by Victorian standards.

Or by the standards of the public schools. The British Empire is being maintained (or otherwise) in the Spartan bathrooms of Wellington and Marlborough. Damn it all, at coll. you had to tub with a lot of other fellows, even though you *were* a pre. But out in India you have a tub all to yourself.

Too much plumbing makes a fellow soft. And what does a fellow want with electric bells? The prefect sahib can go on shouting "Boy!" just as he did at coll., and fairly give the little squirt hell if he doesn't hear.

The British Raj must always be vocal. There is a more agreeable sense of power in the vibrations of the larynx than in those of an electric wire.

You will be told that the introduction of up-to-date comforts would lead to unemployment among the wogs; and so, I suppose, it would. You will be told that anyway "servants cost nothing in this perishing country", so it's cheaper to live that way.

But enquire further and you find that even a bachelor living alone must have about fourteen servants before he can run his perishing bungalow at all. The wog who waits on you at table is not permitted by his religion to clean your boots, the wog who cleans your boots may not empty your bath, the wog who empties your bath may not groom your horse—I know not what all. Fourteen servants at an average of ten pounds a year each. So it all evens up. Except that you still have no plumbing. And no electric bells.

The coincidence, in this respect, of the Hindu caste system with that of the public schools encourages my private belief that the whole thing is a vast conspiracy. The Hindu religion has always been remarkable for the way in which it absorbed other faiths. Animism first, then Buddhism. And now the good old public school system, under which every Hindu boy may have something to do: one fag to sweep out the prefect sahib's study, one to fill his bath, one to clean his boots, and so forth. Division of labour as we knew it at Winchester. "Please, sahib, I'm not boot-fag, sahib, that's Gandhi minor, sahib, I'm bath fag, sahib." And the prefect sahib, fresh from coll., accepts without question so familiar a system, even to the extent, poor boob, of claiming the superiority of sweated to mechanical labour.

It was the day after our arrival at Quetta that I got the telegram for which I had hardly hoped.

Maharaja graciously consents best come immediately Carlton Hotel Lucknow where letter with detailed directions awaits you salaam O'Connor.

Before leaving London I had run across my friend Sir Frederick O'Connor, who was for many years British Envoy in Nepal. He too was on the point of leaving for India, though by a more orthodox route than our own. It was possible that he might be going up to Katmandu, the capital of Nepal, to be invested with a decoration by the Maharaja. If so he could ask for His Highness's permission to bring me with him. But since the plan was nebulous I had thought little more about it beyond wiring him news of my arrival in India.

And now this telegram had come. I was to visit Nepal, an honour afforded to few Europeans but an occasional official. I thanked my stars that the Kabul project had fallen through, otherwise I would have arrived in India too late to take advantage of this magnificent opportunity. I would catch the first train to Lucknow in the morning.

I said good-bye to the party with many regrets, for we had had a harmonious trip, and to the Colonel, in particular, I had become much attached. It would have been impossible to do such a journey in better company than his. Mrs. Christmas was off the following day, and would catch her bateau with ease. Mr. Waters had already gone; he was visiting a friend in Lahore. Manfred would join forces with Quinney until my return from Nepal, and in the meantime, with Mrs. Mock and Miss Gumbleton, they were proceeding to Peshawar with the Colonel. The performance of the Rolls engines had been magnificent, for they gave us no trouble at all from start to finish, and the tyres from Beyrouth, though six years old and not guaranteed, had done us proud.

Before I left I was advised to engage a servant. Processions of them came to be interviewed, some poor, some prosperous, some frank, some shifty. Each invoked the name of Allah to grant me eternal felicity if I would let him be my bearer, and produced well-thumbed testimonials of a glowing nature. I seemed to have fallen upon a storehouse of "treasures". But in the end I decided that I would not really require a bearer until my return from Nepal, and dismissed them all. I was not sorry. The obligation to assume the superiority of a sahib embarrassed me, and I find as a rule that I can best minister myself to my own comforts. (In point of fact, I did without a bearer the whole time I was in India—an unheard-of eccentricity which shocked my friends a good deal.)

So now I settled down to seventy-two consecutive hours in Indian trains, and found that their comforts, like those of India in general, are grossly exaggerated. It is true that the carriages are broader and longer than our own, but their cushions are of shabby and shiny black leather. On these you lay your bedding, for of course none is provided. The chief problem is that of the windows. Each window is in reality three: a glass window, a wooden shutter, and a shutter of gauze to keep out the mosquitoes. There are therefore eight different ways of arranging each window, and since there are usually eight windows to a carriage, a variety of permutations and combinations sufficient to keep you busy for an entire journey. I made every sort of experiment but never, during my whole experience of Indian trains, arrived at a satisfactory combination between the elements of light, temperature, cleanliness and freedom from vermin. In the end the problem resolved itself broadly into two alternatives. Either you shut all the windows and suffocated from heat, or else you opened them all and suffocated from dust. You have only to leave a window open for five minutes on an Indian train for everything in the carriage to be smothered in the dust of the landscape. You can trace an indecent drawing on the seat, like children do on the backs of dusty motor-cars, safe in the knowledge that ten minutes later it will be entirely obliterated.

Indian trains have no corridors. When you want a meal you get out at a station and walk along to the restaurant-car, where as often as not you find yourself imprisoned for two or three hours until the train stops again. When there is no dining-car you eat hurriedly and at great expense in a station restaurant. After a day and a half of these meals I preferred to starve. Course followed course, and each was more tasteless than the last. I longed for the native pilaus of Persia and Afghanistan. But in this Hindu country, with all its food taboos, you never get a native meal (and if you did it would be too strong for your European palate). Thus the food in India, except at the table of an enterprising housewife, is bad to a degree undreamt of by the critics of the English hotel. Naturally catering is difficult; but the chief fault of these horrible meals is their pretentiousness. Quality is sacrificed to quantity. Personally, as far as food is concerned, I am a one-dish man, and this is the general rule in countries which enjoy good eating. Whether it be a cut from the joint and two veg. in a chop-house, a plat du jour in a French restaurant, an Italian risotto, an Arab kouss-kouss, a Persian pilau or a Malayan curry, one staple dish, perfectly cooked, and plenty of it is a meal to satisfy the most fastidious gourmet. Since snobbery affects eating like everything else, it is a safe rule, in travelling, to avoid those hotels and restaurants which advertise a five- or six-course menu. In India, which is Victorian in a gastronomic as well as a sanitary sense, all of them do.

For the first few hours I shared a compartment with a bearded Spanish priest in a white cotton frock. (Mrs. Christmas, seeing me off, said, "Really, it's a bit thick being put in with a native.") He was a charming old gentleman who had learnt his English in Wigan and spoke of the beautiful city of Preston. No, he said, he had no desire to return to Spain since it would mean incarceration in a monastery, while here, with his flock of Anglo-Indians, he was free. He made no Hindu converts, he said, but sometimes he could enlist the poorer Mohammedans in his flock in return for food and clothes. He left me at Sibi, and for the rest of the journey I was alone. The scenery at first was mountainous, but extraordinarily colourless, and after a bit we descended into interminable desert plains, sometimes covered with scrub. The incessant mournful wail of the platform vendors at every station intensified the melancholy of the landscape. This dirge in a minor key, so different from the sprightly "Chokleets, cigarettes!" to which one is accustomed, seems to symbolize above all things the pessimism of India.

I fell to wondering about Nepal. Though its prospect thrilled me I knew very little about the country. I knew that it *was* a country, as independent a kingdom as Persia, China or Japan, though the general ignorance on this point is extraordinary and even the Gazetteer of India (to say nothing of atlases) describes it as an Indian native state. I knew that it was about the size of Portugal, difficult of access, in the Himalaya Mountains, boasting Everest itself, and marching with India on the south and Tibet on the north. I knew also that, unlike any country in the world, it could only be entered by special invitation from its ruler, and that in fact this invitation was an exceedingly rare honour. Even Lord Curzon himself never visited Nepal. As a student of Indian art he was anxious to do so, but no Viceroy of India has ever been invited to Katmandu during his term of office. The Maharaja said that he would esteem it an honour to entertain Lord Curzon as a distinguished statesman and scholar, but indicated that an invitation to the Viceroy was a precedent which he could not create.

I knew that Nepal was the country of the Gurkhas, whose magnificent army the Maharaja had placed voluntarily and unreservedly at our disposal on the outbreak of war, and that in recognition of this generous service a gift of a million rupees per year was voted to Nepal by Great Britain. Otherwise my ignorance of it was complete; and this was one of the rare occasions when ignorance *is* bliss. I could not have anticipated a journey's end more keenly. It is seldom that one visits a place with no preconceived impression of its character; but I should enter Nepal with a free and open mind, like an explorer entering a new country.

It has always been a favourite pastime of my imagination to toy with the idea of mysterious worlds well lost, of forgotten but flourishing civilizations hidden behind ranges of mountains. I knew moreover that the Himalayan range concealed age-old civilizations whose full secrets would never, perhaps, be laid bare. But remote countries prove, as a rule, to be appropriately uncivilized. An Erewhon is only likely to exist in practice through getting the best of both existing worlds, and Nepal, so it seemed from the map, had unique opportunities in this respect. Her geographical position is unique: she is so far and yet so near: sufficiently protected by her mountain bastions to withstand the covetous imperialism of her neighbours, yet near enough in point of distance to assimilate their experience. Thus I felt like Samuel Butler seeking his Erewhon, but with the certainty, not merely the possibility, of finding a vital civilization of some kind or another beyond the range.

At seven o'clock on the second evening I reached Lahore, whose station might have been Leeds, with red North-Western trains like those of the L.M.S. Here I changed on to the East Indian Railway, finding a coupé reserved for me on the Calcutta-Punjab Mail. (Its carriages, by contrast, were green and white.) Next day at midday I reached Lucknow, where a letter from O'Connor awaited me. He had gone on to Katmandu two days before, but had left me detailed directions how to follow him. The slowest railway in India took me up through the plains of Bihar, where the land at last was fertile. Half asleep I contemplated the smooth green landscape with its fields of mustard and thatched villages, and thought that it might have been England on a summer afternoon. But as I awoke and focused my attention I began to see startling things in my English landscape. That thrush had a turquoise tail, the sparrows twittering in the hedge were bright yellow, the starlings had scarlet throats, the swallows on the telegraph poles were twice life-size. Slowly other peculiar features crowded in upon my consciousness. It was like one of those puzzle pictures in which one is told to detect the mistakes: at first it seems faultless, then gradually one begins to notice one thing after another that is wrong; or like a dull landscape in a child's painting-book into which he has introduced a fantastic note here and there for his own pleasure. He has painted vivid scarlet flowers on the shrubs. Those grasses are bright mauve. A coconut palm shoots up above the ordinary woodland or a torn banana-tree among the bushes. A pink saree flashes across the road. The peasants in the fields are dark brown in white loincloths. Here a group of them is accompanied by a piebald horse which, out of sympathy, has adopted their brown-and-white colouring. The crops are lentils and sugar-cane and rice instead of oats and hay and turnips. There are Gandhis by the hundred, minding goats. Sometimes the houses, instead of thatch, have tiled roofs in the Provençal manner. The line crosses wide rivers with mud banks, all flowing towards the Ganges, and everywhere are cream-coloured oxen pulling wagons with great thick wheels.

For I could not tell how many hundreds of miles on either side the country spread flat and smooth and green, without so much as a hillock. In the evening the sun, instead of setting quietly, swelled to ten times its natural size and rolled along the horizon like a gigantic, red-hot disc; and even after it had consented to retire the landscape, seeming to generate light from within itself, got on just as well and just as green without it.

In the middle of the night I changed at Muzaffarpur and sat for two hours in an empty waiting-room. My train came in and I settled myself into an empty compartment. At the last minute a burly, red-faced Englishman arrived with a rush, having kept the train waiting. He kept it waiting again while his servant fetched him some tea, and complained loudly of the inefficiency of the line.

"The hell of a railway. Never starts on time."

"Where are you going?"

"The plug-hole of creation, two or three stations down the line—of all the lousy places—that's where you'll see me for the next five years—only Englishman there—three or four Dutchmen—they come for the sugar when Java closes down, but they don't do much good—can't speak the lingo—well, they've wired for me, and I'll damned well see they pay me my figure or this goddam railway'll see me again to-morrow——"

"Five years seems a long time to have to stay in a place like that."

He seemed surprised at my remark. "But the money's good—six hundred and fifty pounds a year all found, and I'll see I get it—they've done the asking—wire arrived yesterday—chucked the other job—caught the mail train straight away."

"Where have you come from?"

"Bareilly—that's a top-hole spot—stopped for a hand of poker at Patna—best fellahs in the world at Patna—nearly missed the goddam train—lousiest railway in India, never on time—Bareilly, that's the place—nearly snuffed it last year—burning the candle at both ends, that's the form—then the kid I'd been running after at the dances nursed me in hospital—she was a good kid—now for this joint, the plug-hole of creation it is—well I'll see I get an agreement out of them—wired for me, they did—take charge of the mill this morning at eight o'clock—well I'll wait about the station and stroll in there about half past eight—damned if I won't—they wired for me—look at all that cane—first-class cane—best mill in India, this—grow their own cane—that's their advantage—other mills crash because after a bumper year the natives won't bother to grow any cane next year so there isn't any goddam cane to be had—fellah who ran the last mill I was working in filled the machinery up with rotten oil—I knew the stuff was muck, wouldn't have put it into a motor-car—wasn't for me to say—I said to him, 'Why not let me have a sledge-hammer and smash the works up from this end—muck, that oil, smash the works up in a month—smash 'em up from this end', I said, 'doesn't matter which end you smash 'em up from'—bitched up his machinery he did, in six months—rotten oil, wouldn't have put it into a motor-car—know nothing, these fellahs—well, here I am—plug-hole of creation—so long, old man—interested to have met you—see you again some time—where's that bloody boy?"

Six weeks later the whole of this country was devastated by earthquake, and hardly a sugar-mill was left standing. I often wonder what happened to my companion. Perhaps he went back to Bareilly.

At Raxaul, exactly seventy-two hours after leaving Quetta, I was met by a Nepali overseer, who took me to the British Legation bungalow. Here I was to spend the night, proceeding by the morning train over the Nepal Government Railway. I bathed, lunched, and slept till five o'clock. The bungalow was cool and comfortable, in a garden of bright blue columbine and scarlet hibiscus. I browsed among the books left by generations of British Envoys to Katmandu: the Bible, Guy Boothby, a life of Gladstone, *Highways and Byways in Devon and Cornwall*, a map of Tokyo, *Much Ado About Nothing, Gas and Oil Engines Simply Explained*, an Arabic grammar, *Horses and Stables*, by Lieut.-Gen. Sir F. Fitzwygram, Bt., *Androcles and the Lion*, Mrs. Molesworth, Gibbon, Hichens, a Swedish grammar, *Electric Light for Country Houses*, a Russian grammar, Burke. Outside there were sultry smells in the moonlight and crickets chattered. The calm and solitude were welcome after three days and nights in a train and five and a half weeks' incessant motoring.

Chapter II

NEPAL

"HENCEFORWARD," said the overseer, "you are the guest of the Nepal Government. You will put your hand in your pocket for nothing until you leave Nepal." I was given my ticket and an Indian servant as interpreter. The train took us over a little bridge into Nepal.

We were still in the plains; the Himalayas, somewhere ahead, were hidden in mist. We stopped for an hour at Birganj where the native passports were examined. With pride I was shown the engines of the Nepal Government Railway, housed in a shed like animals in a cage, and thought, as I registered appropriate astonishment, of the occasion when the sons of the Emir of Katsina, who owns most of the camels in the West African desert, were taken to the London Zoo. The children, said the newspapers naïvely, gazed "in wide-eyed wonder" at the camels and giraffes. I hoped that my wonder was suitably wide-eyed.

After Birganj we began to climb through the Terai Jungle which fringes the southern frontier of Nepal from east to west. The Terai is the home of tigers, elephants, rhinoceros and every sort of big game; from the train it seemed as innocent as English woodland, on a taller scale.

At Amlekganj, twenty-five miles from the frontier, the railway comes to an end. Here a car was waiting to take me the next twenty-five miles to the bottom of the first pass. The road wound upwards alongside the white, dry bed of a river. Mounds and cones like gigantic anthills rose from the river-bed, and jungle trees clung precariously to their sides. Presently the mounds reached the dignity of mountains and necessitated a tunnel for the road. Everywhere were wayside shrines, smeared with yellow and orange pigment from the pollen of marigolds. An old man handed to my driver and servant a kind of hors d'œuvres plate with dishes of the dye, with which they daubed their foreheads. Suspension bridges took us across the river-bed, and as we mounted there was water in the streams. At one point the motionless figure of a man, dead or dying, lay on a litter with his feet towards the waters, a white flag beside him and a small boy on guard. We passed through mustard-fields to Bhimpedi, a thatched village, where the road ends.

Here a fat grey pony was waiting to take me up the first mountain. My servant-interpreter, a silly Indian with white teeth, wailed that there was no mount for him. Clearly he was a man of the plains. The poor creature had already stopped the car to be sick by the roadside, and as he had never walked up a hill in his life the prospect of the ascent, on foot, appalled him. But I am afraid that I was too exhilarated by the mountain air and by the Himalayan foliage glistening in the afternoon sun to be much concerned with his predicament. Here was none of the barrenness which one associates with mountain country, but rich vegetation and a silver green forest. The Himalayas, below the snow line, are very unmelancholy mountains. As I turned my pony towards that almost perpendicular slope I knew that India was behind me, once and for all, and that I was riding up into a new country.

It was still early afternoon when we reached the rest-house at Sisagarhi. Here I found a clean white room prepared for me, a fire burning in the grate, a meal on the table, a bed with mosquito curtains, and a welcoming note from O'Connor. Poached eggs were brought me for tea; I lay in an armchair and read and felt contented. My bath was brought, followed by an ample dinner. My silly servant came and sat by the fire while I read, and I wished he would go but did not wish to offend him. Every few moments he interrupted me, asking if there was anything I wanted. "I am here only to serve you," he said. His servility irritated me. Finally he asked leave to go to bed, and I was alone.

Next morning I was awakened by a telegram from O'Connor, saying that I must try to reach Katmandu before two o'clock and should start not later than six. It was now six-thirty, but I managed to get my cavalcade off by seven-fifteen. My suite consisted of a pony-boy, a small major-domo, fat-faced

Into Nepal

Above: Women Coolies in Nepal *Below:* Nepalese Children

and military, with a wispy moustache, two coolies to carry my luggage, and an etcetera from the Rest House who wisely did not accompany us further than the top of the pass. The silly servant returned to more accustomed levels. Before he went he hoped he had served me well, and reminded me of my "solemn promise" to give him a testimonial. What should I write—that he "was with me as bearer for twenty-four hours and gave every satisfaction"? Yes, he said, only leave out the bit about twenty-four hours. I began to evaluate differently the innumerable glowing testimonials of their worth which Indian servants accumulate.

From the top of the pass I looked down a sheer slope of three thousand feet to a narrow valley, directly beneath me. Its stony white river was so tiny from this height that I seemed to see it through the wrong end of a telescope. The path was too rocky and vertiginous to tackle on pony-back, and as I stumbled down over great projecting boulders and slippery faces of rock I began to understand how Nepal's geographical situation helps her to preserve a glorious isolation. The journey to Katmandu might almost be described as a penance.

But to me it had never a moment of boredom. The scenery was a joy. Tall rhododendron-trees, huge, broad-leaved evergreen oaks, maples and acacias, with orchids coiling around their branches and ferns in their undergrowth, framed a luxuriant vertical landscape. There was hardly a natural horizontal surface, but the bare parts of the mountain-side were terraced for rice cultivation, tier above tier like the auditorium of an amphitheatre. Banana-trees, so various are the properties of Himalayan soil and climate, grew side by side with pines (imagine a banana-tree in a Scottish pine-forest), side by side too, with oranges, cherry blossom, eucalyptus, bamboo and an occasional cypress.

The valleys were amply populated and an endless stream of people toiled up and down the track. At first I was surprised to find a steep and arduous path so much frequented. Then I realized that this was not merely the main but the only road to Katmandu, and that the traffic represented but the normal comings and goings of a great city. To one in search of Erewhon it would have portended a populous and thriving civilization beyond the range. Moreover it was human traffic entirely, for the slopes are too precipitous for any beast of burden. Coolies carried prodigious loads on their backs, suspended as a rule by a band across the forehead: sacks or baskets almost as big as themselves, full of stones, merchandise, household utensils, heavy pieces of furniture and perhaps a mother-in-law perched on top of the lot. Women carried bundles as heavy as the men, and there were child coolies too, boys and girls from four and five years old. Women passengers travelled in chairs on a coolie's back or reclining uncomfortably in litters with their various possessions and always, I noticed, a bundle of turnips at the feet. But whether the latter had a religious, sexual or purely culinary significance I did not discover. Many of these human caravans were travelling to or from Katmandu, but there were peasants too, moving from village to village on the business of cultivation. And in all their faces I saw, to my delight, that I was once again within the ethnological radius of Central Asia. I had indeed left the Indian peninsula behind me at the foot of that first pass. Here was a Mongolian rather than an Indian race, an attractive, wide-cheeked, narrow-eyed people ready to laugh and smile, to whom my sympathies immediately warmed.

There were Tibetans too, on pilgrimage to the famous Buddhist shrines of Swayambunath and Boddhnath, like people of another world: slit-eyed, weather-beaten, with faces creased and furrowed as hide. By contrast with the lightly clad Nepalis they were dressed like Eskimos, in warm garments of rough cloth (dull red or grey or blue), rugs, fur hats which covered the ears, woollen leggings and boots. They wore pigtails and innumerable bright-coloured ornaments: earrings of a dozen oval rings, each large enough to encircle the wrist, innumerable bracelets, necklaces of filigree silver, turquoises and uncut stones. Some of the Tibetan women were gaunt and solemn and hawk-like; others were fat and coarse and smiling, like Dutchwomen or landladies.

At the foot of the pass I mounted my pony again, and continued for the next hour or so by the winding course of the stream. Here the path undulated gently by mountains which were always imminent. Sometimes it would be forced upwards by the lumbering incursions of some outcrop, descending again when the slopes had retreated to a safe distance. Sometimes we would be ambling across gentle downland of wine-coloured grass, falling away to where the wine-dark terraced earth was spotted with crème-de-menthe green. There were many villages—or rather, one long, straggling village, with small shrines everywhere, garlands stretched in propitiation across the rivers, stacks of corn-cob drying by thatched brick farmhouses.

For an hour or two a journey on pony-back is delightful. When you want a rest you get off your pony and walk; when you want another rest you get on your pony and ride. But I must confess that I am never at home in a horse's company. We have little in common. I find it a stupid and malignant animal, with very little sense of self-preservation, and no intelligent will of its own. I am convinced that it will commit suicide from sheer ineptitude unless I take steps to prevent it. When I am on a horse's back I treat it in my mind's eye as though it were a bicycle. I am never altogether at ease but assume that if I let my attention wander from the road the horse will collide with another, that if I overbalance the horse will fall, that if I feel giddy above a precipice the horse will go plunging down it, that unless I guide it carefully past all sharp surfaces the horse will have a puncture; and if my horse makes a rude noise I blush guiltily, and hope that no one heard. So it was a somewhat nervous and exhausting ride.

We were approaching the Chandragiri Ridge, and it looked as though the horse and I were going to have a pretty tough time of it. The nearer we got the more I wondered how on earth we were going to scale this perpendicular wall of mountain. It seemed to block the way impenetrably. Try as I might I saw no trace of a break in its ramparts. And indeed there was none. Protesting slightly the animal took a look at the ridge, braced itself for an effort, and jerked me up those three thousand feet in a series of the sharpest zigzags I have ever encountered.

At the top I stood still with astonishment. There, spread far below me, was the Valley of Katmandu, a valley so wide that it seemed an illusion. To find this broad, rich plain beyond the tortuous clefts of the road I had covered was utterly unexpected, utterly thrilling, like the discovery of some lost world. It was an ample, soft pile carpet stretched at the foot of the Himalayan crags. It was Erewhon indeed.

Legend relates that this valley was once a lake, which was visited by one of the Buddhas. Finding that no lotus grew there he threw a lotus root into the waters, prophesying that it would grow into a temple and that the lake would become a populous country. His prophecy was fulfilled. The lotus root became the site of the Shrine of Swayambunath. Manjusri, a god from China, visited the valley with a sword carved like the smile of the moon and struck the mountains in two. Thus the lake was drained and the Baghmati River runs through the sword-cut gorge to this day.

The descent seemed interminable in my impatience to reach this enchanted goal. At the foot of the mountain a car awaited me, and as I devoured my sandwich lunch (for it was six hours since I had eaten) it did not at first occur to me to wonder how on earth it got there. But when other cars began to pass us I came to, as it were, and was staggered at the phenomenon. The path behind me, I knew, was the only link between Katmandu and the world where motor-cars are made, and it would of course be humanly impossible to drive a car across it. I gave it up and asked my chauffeur the answer.

"Coolies carry the cars," he said. "For one car you need eighty coolies, with eighty more to relieve them when they are tired."

Later I discovered that there are as many as five hundred motor-cars in the valley, and when, to crown all, I saw a large steam-roller from Rochester, Kent, quietly flattening the roads outside the city, I realized (if I had had any doubts before) that Nepal has the strongest race of porters in the world.

The pagodas of Katmandu appeared before us. Presently we were bowling along formal avenues of eucalyptus and bamboo and emerged into a huge, grass parade-ground, like the playing fields of a school, where Gurkha troops in khaki were engaged in every kind of military exercise. I caught a glimpse of imposing white palaces and equestrian statues (these, weighing four tons each, are the coolies' record load). Soldiers and civilians alike saluted as I passed. The car turned in at a gateway and I saw Sir Frederick O'Connor and Colonel Daukes, the Envoy,* advancing to greet me across the lawn of the British Legation.

Straight from the back of my mountain pony, as it were,

---

* Now elevated to the status of British Minister.

Above: Durbar. Sir Frederick O'Connor with the Maharaja and ruling family of Nepal
Below: Garden Party at Katmandu. The Maharaja (right foreground) escorts the King

Above: Malla Elephant, Katmandu *Below:* Drawing Water in Patan

I was whisked off to a durbar at the Singha Darbar Palace; and it would be hard to conceive of a more astonishing transition. The primitive rusticity of the Himalayan heights switched to the white and golden splendours of a modern palace. A band was playing before its imposing classical façade at the end of a long sweep of formal water; a guard of honour, in scarlet uniforms, presented arms as we drew up. Through an ante-room of distorting mirrors we were conducted to the gallery (a purdah gallery where the women could sit without being seen). Here sat the entire European population of Nepal: the British Envoy, the Legation Surgeon, and a British engineer, each with his wife. Below, in a setting of parquet floors, mirrors, and glittering chandeliers, with a crystal fountain in the centre, the ruling family of Nepal were assembled in full regalia to do honour to Sir Frederick. All wore scarlet uniforms, bespattered with orders and decorations, and jewelled head-dresses, each crowned with a sweeping bird-of-paradise plume. The insignia of the Star of Nepal were brought in on a silken cushion, its bearer supported at the elbows by two attendants.

Presently the Maharaja entered, in long robes, followed by two minute, dark pages, and sat on a silver throne. During his presence mummers gabbled in queer, falsetto tones, to fill up pauses in the ceremonial. With a necklace of huge emeralds he wore a head-dress more magnificent than any of the others. Rising from a thick skull-cap of pearls were two great plaques of diamonds, representing the sun and the moon: to one side a gigantic carved emerald from Arabia, a circlet of emeralds, dropping from the crown, and beneath, over the ear, a great cluster of them, too big to be true (but true) like a bunch of grapes turned into precious stones by a magician's wand. Over all the bird-of-paradise plume nodded in a cascade of shimmering white and orange. The Maharaja rose and made his speech in English, in clipped, emphatic tones, referred to Sir Frederick O'Connor's many services to Nepal, and invested him with the star of the Order. Sir Frederick replied, and the crystal fountain began to play.

It was evident that here was no taint of democracy, but the trappings of an autocracy paralleled nowhere else in the world to-day for its absolutism, its pomp and state, and the magnificence of its entourage. Maharaja Sir Joodha Shumshere, of fine Rajput stock, is an imposing figure, well built, dignified, with a sweeping moustache. His full style and title is His Highness Projjwal Nepala-Tara Ati Pravala Gorkha Dakshina Bahu Prithuladheesha Sri Sri Sri Maharaja Sir Joodha Shumshere Jung Bahadur Rana, G.S.SS. Maurizio e Lazzaro, G.C.I.E., Prime Minister and Supreme Commander-in-Chief of Nepal. He is a despot—but a benevolent and enlightened despot with an infinite capacity for hard work and the interests of his country very much at heart. He rarely leaves Nepal; nor is any member of his family permitted to do so without his special permission; and this, except for urgent or official reasons, is seldom granted. The gods Siva and Vishnu are explicit in their veto against crossing the "black water", and a member of the ruling family of Nepal has only visited Europe on three occasions: the first in 1850 when the Maharaja Jung Bahadur visited the Court of Queen Victoria (and it was considered, at that stage of Nepal's history, a unique testimony to his power and the security of his rule at home that he should be able to do so); the second in 1908 when the late Maharaja Sir Chandra Shumshere visited King Edward; and the third in 1934 when General Sir Bahadur Shumshere Jung Bahadur Rana, eldest son of the present Maharaja, came to England as the guest of the Government to present a decoration to the King, and remained to establish the first Nepalese Legation in London. There are upwards of twenty-five modern palaces in Katmandu, and here the members of the ruling family live.

But they are not princes. At the most they are generals in the Nepalese Army. For Nepal has also a king. The Maharaja is officially no more than hereditary Prime Minister, through a system whereby not the eldest son but the eldest surviving member of the ruling family succeeds (and thus dangerous minorities are avoided). The King, politically, is no more than a cipher. His importance is purely religious; he is a figurehead, like the Mikado. He is seldom seen but remains, as a rule, within the bounds of his palace. I had the honour, however, to see and be presented to His Majesty, the day after my arrival, at a garden-party given by the Maharaja for Sir Frederick O'Connor. He arrived, walking quickly, his arm supported by the Maharaja: a pale young man in pince-nez, with a tendency to embonpoint, in a frock-coat and white jodhpurs, black hair curling from beneath a round, Astrakhan cap, and a huge white flower in his buttonhole. He sat in silence throughout the afternoon, as befitted a semi-sacred figure, and no one but the Maharaja addressed him.

The chief item of the garden-party was a shooting display, in which the Maharaja, his guests, and other members of his family took part. Maharaja Sir Joodha Shumshere is a first-class shot, and had recently bagged thirty-one tigers in twenty-seven days. A tiger-shoot in Nepal is staged on a tremendous scale: roads are cut for miles through the Terai jungle, where even tracks never existed before, two or three hundred elephants are assembled, and a camp arranged to house many hundreds of people: for the Maharaja, on a tiger-shoot, travels with an enormous suite, his wife, and almost all his relatives. The tigers are shot from elephants, splendidly caparisoned, forming a huge circle round the spot where the animal has been lured by a "kill", and the spectacle is the nearest approach to the magnificence of an ancient gladiatorial show to be found anywhere in the world to-day.

On this occasion, however, the animals were of cardboard, sliding across a range and returning backwards, the hits marked with spots of paper. The programme, printed in gold on a pink ground, read as follows:

(1) Shooting at: Wild-buffalo.
Tiger.
Rhino.
Spotted Deer.
Leopard.
(2) Snapping at a vanishing bear.
(3) Picking off a wily Ghazi.
(4) Bursting balloons on a flying goose.
(5) Bursting balloons on a dancing peacock.
(6) Bursting balloons on a flying kite.
(7) Bursting balloons on pitchers.

This was followed by a display of gymnastics and sports by the Army, very reminiscent of a similar display at Aldershot or Tidworth. We watched from a marquee, while a band played European music with a preference for *Her Mother Came Too*.

The Gurkha is a wiry little man and a splendid fighter. On the huge Maidan, which is a mile and a half in length and is said to be the biggest parade-ground in the world, you can watch troops drilling all through the day, and it is easy to guess at the important part which her Army plays in the life of Nepal. Since her conquest by the Gurkhas in 1768 she has boasted one of the finest national armies in Asia. Apart from the Gurkha troops which form a unit of our Indian Army, there is a regular Army of some forty thousand troops in Nepal itself, and on more than one occasion since the war their services have been offered to the British Government in case of crisis in India.

That the Nepalese have always been a warlike race is evident too from the Katmandu museum, whose principal exhibits are arms and armour. Hundreds of rifles, of every date, are arranged star-wise on the walls, and room after room is filled with guns (including a leather gun), knives, swords and every kind of murderous weapon, down to modern pistols bearing the name of a famous London gunsmith.

The Maidan is fringed with palaces. Overlooking it is a pointed column, two hundred feet high, which was erected by General Bhim Sen in the nineteenth century, and is known as Bhim Sen's Folly. It indicates in him an unexpected sophistication: for the tower, together with its cloister of arches at the bottom, is pure Gothic in style, inspired, presumably, by the Ruskin Gothic in Calcutta. Maharaja Jung Bahadur is reputed to have jumped on horseback from the top of Bhim Sen's Folly to the ground. His horse was killed but he himself remained unhurt.

At the opposite end of the Maidan is a tank, under whose waters trial by ordeal used to be carried out. Overlooking it is a huge stone elephant, beautifully carved, mounted by three figures leaning slightly backward. This was erected in the seventeenth century by King Pratapa Malla, as a memorial to his son, and must surely be one of the finest pieces of animal sculpture in the world.

Sir Frederick O'Connor left Katmandu after a couple of days, but the Maharaja very kindly gave me permission to stay on and put a bungalow at my disposal, so that I need not trespass further on the kind hospitality of Colonel and Mrs. Daukes. Since, in his own interests, no visitor is permitted to walk through the streets alone, a car awaited my orders each morning, and a guide in the shape of a young Nepalese artist, called Maskay. He was a gentle creature, with a discriminating love of his country's artistic treasures, and showed me every corner of the three cities of Katmandu, Patan and Bhatgaon—the two last once capitals of Nepal as Katmandu is to-day. It would have been impossible to see the wonders of Nepalese architecture under more sympathetic auspices.

CHAPTER III

NEPAL (*continued*)

THE East is apt to disappoint the traveller because no Oriental city, as a whole, quite reaches his expectations. Too much drabness goes hand in hand with the sublime. This is not due simply to the imperfections of creative man: there are other reasons.

First, that the East, more even than the West, has throughout history been despoiled to a fantastic extent by warfare. There was always something particularly violent about the Oriental conqueror. Periodically, ruthless hordes would sweep across Central Asia, in the name of empire or religion, decimating the countryside, sacking every city in their path, leaving no stone upon another. They would build new cities in their place, often as fine as those they had destroyed, but these in their turn would perish at the hands of another victorious army. Hence many Oriental cities have changed their identity so repeatedly as to have little identity left beyond a few surviving monuments.

Secondly the East has at no time had any appreciable domestic architecture. Palaces apart, all her architectural genius has been poured into religious buildings. While Europe had begun to beautify her dwellings, Asia, whether Hindu, Buddhist or Mohammedan, still lived in featureless hovels and afforded beauty only to her temples and mosques. Thus it is that so many of the world's wonders rise from surroundings of unmitigated drabness.

In Teheran I had doubted the existence of the Oriental city of the fairy-books. But then I had not seen the cities of Nepal.

Nepal is in a unique position. Her geographical situation has preserved her throughout history from foreign conquest. Moreover, what is more important still, she has kept entirely free from religious strife. Not only did the Mohammedan Conquest fail to penetrate these mountain fastnesses; but when Buddhism from the north and Hinduism from the south met in Nepal no breach occurred. Instead of fighting, they shook hands. Here, as in no other country in the world, the two religions dovetail one into the other in a perfect blend.

That this Hindu-Buddhist marriage has been a happy one is evident from the demeanour of the Nepalese, and accounts to a great extent for their very distinct national character. For combined with the vitality of Hinduism in its prime they have the Buddhist's calm and contemplative philosophical spirit. They are an essentially human race, and a proud and vital race into the bargain.

But if the alliance has left its mark upon the people, its effect upon their art and architecture is little short of incredible. The combined inspiration of the two religions, poured into the art-blood of Nepal, has produced what I have little doubt are the most beautiful cities in all the East. Moreover they are completely intact: not a ruin is to be seen.*

Religion alone does not necessarily produce great art; it requires to influence a race of naturally great artists. The Nepalese are born of another contradictory union besides the religious: the racial. They are, broadly speaking, part Gurkha (since the eighteenth century) and part Newari. And if the Gurkhas are a race of fighters the Newaris were among the greatest race of artists that the world has ever seen. Very little is known of them beyond a presumable Mongolian origin; very little, owing to the closed state of the country, has been seen or written of their art, and nothing had prepared me for the wealth of artistic and architectural genius which now met my eyes. For it is confined to on isolated buildings; it is everywhere, in the great squares and mean streets, the noble temples and small shrines alike.

Moreover, though religion is the chief source of its inspiration and provides the principal decorative motifs, the Newaris extended their creative genius to domestic as well as religious architecture. Their private houses, even in the poorest quarters, are as beautifully designed, as finely carved

---

* A few weeks after my visit incalculable havoc was wrought in the valley by earthquake. "The loss", the Maharaja wrote to me later, "has been very, very heavy indeed, and is, I am afraid, irreparable in some cases."

as their temples. Thus the great religious buildings of Nepal, unique in the East, stand out from architectural surroundings which are themselves of unexampled richness. All Katmandu, not merely the Taleju Temple, all Patan, not merely the Temple of Krishna, all Bhatgaon, not merely the five-roofed pagoda, are, in my eyes, worthy to rank as wonders of the world.

If you wanted a neat phrase to summarize Nepal you might describe it as "the Italy of Asia". Artistically (to give a loose definition) Nepal is to Asia as Italy to Europe. Even this is an understatement of Newari inspiration; but only in Italy or Spain, and then in a lesser degree, do you come upon works of art hidden in odd corners and back streets to anything like the extent that you do in Nepal, and incidentally the periods of the two countries are similar. Though some of her buildings go back to a far more ancient date, it is assumed that the majority of Nepalese architecture dates from the sixteenth and seventeenth centuries, when a great architectural renaissance seems to have spread throughout the world.

There are two thousand seven hundred temples in the Valley of Nepal, and each single one is worth a visit for some miraculous piece of carving or design which you may find there. Needless to say, despite Maskay's zeal, I only visited a fraction of the total. Indeed, my time in the country was so limited that I cannot presume to give more than a vague and general impression of three cities which deserve years of detailed study—and which even then would remain indescribable.

It says much for the enlightenment of the Rana family that the new city of Katmandu, with its palaces, barracks, parade grounds and so forth, has nowhere been allowed to impinge upon the old. The two stand side by side, representing distinctly an ancient and a modern civilization. Thus it was not until my third day in Katmandu that I saw the old city at all, and my first sight of it was the more striking in that it was so completely unexpected. It is an essential feature of the Oriental city of the fairy-books that its buildings should be fashioned in a form unrelated to anything in one's familiar world. In this respect I had until now been disappointed, for Moslem architecture, after all, is much akin to classical. But here I was met by a combination of shapes utterly foreign to all previous experience, and the moment when I first beheld the Darbar Square of Katmandu was one of the most

The Great Garuda, Katmandu

exciting I can remember. I stood astonished at the zigzag of roofs which cut up into the sky. In the world I knew, the roof was little more than an incident, necessary to finish a building whose walls were its predominating feature. But here the principle was reversed: the roofs meant everything, the walls nothing. The diagonal planes which dwarfed, instead of modestly surmounting the vertical, staggered all my preconceived architectural notions. But miraculously enough, they did not look like hats too big for their wearers. Here was an utterly new world of building, which negatived every known principle, yet amazed me by the beauty of its proportions.

There are, broadly speaking, two forms of Nepalese temple. There is the two-, three- or five-roofed pagoda, recalling (and said by some to have originated) the Chinese; and there is the Hindu sikra, or cone-shaped tower.

Despite its effect of fantasy the pagoda is geometrically perfect, with an admirable simplicity of form. The neatness of its joinery recalls an exquisitely fitting toy; but a toy from an antique-shop rather than a toy-shop, kindergarten that has soared into the realms of art. As a rule three square, sloping roofs, one big, one middle-sized, one small, fit neatly one above the other, in perfect symmetry. They project almost to hide the cubes of brick, of proportionately diminishing size, which form the nucleus of the building. They are supported at an angle of forty-five degrees by struts completing a triangle (usually equilateral) with the roof and the wall. Wooden windows, overhung by the roof, underhung by the struts, are let neatly into the wall on each of the four sides, with doors on the ground storey. A golden bell and trident, or perhaps the figure of a Buddha is placed on top to complete the effect. Sometimes a smaller cube forms the ground storey, and the extra space is filled out by a square colonnade whose number of arches is proportionate to the number of roofs. In every case the central shrine is tiny by comparison with the sweeping canopy which frames and protects it. As a rule the whole building stands on a plinth of steep, brick steps.

Such, baldly speaking, is the Nepalese pagoda. Its beauty, however, rests not merely in the soaring regularity of its design, but in its materials and above all in its detail. A Chinese traveller who visited Katmandu in the seventh century wrote of a "city of glorious temples in brick and carved wood". Nepal to-day is still an architectural epic in wood and brick; teak-wood which weathers from natural brown to silver-grey or the colour of black oak (sometimes it was painted, and the paint has now faded to attractive dull shades); brick of rich and subtle hues, varying from terra cotta to plum-colour and coral pink. Above, the roofs are of red-brown tiles, often so small and round and closely fitting as to give the impression of cobbles in a street.

And then the carving! There is no part of the wooden structure unornamented, yet no ornament which is not structural: no excrescent decoration to detract from the functional simplicity of the design. Each wooden strut supporting the roof is in itself a work of art, wonderfully carved with sacred animals, or deities with many twirling arms. Windows let into the brick wall are masterpieces of woodcarving, in which the artist, unable to stop, has elongated the lintels and sills beyond the window itself, to cover almost an entire wall with his handiwork. Sometimes the windows lean forward to meet the struts of the roof, and then you get a carved grille or trellis-work flush with the central frame. Plinths, corbels, eaves, capitals, cornices, architraves, spandrels, pediments, bosses are all similarly carved; nor does this apply only to the temples, but to all the private houses, which rise to three or four storeys.

The carving, moreover, is not merely ornamental, but of deep religious significance; nor are its subjects floral or geometrical, as in Mohammedan carving, but human and animal. Of all religions none has more living symbols than the Hindu, hence Hindu carving is always vividly alive. In Nepal the Hindu symbolism is enriched by the innumerable attributes of Buddhism, so that each artist had a fantastic wealth of subject matter to draw upon for his inspiration. There is no end to the variety of sacred and mythical animals, of legendary scenes, of Hindu deities and manifestations of the Buddha which figure in Nepalese carving. Most decorative, perhaps, are the ornithological symbols. You will see cornices which on closer inspection prove to be hundreds of carved birds facing towards you, while the peacock windows, where the tail of the bird spreads into an exquisite trellis-work, are among the minor gems of Newari art.

The Newaris were a people who could not see a piece of

wood, stone or metal without fashioning it into life. Palaces have wonderful gateways of elaborate gold or bronze. Stone-carved animals: gryphons, elephants, lions, garudas and other mythical figures guard the temple steps in pairs. Each temple is surrounded by a galaxy of images in stone or copper gilt, statues, carved plaques, bas-reliefs and a host of minor shrines. Perched on a pillar of grey stone or polished granite before a temple is the effigy of some Nepalese king, a Buddha or a garuda (complete with umbrella or the canopy of a snake), two figures, perhaps, seated back to back, or a peacock with tail outspread—moulded nearly always in shining copper gilt. These pillars are said to be entirely peculiar to Nepal.

A paraphernalia of non-architectural oddments adds to the decoration. Golden pennons stand beside the gods. A wide brass "strap" stretches from the topmost roof to hang over the entrance. Figures, as in a Punch and Judy show, but of gods, look out of the window of a temple. Little bells dangle from the roofs. Often a garland of bunting, edged with silver, is draped round the edge. A tall bamboo with a faded flag is stuck up in front. Strings of flags are stretched across the streets. Votive offerings—pots and pans, effigies of animals and gods in plaited straw, papier-mâché elephants or horses, little children's toys—are scattered about the roofs or beneath the eaves of the principal temples.

Though wood and brick predominate other materials give variety to the buildings. Sometimes white plaster covers the brick. Sometimes, as in the Great Taleju Temple in Katmandu, the roofs are of gilt. (This is the temple reserved exclusively for the Royal Family, and when the Gurkha conqueror offered human sacrifice to its goddess she signified her displeasure in a dream.) The Temple of Machendranath, in Katmandu, which stands in a courtyard crowded with statues and carvings, has beautiful brasswork. The Temple of Cwabahal, in Patan, is a mass of gold and silver, where the embossed metal, welded into all kinds of shapes, sometimes black with tarnish, sometimes shining brazenly, forms an astonishing frontage. Sometimes, in the grander houses, carved ivory is inlaid in the woodwork. Sometimes temple windows are entirely of beaten brass. Sometimes, again, their walls are paved with white marble.

In the Darbar Square of Patan (perhaps the most beautiful, certainly the most spacious of the valley's three great Darbar squares) stone temples vary the architectural landscape. Grey Hindu cones rise straight and simple amid the kaleidoscope of jagged pagodas. Two great octagonal erections of kiosks in grey stone provide yet another style, which recalls certain phases of the Mogul. One, the Temple of Radha-Krishna, is encircled by a frieze, no more than six inches high, of exceptional beauty, ·recording in carving the life of the god. Opposite the great Darbar Palace, with its countless roofs, which occupies an entire side of the square, is a bell, five feet in diameter, towering as high as a small temple.

On the steps of temples Nepali shopkeepers have spread out their wares. Coolies are resting their heavy loads, children are winding wool. Sacred cows wander unmolested about the square. Doves and hens peck among the temples and rooks wail overhead. Men with shining legs of bronze wash themselves at delicately carved fountains and women come down to draw water in their pitchers of brass. Nearby, squatting on the ground, the hairdressers ply their trade, shaving the heads of the men. The people are small, in round caps and cotton jodhpurs and long, soft scarves of goats' wool; and on doorsteps men and women sit almost naked in the sun and are massaged with oil (sun-bathing is not confined to the Mediterranean). Children scramble ecstatically around you, and in a side-street you may meet an amateur children's band of drums and cymbals.

In the side-streets of all the three cities you will come upon minor shrines, sandwiched between dwelling-houses, guarded perhaps by brazen images of rats or elephants. There are small courtyards with fountains and temples like those in the Darbar Square, but in a miniature design. In a pleasant quadrangle of grass surrounded by eucalyptus trees and houses is Patan's Temple of Machendranath. A national deity of Nepal, he is taken out once a year in his car, sixty feet high, and acclaimed by the people in the hope of rain. In a yard which is sordid by contrast, a beautiful pagoda grows, as it were, from the roof of the surrounding houses, the usual pillar and effigy standing in front of it, amid the refuse. There are big, square lotus pools, here and there, within and without the temple precincts, and from the centre of one protrudes the enormous brazen head of a snake.

The symbol of a religion of fear ? Yet they are a contented

Above: Palace in Darbar Square, Bhatgaon   *Below:* Darbar Square, Katmandu

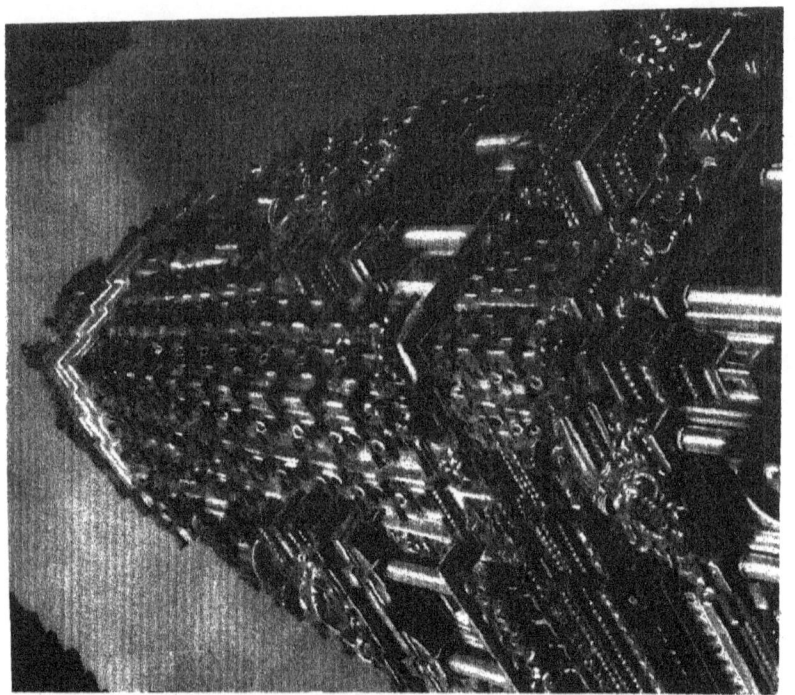

Mahabuddha Temple, Patan

Window in Patan

people, in no way crushed, like the Indian, by their superstitions. The Buddhist element would seem to have a rational, calming effect. In the Darbar Square of Katmandu, carved in bas-relief, is a huge human monster, some twelve feet high. He has six arms, each brandishing some instrument of destruction, and he tramples on a prostrate body. He is the god Kala Bhairab, and worshippers have smeared him in propitiation with black and red and yellow pigments. A few yards away, before the house, made from the wood of a single tree, which gave the city its name, is a statue. It is known as the Great Garuda and represents a human figure, several times life-size, with the wings of an eagle, kneeling on one knee. The figure's hands are clasped in prayer; he wears an elaborate headdress, and a snake is coiled round his neck. His face is strong and proud, but calm, cultured, beautiful. It is as fine a piece of sculpture as the Greeks ever produced and deserves to rank high among the great statues of the world. It is the Great Garuda, worshipped by Hindu and Buddhist alike, and not the fiendish Kala Bhairab which seems to me to contain the spirit of Nepalese civilization. Here is epitomized the character, culture and religion of the Nepali: his nobility of race, his warlike strength coupled with his love of art and his contemplative spirit.

Buddha sits side by side with Vishnu and Siva on many temples. His figure may be seen incongruously seated upon the Hindu symbol of the lingam. The lovely Mahabuddha temple in Patan, built of terra cotta, with countless thousands of representations of Buddha carved on its sides, is built in the conical style of a Hindu shrine. Elsewhere a single image is worshipped as Siva by the Hindus and as Avalokitesvara by the Buddhists. Nevertheless there are two famous shrines in the valley which are almost exclusively Buddhist, and where Buddhist pilgrims come from all over the East.

The first is Swayambunath, which crowns a hill some miles to the west of the city. Past three gigantic figures of Buddha you climb three hundred feet of stairway. At the top is a great white hemisphere of masonry: the stupa. A tower surmounts it, gilded to look as though it were built of golden bricks. On each of its four sides are painted two huge and realistic eyes, with a question mark where the nose should be. Their all-seeing gaze surveys the whole Valley of Katmandu. Above is a spire of thirteen golden rings crowned by an ornamented umbrella and finial. In front the golden vajra, or thunderbolt, rests on a circular stone pediment, carved with the animal symbols of the Tibetan year. Round the stupa are five golden shrines, dedicated to the five divine incarnations of the Buddha. Among the innumerable votive offerings which surround the temple is a very lovely gilt statue of Tara, the Nepalese goddess who introduced Buddhism into the country. Through a forest of images you pick your way to a building where Buddhist priests keep alive a sacred flame.

But even at Swayambunath, stronghold of Buddhism as it is, a Hindu tower, of late date, stands on either side of the stupa, and a Hindu Temple of Harati, the goddess of smallpox, is in the background.

Boddhnath, the other place of pilgrimage, is in the valley itself, and is surrounded by a cloister of lodgings for the pilgrims' benefit. Here Buddhist pilgrims come from Tibet and even from China, often taking years over their journey, and climbing the terrific snow wall of the Himalayan Range to get there, for to the Buddhists of the north it is the holiest shrine out of India. Sometimes they impose fantastic penances upon themselves and do the whole journey on all fours, hopping on alternate legs, touching the ground with their heads every few yards, or in other uncomfortable postures. When they first see the eyes of Boddhnath from the mountain-top they emit a cry and run the rest of the way down to the shrine. Every twelve years water gushes from beneath the stupa of Boddhnath. It is held to be sacred nectar and the first draught is sent to the Dalai Lama of Tibet.

Buddha himself visited the Valley of Nepal, and in his honour the Emperor Asoka, about 250 B.C., built four stupas in and around Patan. These still remain, among the oldest monuments of Nepal. But what they contain in the way of relics will probably never be known.

One afternoon we drove to Pashpati, one of the most sacred Hindu shrines in the world, which has as little connection with Buddhism as Boddhnath with Hinduism. It is dedicated to Siva, who visited Nepal in the form of a gazelle. Here the narrowed Bagrati river emerges from a deep green gorge. Temples and stone steps fringe the waters, and round stone platforms which are the burning ghats. On one were the remains of a funeral pyre, still burning, so that from the bridge where I stood I could see the charred shape of the corpse. One relative watched it burn; others were shaving their heads in mourning in the background. Then a dying man on a litter was carried down to the water's edge. I thought it gruesome that he should have to die with corpses around him, in the knowledge that he too would soon be burning on one of those pyres. But to him death was a matter for rejoicing and, as a good Hindu, he considered himself fortunate that he should be privileged to die with his feet in the holy river. Because of this attitude to death Pashpati was not macabre, though the monkeys might easily have made it so.

A positive circus of these sacred creatures scampered about the temple roofs, which they have so torn to pieces that the tiles have had to be replaced by corrugated iron, and only the gold-roofed temple, with its carved silver doorway and windows, remains unblemished. In the seventeenth century a Nepalese queen set such store by its holiness that she had a two-mile rope attached to its roof, that it might extend to her palace in Katmandu. On a more recent occasion an offering of 125,000 oranges was brought by a raja and stacked in the courtyard.

The antics of the monkeys were obscenely comic; they made a variety of piercing sounds, for, like human beings and unlike other animals, they are not confined to one. A crowd of children laughed delightedly; the sick man died on his litter beyond the bridge. We bought nuts, and as soon as the news got about hundreds upon hundreds more monkeys appeared from nowhere and came pouring down a stone staircase as noisily and excitedly as schoolboys in the midday break. They barged each other and fought and yelled and ran helter-skelter for the nuts. No matter in what direction we looked monkeys were leaping towards us in hundreds. It was as if a zoo were to be inaugurated in the London Necropolis at Brookwood.

Looking back for a moment over the bridge I saw that they were trailing the newly dead body in the shallow water. Its wooden pyre was ready, and presently it would be a charred and flaming mass. My attention was diverted by shouts of merriment from the children, for one of the monkeys, whether or not it had sore feet, was walking about on its hands on the parapet of the bridge, and very ludicrous it looked.

There are thirty or forty small shrines at Pashpati, lining

the river and proceeding in tiers up the hill; small square shrines of stone, with stone bell-roofs, each dedicated to some particular mortal. They date, for the most part, from the eighteen-sixties, and the excellence of their stone-carving is encouraging. For it indicates that Newari art has continued to flourish since the Gurkha conquest, and even in modern times.

Returning in the evenings we would often be in time to see the post leave. This was an impressive sight. The mails are carried by a runner, in a smart red and blue uniform, with shorts. He holds a staff in his hand, with a bell which rings as he runs. He goes at a steady trot, and out of the city is accompanied by a guard of police. At a fixed point in the route he is relieved, and the mails proceed by a kind of relay race to Raxaul. There are two despatches and deliveries per day, and the Indian newspapers arrive no more than two days late. It is said that the mail-carrier is respected even by the tigers in the jungle, who will always treat him as sacred, much as they may molest the peasants.

At the bungalow we would usually find a crowd of vendors awaiting us. They brought many beautiful things: Nepalese paintings mounted, like the Tibetan, on embroidered banners, bronzes, precious stones, carved ivory and conch shell and rhinoceros horn, Chinese jade and porcelain, old brassware and stone-carved images. There are two currencies in Nepal: Nepalese and Indian rupees, and the latter, as in the days of the East India Company, are still referred to as "Company rupees".

Then we would sit round the fire, and Maskay would talk. His wife had died quite recently, but personal ties are slight in the East, and her loss did not weigh on him heavily. He preferred, indeed, to be free, as befits an artist. He spoke of his small son, two years old: a strapping child, with a precocious passion for meat. Maskay's family urged that he should marry again, but he preferred to listen to his son, who gave him the strongest advice against matrimony.

One evening we went to Balaji, which is a kind of sacred garden outside the city. Here is a lovely recumbent statue of Vishnu, lying in the water on a bed of snakes, submerged except for the head, its pillow of serpents' heads, and the hands and knees. Fish dart here and there in a long tank of water, with bamboos nodding above. There are waterfalls, and a dozen carved stone dragons' heads which spout water into a lower pool. It was strangely like some garden in Italy.

By a spring Maskay showed me a stone, daubed by worshippers, on which it was possible to trace the image of Buddha.

"No one carved it," he said. "It has grown of its own accord, out of the rock. It is a holy stone. Often gods do that. You see them gradually forming themselves. Ganesh especially, with his elephant's trunk. You see the outline of the trunk first, and in time the whole figure of the god appears."

Apart from the sacred significance of certain flowers and animals, the propitiation of rivers and so on, nature worship is an integral part of this religion. You will see, for instance, a shrine which is split almost to pieces by a tree growing from its centre, swollen with age; and here it is the tree itself, not the figure in the shrine, which is the object of worship.

The old city of Katmandu was quiet and busy in the evenings, and we would often wander through the streets, where no wheeled traffic broke the silence. One night I heard, intermittently, a small bell, and, so are our reflexes tuned, I automatically said to myself, "Tram." It was a moment or two before concentration returned, and I realized that it was a temple bell. It is distressing how lovely sounds have come, in modern life, to be associated with unromantic things: the ripple of a fountain recalls immediately a lavatory cistern, the cry of a bird is like the whistle of a steam engine. If only our reflexes worked the other way and the tram-car reminded us of a temple bell, the cistern of a fountain, the steam whistle of the cry of a bird!

Beautiful as Katmandu and Patan are, neither has quite the consummate air of Bhatgaon. Built in the eighteenth century, it would seem to be more elegant, more "baroque" than the other cities. The carving is more profuse and there is a freer variety of designs. The Darbar Square is smaller than that of Patan, but more exquisite. It is paved with brick, in a herring-bone pattern. There is a long white plaster building, with windows and decorations in wood that is almost black, guarded by two great monsters. There is the superb golden gateway, in an insignificant wall, which is said to be finer than anything in China. There is the great bell. There is the palace of the kings, which is the loveliest of all Nepal's domestic buildings, of crimson brick with an unbelievable wealth of carving in sandalwood, so that in the sunlight it breathes a gentle, aromatic smell.

Maskay showed me a house built all in terra cotta. There was no sign of cement and the bricks had a dull, chestnut glaze, mellowed by delicate carving. It was earlier than the houses of brick. Crowds of children followed us through the streets. We stopped to listen to an old man playing a string instrument like a shoe and singing. Surrounding him a swarm of dark little childish faces, punctured with bead-like eyes, looked up at us. Now and then they burst into peals of laughter, as if, unbeknownst to us, a highly entertaining cinema film was being thrown on the wall behind our backs. Further down the street a crowd gathered round the temple dancers: children weighted with bracelets and jewellery, with huge, grotesque masks of the gods. We might not touch them, but could give them money when they begged. Then we came to the lovely five-roofed pagoda which is the gem of Bhatgaon and, perhaps, the most beautiful of all the temples in Nepal. It was built in 1700 by the Raja Bhupatindra Malla, who himself brought bricks to the site. His subjects followed his example and within five days he had sufficient material for the whole temple. It stands on a plinth of five steps more than half as high as the pagoda itself, and each is guarded by two gigantic stone figures: first two squat, moustachioed warriors, Jaya Malla and Phatta, whose strength, according to legend, was as the strength of ten; then two elephants, ten times as strong as they; lions, ten times as strong again; dragons, ten times stronger than the lions; and the tiger and lion goddesses, Baghini and Singhini of strength supernatural. The temple soars upwards in a wonderful cadence, like five pure notes of the tonic scale. The unity and proportions are so perfect that it gives the effect of curving unbroken in its upward lilt: it makes a harmonious whole, of which you cannot distinguish the parts. But each roof, in reality, is as straight and pyramidal as ever, fitting on to the roof below it with neat and geometrical precision.

The more space you cover, in the East, the further do you recede in time. As you travel forward in geography you travel backward into history. Here in Nepal I was living in the sixteenth century. The face of the city of Katmandu, the life of its inhabitants have not changed substantially in a period of time which to a European, seems prodigious. As I walked through the streets and the people stepped aside from my path, making way for me with respectful obeisance, I felt that I was regarded by the populace much as an Engish aristocrat in the reign of Queen Elizabeth. For the absolute rule of the Rana family in Nepal to-day compares very easily with that of the Tudors in England, before the days of a bourgeoisie, industrialism and democracy. This was no dead city of the past, as ancient places so often are, but a city filled with life, of men living still as they lived four hundred years ago, dressed in the clothes, worshipping in the temples, living, sleeping, eating in the houses, trading in the shops of those days.

Moreover the comparison went even further. Walking through these narrow, twisting, cobbled streets of warm brick, adorned with carved windows and an irregular outline of eaves and roofs above, I had some inkling of what England may have looked like in the reign of Queen Elizabeth. For though the architectural styles are so different the materials used were the same. London in the sixteenth century was a city of wood and brick. Moreover the occasional buildings of black and white and the temples with their courts like the courtyards of a Tudor inn or mansion fostered the illusion. Fantastic as it may seem it was possible here, in the wilds of Asia, among people still unspoilt by civilization, to imagine oneself in London long before the Great Fire, five hundred years ago, five thousand miles away.

At dusk we drove home across the plain, across a bridge of brick with carved wood piles, to Katmandu. As we entered the city a car approached with a cavalry escort and a couple of armed soldiers, running behind. We quickly stopped, got out of our car, removed our hats, and stood at attention as it passed. Inside was a member of the Maharaja's family.

Just so must the English populace have stood in homage when the coach of an Elizabethan nobleman passed their way.

I had an audience of the Maharaja before I left Nepal. His Highness received me in his private palace which I had not yet seen: an imposing building outside Katmandu. The word "WELCOME" was emblazoned on the doormat where I entered. The Maharaja, who wore a fine purple overcoat and a sealskin cap, with plume, received me very genially. In reply to his questions I said that I had been astonished to find so many of the amenities of civilization in so remote a country.

"Yes," he said, "a few years ago there were only a dozen cars in the valley. Now there are five hundred. Formerly only five or six newspapers daily were delivered in Nepal. Now there are five hundred per day."

But he did not speak as another Oriental monarch would have done, boastful of the go-ahead Western methods of his country. On the contrary, he spoke with regret. The increase of cars and newspapers was a thing to be deplored. Nepal must at no cost be undermined by the luxuries and the standards of the West.

I expressed my admiration for Nepalese architecture, and my joy at finding so much art and beauty in so small a space.

"I am making efforts," said His Highness, "to keep alive the old traditions of painting and carving in Nepal. I am founding schools where the young will be instructed in these arts by the old craftsmen, and I hope that, if you return to Nepal in three years' time, you may see completed a room in the Singha Darbar Palace which I am having redecorated entirely in the ancient national style of Nepal.* Recently, too, I have passed laws to prevent our art treasures leaving the country."

The Maharaja then presented me with three precious gifts: a piece of musk, from the sexual organs of the musk-deer, which is rare to come by and much prized by the Nepalese; a Gurkha knife, or kukri, in a sheath finely embossed in gold; and a signed photograph of His Highness himself, in a frame carved in Nepalese style.

Before I took my leave he was kind enough to express a hope that some day I might return to Nepal.

"We have been described as a 'forbidden country'," he said. "But we are not a forbidden country. We do not invite everybody to come here, it is true, but we are always honoured to receive people whom we know."

His words, I think, sum up very well the attitude of Nepal towards the foreigner. She is no more and no less forbidden than, say, Chatsworth, and is perhaps best described as a "private" country. At the frontier of Nepal is a metaphorical notice:

---

* The Singha Darbar was very badly damaged in the earthquake.

PRIVATE.
TRESPASSERS WILL BE PROSECUTED.

But the notice is due to no hostile intention, far less to any fear that trespassers may spy out "the nakedness of the land"; it is intended simply to keep out undesirable interlopers and despoilers, to avoid the more insidious forms of Western penetration. The commercial traveller and the uncommercial tourist, the political exploiter and the impolitic explorer, each more distasteful to a true Erewhonian than the last, are firmly and sensibly barred from Nepal. But whoever is privileged to cross the frontier finds a country remarkable for its hospitality and good will.

The Maharaja will not build roads to his capital; for roads mean engineers, and engineers mean Europeans, and Europeans in the East are like bailiffs: when once you get them into a country it is the devil's own job to get them out again. There is a single European engineer in Nepal, and the work he does in the way of bridge-building and electrification is quite sufficient to a people which seeks the mean between comfort and seclusion.

With the assistance of her formidable mountain ranges, Nepal preserves a unique and triumphant independence, political, cultural, and spiritual. Yet as the crow flies, and as the Nepalese mail-runner runs, she is near enough to India to be closely in touch with the affairs of the world at large, and to provide herself with such amenities of modern life as, in the opinion of her ruler, imperil neither her soul nor her stamina.

Next morning I rose at half past four, with the intention of reaching Raxaul within the day. It was still dark when I met my pony and syce and began my ascent of the Chandragiri Ridge. The half-moon was still high, and the landscape was dim and grey, like an under-exposed photograph. But as I rode it grew slowly lighter. First it seemed as though the moon were giving an intense light: for moonlight and the dawn have much in common. Then I became aware that the trees, which were colourless ten minutes ago, had begun to glow green, while pink and yellow flowers shot out their colours from the undergrowth. My syce, whose muffled figure in the darkness I had taken to be that of an elderly man, proved to be a youth of sixteen, with a face like a Jap.

Then I chanced to look back, and stopped in amazement. The valley was enveloped in a sheet of blue-grey mist, so that the horizon ended with a low foothill in the foreground. But right above the sheet of mist at an inconceivable height, appeared two peaks. At first I could not believe that they were real; nothing earthly could be so high. But slowly they began to reflect the rising sun as the expressions of an audience indicate the course and nature of a play; more peaks appeared, as the house began to fill, and all glowed pink in an unbroken line. To the west a spur shone white, to the east the ridge trailed away to a flimsy roseate silhouette. During my stay in the valley the Himalayan snow-line (upward of 20,000 feet high) had always been hidden in cloud; now, just as I was departing, it had laid itself bare to me, unbroken and glorious. I saw no more than the peaks planted on a dead-straight line of emptiness. To the east the mist was quite white, so that they seemed to rise from the sky itself; everywhere it was so thick a curtain as to remove them entirely from contact with the earth. Presently, as it began to roll up from below, the spectacle was even more astounding; for the lower mountains came into view, the snow-line above them rested still on a different plane, and I seemed to be looking at two separate worlds, one above the other.

It was a phenomenon such as words and similes cannot describe, an experience transcending all comparison, touching the absolute. I literally trembled, I wept at its majestic immensity. Never in my life had I seen a sight to touch that unearthly range, never again do I expect to see its like.

Many things were suddenly made clear to me. I seemed at once to understand the nature of the supernatural, of mystical visions, of religious ecstasy in all its manifestations. I was looking upon the difference between earth and heaven, between body and spirit, between the beauty which is of man and the beauty which is of God. I saw the distinction between sublime love, to which man sometimes attains, and the affection which passes for love among ordinary mortals.

But just as in love a man may catch for a moment a glimpse of the sublime, only to see it slip from his grasp, so, as I reached the top of the ridge, this marvel began to fade. The veil descended : it was not good that man should see too much of heaven : the snows returned to their purdah.

Had it not been for the mist I might have seen the Himalayan peaks planted firmly on the ground, like a gigantic Arthur's Seat or Rock of Gibraltar, a phenomenon of the material rather than the infinite world. Just so do many never see true love, for want of a mist to shroud worldly distractions.

Over the ridge I returned to a world of earthly beauty : of rushing water and rich, red earth, where big trees glistened in the morning dew and sunshine lit the cherry blossom into a blaze of pink. The road, now that I knew the landmarks, seemed shorter than when I came. My modest baggage—bedding and suitcase—followed by the ropeway which links the mountains with the plains : I saw it swinging through the air, thousands of feet above me, as I wound my way through the Valley of Khuli-Kani, and I envied its mode of progression (but if the machinery broke down it would be unpleasant for a passenger to be stranded for days in mid-air, thousands of feet above the ground !) I changed horses half-way and was at Bhimpedi in less than seven hours from the Valley of Katmandu. A car met me. We stopped at the ropeway station for the luggage. My suitcase and bedding, they said, had arrived, but the other seventeen pieces were still on their way. Loftily I said I would not bother about the other seventeen pieces. I caught the daily train from Amlekganj and was in Raxaul before dark.

Chapter IV

INDIA

BENARES

INDIA depressed me, after the exhilaration of Nepal. I had a long day in the train, crawling over endless plains towards the Ganges. I crossed the river by ferry, in the evening: a river of fire, of burnished metal which after sunset suddenly turned to coldest steel. In the foreground were dank green flats, and far away lights pierced a belt of red fog to indicate the opposite bank of the wide, sluggish stream. The pandemonium on the ferry boat and in the railway junction was indescribable. Coolies fought (literally) for my baggage. Natives shouted and gabbled and argued in plaintive exasperation; they struggled and swayed and banged against one another for places: pilgrims, mostly, en route, like myself for the Holy City of Benares. I had five hours to wait at the junction: ate a tasteless meal and tried to sleep in a chair in the waiting-room. Natives slept in heaps on the platform like sacks, so indistinguishable from their luggage that I was surprised to see them stir and assume human shape when the train came in.

We reached Benares early in the morning. I took a car and drove to the Ganges. Threading my way through excrement I found a rickety boat, and from a rickety basket chair on its deck I watched the Aryan race salute the sunrise.

The river bank was composed of steps. At the top were the rest-houses of the various Maharajas, where their subjects lodge during the five days of the sacred pilgrimage. The windows of the buildings were far above the ground, because of the phenomenal height of the Ganges in flood, and their lower walls, punctured with holes to house the sacred doves, were like bastions. One was the rest-house of the poor widows, who, night and morning, receive a pound of rice—thanks to a

Pashpati
Above: Sacred Monkeys *Below:* Burning Ghat

Hindu Holy Men
Left: **Benares**   *Right:* **Nepal**

Maharaja's benefaction. Here and there the cones of temples rose from between the buildings, and in one place, where the foundations had fallen away, temples and platforms lay wrecked and half submerged, protruding from the water at an angle.

But it was not the architecture, it was the life on those steps which gave point to the river front. Hundreds of high-caste Hindus (for whom the hours of seven to nine a.m. are reserved each morning) were coming down to the river to wash themselves. Each wore only a loincloth and carried his brass pot, and, as it were, his tooth-glass, also of brass. At the water's edge they performed every kind of ablution. They immersed themselves in the water, they ducked their heads, they washed their bodies all over, they cleaned their teeth and blew their noses and cleared their throats and spat and combed their hair: then they washed their clothes and slapped them down on the stones to wring the water out. Gurgitations mingled inextricably with religious chantings. Women, who might not undress, sat in the water in their sarees and wailed.

There were Hindus of all ages, shining brown in the morning sunlight, but all were lank and gaunt. Some were aged and thin like skeletons. Brahmins sat cross-legged under big umbrellas, and imprinted caste-marks on the foreheads of the pilgrims. There were fakirs caked in ashes, holy men with mauve hair and in garments of ochre. Sacred cattle lazed and wandered everywhere. Women with shaved heads—widows forbidden by laws of caste to remarry—sat among them. Nearby stones recorded occasions, up till a hundred years ago, when such women were burnt alive with their dead husbands. Men sat cross-legged at the water's edge, pouring libations into the sacred river, making obeisance to the sun which rose above the mud flats opposite.

The women's sarees—peacock blue, crimson, canary yellow, orange, olive green—shone gaily in the sunlight, which was not yet bright enough to drain all colour from the scene. It was pleasant to watch this Aryan zeal for cleanliness, this delight in a bathe before breakfast. Only on close inspection was the true nature of the bathing-party evident, did automatic, ritualistic movements and continual chantings testify to a religious rather than a disinterestedly hygienic motive.

Through stagnant water, thick with scum and rotting

flowers, we drifted towards the burning ghats, where a coil of smoke rose into the air from a mass of ashes no longer recognizable as a body. One pyre, neatly stacked in a rectangular pile, had just been lit, and the corpse, swathed in white, protruded from the middle. An old man, surrounded with marigolds, sat cross-legged on the step above. Men were supporting him and rubbing him with oil and sand. He submitted limply to their ministrations, staring, wide-eyed, towards the sun.

"Why are they massaging him like that?" I asked the guide.

"Because he is dead."

And then I saw them unfold him from his limp position and carry him towards the stack of wood. Yet he looked no more dead than many of the living around him. They put him face downwards on the pyre, turned his shaven head towards the river, piled wood on top of him and set it alight with brands of straw, pouring on him butter and flour and rice and sandalwood.

The ceremony was performed with despatch and a good deal of chat, while uninterested onlookers talked among themselves. When I drifted back, some ten minutes later, the head was a charred bone, and a cow was placidly munching the marigold wreaths.

Later in the morning I returned to explore the city. In the filthy streets behind the waterfront I found that in Benares nothing is what it seems: nothing is done for its own sake. Though the Hindu may bathe each morning, his ablutions, qua ablutions, are perfunctory, arguing no love of health or clean linen. Stalls are bright with flowers, but flowers destined only to putrefy in shrines. Bulls stand insolently in your way, scattering the streets with excrement, unmolested from no love of animals but from fearful superstition.

The stink was worst in the temple precincts. The noise was like a zoo. Holy men, smeared with ashes, clamoured around me for baksheesh. (I considered by contrast the clean dignity of a Hindu holy man with whom I had talked in Nepal.) Open drains poured through the alley-ways. Dirty little votive offerings, remains of rice and wax-lamps and decaying flowers disfigured the shrines, so that each place of worship was hideous and stinking with the apparent remains of a nasty meal. Wood and brasswork were so coated with pigment and dirt as to be indistinguishable. Hindus were shaving each other's heads, or quarrelling raucously about their food. The surrounding bazaars were stacked with horrid objects (pots, cigarette-boxes, stationery-racks) in Benares brass, with phallic idols of startling realism, with garish papier-mâché toy gods, with a peculiarly ugly kind of dark brown glazed pottery. Guides attempted to lure me into emporiums which sold silks and carpets and sham antiques at prodigious prices, or offered, in an undertone, to show me the smutty carvings on one of the temples. The mercenariness of the place was worthy of a Mediterranean port.

The temple architecture is debased. The Golden Temple of Vishwanath was built a hundred years ago and gilded in a crude design by Maharaja Ranjit Singh. The Monkey Temple of Durga is stuccoed, or painted, an ugly dark red, and on a notice-board "Gentlemen not belonging to Hindu religion are requested not to enter the temple." Here a gaunt, spectacled Hindu like an elderly Oxford professor in the nude followed me about and leered till I gave him some annas. A child with a half-closed eye, which protruded loathsome and yellow from its lid, pestered me for alms. Finally I gave in, at which he opened the eye and smiled with avaricious delight. (It was the first time I had ever seen someone wink by opening instead of shutting an eye.)

I drove back through ugly streets. Advertisements for patent medicines glared at me by the thousand ("Sexol, for Birth Control, Sold Here", "The Ideal Homeo Hall", "Dr. Chatterjee's Unique Specific for Asthma and Diabetes"), but advertisements testifying mostly to the prevalence of diseases beside which the sinister ailments remediable by the European advertiser are but childish complaints.

I stopped by the Mission Church at Sigra, which is nineteenth-century Gothic of the simplest kind, and found it by far the best bit of architecture in Benares. I walked on its lawns and took shade beneath its trees and observed that the sacred bull is no respecter of religions, since in these Christian precincts too he wandered where he liked. I watched the little Indian girls parading in cotton frocks and the little boys in shorts; I watched Indians in a cantonment playing hockey; I breathed air which, at last, was pure, and for the first and only time believed myself in sympathy with missions.

LUCKNOW

From the squalor of Benares to the elegance of Government House, Lucknow, was a sharp transition, and I began to understand why so many English visitors find everything in the Indian garden to be lovely. If in India you travel exclusively from one Government House to another you carry away the impression of an enchanting country. The quiet luxury of the rooms, as in an English country house; the shade of banyans and green lawns, with fountains playing and scarlet cannas blazing in the flower-beds; the dusky, turbaned servants in their picturesque red uniforms; the attentive A.D.C.'s who order cars for you whenever you want them and organize anything you may wish to do; the cool verandahs with well-appointed writing-tables and an ample supply of illustrated papers; the excellent meals, the drinks, the freedom to do what you like; all this combined, at Lucknow, with the charm and wit and easy manners of Sir Malcolm Hailey showed me a very different aspect of India to what I had seen in dak bungalows and railway stations and the sordid temple purlieus of the Holy City.

"I'm afraid," said Sir Malcolm, "I'll have to put you in a tent. We're rather full up. I hope you don't mind."

A tent, so inured had I become to Asiatic discomfort, was nothing to take in my stride; but to my astonishment I was shown into a huge marquee containing a suite of rooms—bedroom, dressing-room, sitting-room, bathroom—all for my personal use. A printed slip on my writing-table, amid an immense variety of regal stationery and order forms for whatever I might require, informed me amongst other things that I was arriving to stay at Government House, gave a detailed programme of Their Excellencies' movements during the day and appended a list of the guests expected for dinner.

But the atmosphere was delightfully informal. At breakfast each morning Lady Hailey's pet donkey moved about among the guests, and asked for eggs and bacon. A crowd of little dogs yapped around its feet until it lost its temper, went for them, and had to be removed.

One evening there was an investiture in the glittering Durbar Hall, at which Sir Malcolm and Lady Hailey sat enthroned on a dais amid a galaxy of uniforms which would

Benares
Above: Burning Ghat   *Below:* Bathing Ghat

Above: Taj Mahal, Agra   *Below:* Humayun's Tomb, Delhi

have thrilled the susceptible hearts of Jane Austen's young ladies. An unending sequence of Indian gentleman, nervous, perplexed by the problem of keeping their heels together, but bursting with pride, processed in turn to the dais where they were turned into a variety of things I hardly knew existed: Khan Bahadurs, Khan Sahibs, Rai Bahadurs, Rai Sahibs. His Excellency, in white silken knee breeches and a braided, dark-blue uniform straight from the eighteenth century, made a different speech to each one, extolling his virtues and his loyalty to the Empire. Moreover, according to the habitual practice of Sir Malcolm Hailey, decorations were even conferred on the "untouchables".

Afterwards there was a reception, with cakes, coffee and lemonade, while the band played in the courtyard. India's social functions are purely Victorian. You would have to go back a good fifty years to parallel the atmosphere of Government House in full dress: the solid pomp and state and formality, the blaze of uniforms; the garden-parties, discussed by young and old in a thousand cantonments for months before and after, where a brass band plays on a bandstand and gentlemen stroll decorously with their consorts beneath the trees. The Indian Empire was at its heyday in Queen Victoria's reign and Victorian it has remained. The Great Queen still reigns over India; you expect to sing *God Save the Queen* and to see her portrait everywhere in the place of honour.

Moreover her spirit animates the whole of Anglo-Indian social life, and is at its most pronounced in remoter stations. Everybody in India is "looking down" on somebody else. The ladies of the I.C.S. look down on those of the Army, the colonel's wife looks down on the wife of the Commissioner, but both condescend to accept Mrs. X, though only the wife of a junior official, because her father was a lord. ("I don't know if you've met," they will say, "the Honourable Mrs. X.")

The British Empire would not be the British Empire without the cavalry looking down on the infantry and the infantry looking down on the cavalry; without the whole lot looking down on the commercials ("My *dear*," you almost expect to hear them say, "they're in *trade* !"). While in the ranks of the commercials themselves (looking down both on the Army and the I.C.S.) an even stricter hierarchical system prevails, depending on the status of a man's firm, the extent of his salary, and whether he is a burra sahib, "Number Two", or merely a junior clerk.

"What are you?" asked a supercilious young man of a stranger on board a P. & O. "Are you I.C.S.?"

"No. I'm P.W.D.F.M.S."

The supercilious young man walked off without a word.

(They like you to have initials, provided they be the right ones. Initial-less they cannot place you. A major, after puzzling for a long time, said to me:

"I suppose you're F.O."

"No. I'm just travelling for amusement."

He was disappointed, and still mystified. "You look F.O. Just the type. I'll think of you as F.O., anyway.")

But most Victorian of all is the card game: the box outside each bungalow with "Mr. & Mrs. Tattle, I.C.S. Not at Home": the afternoons which well-bred ladies and gentlemen spend dropping cards into the boxes of the ladies and gentlemen with whom they dined the day before or with whom they hope to dine in the near future.

Such snobberies, however, are not confined to the British. There are Indians who will sell their souls for a title, and are always dissatisfied when they get them because they ought to have been higher. A Governor of my acquaintance told me that he knew of a man who was prepared to pay a kra of rupees to become a maharaja. Another said he would pay a large sum to a hospital if he could be made a Khan Bahadur. The Governor refused. The man went to the Viceroy, and gave money to a hospital in Delhi. The Viceroy applied to the Governor to discover whether he would be a suitable recipient of the honour. The Governor replied with heat: "X seems to think that the fountain of honour is the village pump."

When it comes to harassed A.D.C.'s grappling for hours a day with problems of Indian precedence Thackeray isn't in it. Maharajas jostle each other into dinner at Government House in the most undignified fashion lest a rival get in first. There is a famous story of the Maharaja of B (as I will call him) who declared that he would only attend Lord Curzon's Durbar on condition that he should precede the Maharaja of A. Lord Curzon replied that this was out of the question, and peremptorily commanded him to attend the Durbar none the less, indicating that his absence would be considered an act of grave disloyalty to the Crown. The Maharaja gave in. But two days before the Durbar his brother died. He regretted that owing to mourning he could not attend.

His brother died of poisoning.

Some years later, at the Royal Durbar, the same difficulty arose. The officials were much exercised how to deal with it. They could not have a relative of the Maharaja of B taking poison every time His Highness was summoned to appear before his sovereign. Finally someone hit upon a brilliant solution. The Maharaja of B was attached to the royal suite: thus ex officio he had precedence over the Maharaja of A, and the problem was evaded.

This Maharaja of A on an official visit to some military station, once refused to get out of his train because his salute had not been fired. It was pointed out to His Highness that it is not the custom of the British Army to fire salutes on a Sunday. But he was taking no risks. He remained in his train till Monday morning, when he duly received his salute—and the entire programme of events was disorganized.

There is another, and different, story of the Maharaja of A, concerning the occasion of an important religious ceremony in his state. While heading a procession through the streets the Maharaja noticed an attractive girl at an upper window. He stopped the procession and entered the house. The procession had to remain outside at a standstill until His Highness's return. It was there for ten days.

Lucknow is full of fantastic palaces which date from the eighteenth century and represent the ultimate debasement of Moslem architecture. But the extravagance of their style and the immensity of their proportions make them entertaining to visit. They represent for the most part the eccentricities of the old Nawabs of Oudh; but it is with the name of Claud Martin that I shall always associate them in my mind. Martin was a French adventurer, the son of a cooper in Lyon, who enlisted in the Lorraine regiment at the age of sixteen, and arrived in India at the time when Dupleix seemed likely to sweep the board. But within a very few years the tables were turned, Clive overthrew Dupleix, and after the fall of Pondicherry Martin opportunely changed sides, rising to be a captain (and ultimately a retired major-general) in the service of the British. In the course of his duties he came to Lucknow and ingratiated himself so successfully with Asaf-ud-Daula, Nawab of Oudh, that he spent the rest of his life there in his service as a glorified major-domo and Court favourite.

Asaf-ud-Daula, we are told by an English traveller,* expended every year about two hundred thousand pounds in English manufactures. This Nabob had more than a hundred gardens, twenty palaces, twelve hundred elephants, three thousand fine saddle-horses, fifteen hundred double-barrel guns, seventeen hundred superb lustres, thirty thousand shades of various form and colour; several hundred large mirrors, girandoles and clocks; some of the latter were very curious, richly set with jewels, having figures in continual movement, and playing tunes every hour; two of these clocks cost him thirty thousand pounds. Without taste or judgment . . . his museum was so ridiculously displayed that a wooden cuckoo clock was placed close to a superb timepiece which cost the price of a diadem; and a valuable landscape of Claude Lorraine suspended near a board painted with ducks and drakes. He sometimes gave a dinner to ten or twelve persons sitting at their ease in a carriage drawn by elephants. . . . His jewels amounted to about eight millions sterling. I saw him in the midst of this precious treasure, handling them as a child does his toys.

Amid such lavishness it is not hard to understand how Martin accumulated an enormous fortune. He was, as we should say to-day, "in on a good racket". His commission on all these fantastic European treasures must have been prodigious; he netted more pickings as Superintendent of the Arsenal, fitting out the East India Company's contingent which protected Lucknow; he made a tidy sum from bribes for his good influence at Court; he became a moneylender on an enormous scale and a pawnbroker on a lesser one; and finally he drew a respectable income from the manufacture of indigo.

Martin was a versatile eccentric, as eccentrics go, and spent his fortune in a variety of ways. He was of a mechanical turn of mind. He had a mint of his own, a printing press, a distillery of scent; he amused himself (with profit) as a watchmaker, a gunsmith, a horticulturist and a horse-breeder; he experimented with balloons. But he had cultured interests as well. His library of four thousand books included Sanskrit and Persian manuscripts; his gallery of two hundred pictures contained forty-seven Zoffanys and a number of Claude Lorraines; while his fantastic architectural creations, in which

---

* Lewis Ferdinand Smith. *Oriental Memoirs*, by James Forbes, 1813.

his own designs played a prominent part, survive in Lucknow for all to see.

Chief among these is the Palace of Constantia, now known as La Martinière and converted into a school for Anglo-Indian children. Martin left the bulk of his money (amounting in all to forty lakhs of rupees) for the establishment of three such schools in which children were to be educated "in the English language and religion", a curious stipulation from a Frenchman and a Catholic. The other two are at Calcutta and Lyon respectively. He made especial provision in the will, a fantastic document of thirty-four articles in a curious hotch-potch of French and English, for an annual commemorative feast at which each boy should drink a glass of sherry.

La Martinière, which cost £160,000 to build, is a palace as big as Blenheim, standing on an imposing terrace. It overlooks a huge park and an artificial lake from which there rises a fluted column, 125 feet high, built, we are told, "apparently with no other object than that of exciting the admiration of Nawab Asaf-ud-Daula, to whom it is said that the general had tried to sell the palace".

The portentous mock classical façade is flanked with wide, semicircular colonnades, while the central block is piled high in a fabulous sequence of pediments, battlements, Italian balustrades and Indian cupolas. A gigantic Hindu lion grins from each corner of the roof, and crude Italianate statues are perched precariously on kiosks: a pair of overgrown cherubs gawkily intertwined, a knock-kneed Roman Emperor, very short in the leg, a rakish Britannia with a tilted helmet, a Muse striving frenziedly to restrain her companion from suicide (or perhaps merely controlling her in a fit of vertigo). The interior is profusely decorated with rococo Italian plasterwork: arabesques and bas-reliefs on a ground of pink or pale green, the work of imported Italian artists. A great bell, cast by Martin himself, stands in the central vault, and beneath is his tomb, designed by himself and surmounted by his bust.

Elsewhere in Lucknow are the even more eccentric palaces, mosques and mausoleums of his patron, in which Martin himself must certainly have had some hand. The roof of the Great Imambara is an orgy of onions: prize onions, middle-sized onions, spring onions forming a balustrade. The precincts contain a mosque and other gigantic buildings adorned with every imaginable excrescence. One, besides its onions, has a semicircular roof studded as it were with big, stone nails. On one side of the courtyard is the largest vaulted hall in the world, which has no wood whatever in its construction. In side-aisles are models of famous shrines, in wax or sandalwood, reminding me of that advertisement which portrays the Scott Monument in Edinburgh built of jampots. The interior of one of its domes imitates the design of a melon, and the building, which is poorly plastered inside, contains a maze. Husainabad has a garden containing, among other oddities, a model of the Taj Mahal in plaster. The main hall, or Palace of Lights, plastered black on the outside, contains nothing but chandeliers. Hundreds of them, heavily ornate, of every conceivable colour and size, hang from the ceiling or sprout from the floor, and the effect is like that of a mammoth electrician's showroom in the Tottenham Court Road.

Elsewhere is a picture gallery in which, among miniatures of flowers, military scenes, and cockfights, are the portraits of the Nawabs of Oudh. It is instructive to watch the gradual degeneration of their features. The first is manly enough, but each successor is fatter and flabbier until you reach the last: an obese, yellow monster like an overfed Levantine, with thick black, silken, curling hair, and a pendulous naked breast protruding from his robes.

Lucknow has an iron bridge, designed by Rennie, similar to that which he built at Boston, in Lincolnshire, and one of the oldest of its type in the world. It is not beautiful, and one can only be thankful that iron, as a bridge-building material, was not yet prevalent during Rennie's career. Had it arrived earlier Waterloo Bridge would have been destroyed without fuss or regret.

But of all the monuments in Lucknow the ruins of the Residency stand out as the finest and most moving. Built of sandstone in a fashion far more solid than the modern colonial building, fragments of its classical columns and fanlights survive. Of an admirably proportioned design, it was planned on a spacious, eighteenth-century scale which rendered it all the more vulnerable to bombardment. There is something especially poignant about an eighteenth-century ruin, and the residency at Lucknow is the more so since the Mutiny is almost within living memory. I could not help visualizing, as I walked through its grounds, the picture of some Government House of to-day subjected to a similar fate.

AGRA

It is one of my misfortunes that I can rarely contemplate white marble without recalling mutton fat. It was therefore with some misgiving that I approached the Taj Mahal, which I knew, moreover, to be late and debased in style.

I had already visited the Agra Fort, which only increased my apprehension. I found a strong suggestion of the ham sandwich in its alternate layers of marble and red sandstone while the greater part might have been made of pressed beef, its fat carved in ornamentation as if for an exhibition of Empire produce. The gatehouse of the Taj itself is hardly more encouraging; it represents a style which I can only describe as "Debased Galantine".

But when I first set eyes on the Taj, framed in this archway, I forgot about mutton fat: I saw a vision of rapturous whiteness. I could not help being impressed by its size, its simplicity, its perfect proportions, for the Taj is geometry raised to the kingdom of art; but above all I was soothed by this miraculous effect of whiteness.

The Taj Mahal owes much to its setting. It is surrounded by the loveliest of gardens, laid out formally in the Italian style. A wide channel of water, enclosed by an avenue of cypresses, leads to the mausoleum, whose western terraces give on to the River Jumna. Stone paving encloses lawns, where there are flower-beds of cannas and shrubberies of scarlet hibiscus, and birds abound in the trees.

But the nearer I approached the tomb the further did the vision fade, and I never recaptured my first impression. The four minarets, at the corners, stalked up through the trees like ill-proportioned lighthouses of white glazed tiling. For some reason I had expected to find that the building was much over-decorated. But the reverse is the case. At close range the decoration seemed to me inadequate to the immensity of the tomb. The bays are carved with shallow recesses which look like empty niches. A pretty little floral design in coloured stones surmounts the archways, framed in a black belt of Arabic lettering; pillars have a herring-bone inlay; there are blank panes of marble with a zigzag border in stone of another colour; but of carving there is none, save in the lower panels which are bas-reliefs of flowers, woven into no design, but standing upright in the Persian fashion, like plates in a book of botany.

I could not help seeing a paucity of inspiration in the simplicity of this décor. But it may be the nature rather than the quality of its workmanship which is at fault. Marble, unlike other stones which weather and take on lights and shadows and live of themselves, is a dead stone, it *is* like mutton fat, unless it is carved into life or ingeniously combined with some of those other stones to give it point. The Greeks understood marble. In their temples it is always carved, in the form of fluting, perhaps, or a frieze. But the marble of the Taj stands up in unrelieved slabs : hence there is a deadness, an inadequacy about the building which its fine geometrical proportions do not at first sight suggest.

The truth is that the Taj Mahal is primarily a sentimental and theatrical structure. Its appeal is in its "story". As you contemplate it you think of the Emperor Shah Jahan mourning for Mumtaz Mahal, his beloved wife, and resolving to build to her memory the costliest and most splendid shrine ever known. The Taj Mahal, enshrining their tombs, is what the newspapers would call a "Monument of Love". The interior, with its open-work marble screens and the pattern of genuine precious stones inlaid in the marble of the tombs, has a certain exquisite delicacy and gives no impression of ostentation. Nevertheless it is a work of splendour rather than a work of art : it is precious rather than beautiful. The fervid inspiration of religion gives to other Mohammedan buildings a vigour which is lacking in the Taj; maybe the inspiration of a living god is stronger than that of a woman mourned.

I was told afterwards that I should have seen the Taj by moonlight. But I have as little use for a building as for a woman whose beauty blossoms only by the light of the moon.

In Agra I found Manfred and Quinney, and learnt that the adventures of the expedition had by no means ended at Quetta. On the way to Peshawar the Colonel drove into a river, was engulfed in quicksands and took five hours to get out. In fact it was largely due to the determination and efficiency of Mrs. Mock that he did so at all. Bits of the road had proved worse than anything in Afghanistan, and the Dowager had arrived in Peshawar without a single mudguard.

Manfred and Quinney left the morning after my arrival for Bhopal and Udaipur, but that night, to my surprise, Miss Gumbleton appeared. She had been to Kashmir, which was enveloped in snow, its houseboats languishing untenanted on a wintry river, and was on her way to Poona, where she intended spending Christmas alone. Together we hired a car and visited Akbar's capital of Fatehpur Sikri.

Fatehpur Sikri is some twenty miles from Agra. Big milestones of phallic appearance punctuate the way to the city, which is built entirely of red sandstone quarried on the spot and towers above the plain. Founded by Akbar to celebrate the birth of his first son, it was only inhabited by him for fifteen years, and then abandoned for some reason which has never been properly explained. As a result, though dating from 1569, it has still a strange effect of newness : it is the fact of being lived in, rather than the wear and tear of the elements, which ages a city. Empty since 1585, Fatephur Sikri looks unfinished, for its style is relatively simple ; it has few of the additions and embellishments which enhance the decoration of a city throughout the ages, few of the refinements which I was to find in later Mogul architecture. It is unique among cities in that it is wholly of a single period, and a period, moreover, of a very few years.

It is interesting also in its marked fusion of the Hindu and Mohammedan styles. Akbar was centuries ahead of his time in his extraordinary religious toleration. He treated Hindu and Moslem alike and earned unpopularity from the Moslems through his repeal of the tax on Hindu pilgrims and the polltax on adult males who were not of the Moslem faith. Though at first Persian artists predominated at his Court, Hindus ultimately outnumbered them, and their architectural influence is apparent. The Jama Masjid, or Great Mosque, though built, with three great domes, after the plan of a famous shrine at Mecca, has pillars broken by Hindu decoration and a square instead of a vaulted ceiling. But it is a conventionalized Hindu, where the elephant's trunk of Ganesh has become a mere scroll and the lotus bud is no more than a formalized corbel.

Of all the buildings in Fatehpur Sikri the most remarkable is the hall of private audience, for here you feel that the ghost of Akbar still persists. Though illiterate, the Emperor possessed a library of twenty-four thousand volumes, which would be read to him continuously. He surrounded himself with wise men, and liked in particular to dispute on theological questions. Every religion interested him, and at his Court were Hindus, Buddhists, Mohammedans, Jains, Zoroastrians and finally Christians, in the shape of Portuguese Jesuit fathers from Goa. (On one of the gateways to the Jama Masjid a quotation from the Bible is carved in Arabic lettering below an extract from the Koran.) He would summon the representatives of the various faiths together in the Diwan-i-Khas, debate with them and listen for hours to their arguments. The building is of unique design. Inside is a huge pillar, from the top of which four bridges radiate to connect with a gallery round the walls. Akbar would sit on this isolated throne in the centre, while the disputants were gathered round the edge, the people remained below and ministers could approach the Emperor from each of the four corners. In a building nearby is the Astrologer's Seat, where he would commune with Yogi philosophers. Akbar saw good in every religion, and the representatives of each continually believed themselves on the point of converting him. But he could not accept their mutual intolerance, and finally promulgated a divine monotheism of his own. This, much to his grief, was accepted by none.

The Jesuit fathers must have been sadly shocked by the Emperor's harem of three hundred women at Fatehpur Sikri, albeit it was drawn impartially from all religions. It is hard to imagine these saints and ascetics in the midst of the lavish Oriental surroundings of which one can still see the framework to-day; among the magnificent buildings of the harem, the Sultana's houses, the Turkisk and Zenana baths, the places where the ladies played hide-and-seek, the stables for thousands of elephants and camels which the Emperor would inspect himself each day. (So thorough was he in such respects that he would often move about in disguise among the common people, to discover their way of life and their ideas.) Most noticeable among these buildings are the hospital, whose existence one would hardly have expected in sixteenth-century India, and the Panch Mahal. This is a five-storeyed building of kiosks piled one above the other, and reminiscent of the Temple of Krishna in Nepal, save that it is shaped like a right-angled instead of an isosceles triangle. The merchants who, in the reign of Queen Elizabeth, visited the Court of Akbar, establishing Britain's first connection with India, must have been astonished by the splendour and the up-to-dateness which they saw in this barbarous country beyond the seas.

A Mohammedan guide took us round, and seemed refreshingly human compared to the impersonal Hindu guides in other places. It is a relief to meet a Mohammedan in India. To talk to him is, by comparison, like talking to a Christian, to someone of one's own flesh and blood. The company of our guide was a tonic : he was lively, sociable, intelligent, amusing, and told stories with relish, indulging in sly witticisms on the subject of Akbar's ladies. But he referred to the Hindus as "savages" : the intolerance which so saddened Akbar is as rabid as ever.

On the way back we stopped at Sikandarah to see Akbar's tomb. Standing in an ample garden it is a striking but not a beautiful building. The gates are as though panelled with various kinds of salami sausage. The tomb itself is the usual orgy of kiosks, but Shah Jahan, with his incorrigible mania for marble, substituted it for red sandstone on the top storey.

Beyond Sikandarah we passed a statue of a horse, in red sandstone. It is said that the animal, carrying mails, galloped from Agra to Delhi and back to this spot (close on two hundred and fifty miles) in a single day. Here, within two miles of Agra, it expired from exhaustion, and the rider was subsequently buried in the same place. Sandwiched between the road and the railway the horse seems to challenge more modern methods of transport. Evidently the pursuit of such "records" is no new craze, and the Moguls were as devoted to speed-worship as ourselves.

CHAPTER V

INDIA (*continued*)

DELHI

DELHI, as I approached it, looked oddly like a European capital; the white backs of buildings in New Delhi might almost have been modern tenements in the suburbs of Berlin. It was pleasant, after so long in the "wilds", to find the appurtenances of European civilization. The taxis had real taximeters. There were haberdashery- and antique-shops (or perhaps there was only one of each) as smart as in the Rue de Castiglione. There was a bookshop in which I could dawdle as contentedly as in Oxford. *The Private Life of Henry the Eighth* was on at the principal cinema.

I stayed at the Cecil Hotel, a pleasant place consisting of several white buildings, covered with purple bougainvillea, and standing in an ample garden. It is run by the Hotz family, who are the Ritzes of India and own all the hotels worthy of the name. The original Mr. Hotz was a Swiss photographer who had strayed to India. Mrs. Hotz did not see her large family getting fat on photography, so set to work to make their fortunes herself. She bought a hotel in Simla, made it an immense success, and sold it at a profit on condition that she refrained from opening another hotel within eight miles. She opened another, ten miles off, and made a success of that too. To give occupation to her staff of servants in the cold weather (as the heat of an Indian winter is called) she opened the Cecil at Delhi, which is run by Miss Hotz. On the snowball principle, the Hotz hotels increased; each member of the family was sent home to Switzerland to learn the trade and found on his return a nice new hotel, ready for him to run. So now the Hotzes are rich, but not from photography.

There were many visitors in the Cecil Hotel. For though the

Viceroy and his Court were on tour, Christmas was approaching and the climate by Indian standards was pleasant. Hawkers of postcards, jewellery, brassware, silks and embroideries, Tibetans with treasures from their native land camped in the gardens and pestered you to buy.

One day a snake-charmer turned up. He emptied snakes out of bags, disentangled them, sorted them out, throwing them about like bits of rope, and tied them in knots, all with complete unconcern. A hooded cobra watched the proceedings from a basket, like an old ram. The deadlier snakes were in little round boxes, whence he stirred and baited them with sticks. The Russell viper reared up out of its box, hissed with fury, coiled itself round and round in spirals, making a noise like a chain, darted a little red tongue in and out.

"Cobra chicken bite five minute dead, krait chicken bite three minute dead, Russell viper chicken bite one minute dead," he announced with matter-of-fact relish. Fascinated, I watched this tiny king of poisoners, which could kill so quickly by a mere lick of the tongue, death coiling and uncoiling in lovely stripes of brown and yellow and grey. The fascination of contemplating death within one's reach never palls, whether at the top of a precipice, in front of a train, by the pistons and wheels of a factory. A snake is its most beautiful, hence its most fascinating instrument. The krait was a harmless-looking white-bellied thing, no bigger than a very large worm. With the scorpion, a venomous little black lobster, the charmer was less at ease. He picked it up gingerly by the tail and threw it down again quickly: the ugliest instrument of death.

"Cobra chicken bite five minute dead, krait chicken bite three minute dead, Russell viper chicken bite one minute dead." He forced them, twisting with protest, back into their little boxes.

Around the Cecil Hotel is a kind of park, like the Bois de Boulogne. Here, I thought, it would be nice to take an occasional stroll. But before I had reached the end of the drive I was pouring with perspiration. Outside in the park I was choked with dust, the grass was parched, the litter and stench were appalling. I soon realized why no one in India ever walks, reluctantly gave up all idea of gentle exercise, and in future hired a tonga. This is a sort of pony carriage with seats back to back. The front seat tilts comfortably backwards: the driver sits on that. The back seat tilts uncomfortably forwards: you sit on that.

In this way I covered the surrounding country of Delhi. Distances, in India, are considerable. The country is so flat that no one need stint himself in the matter of space, and the cantonments of a town, where the British population is quartered, are not only extensive in themselves but often four or five miles from the native quarter. Delhi has seven cities, each representing a different era in her history, each testifying to the inability of India to govern herself. In the West the site of a city is directed by geographical features. Contour lines impose natural limits and necessitate compression, so that each new era must to some extent destroy or alter the buildings of its predecessor to find room for itself. But within the ample proportions of India you can spread yourself in architecture to your heart's content. Here, instead of destroying old buildings, each dynasty has simply built its Delhi a little further along. Thus intact examples of the architecture of every period survive, and you proceed from one era to another across a deserted landscape of thorn and scrub and sand.

In the centre of the existing city (which in its turn is being superseded by New Delhi) is the Red Palace of Shah Jahan. Here I spent many happy, shady hours, and blessed the name of Lord Curzon. Lord Curzon is a man, unpopular in his lifetime, who is held in increasingly affectionate memory. His restoration and preservation of ancient monuments, relatively unnoticed at the time, is since his death, a living monument to him, inspiring all one's gratitude. It is impossible to exaggerate the value of his work in India; for besides rescuing masterpieces of Mohammedan architecture from decay and destruction, he has created for them surroundings worthy of their beauty, and Delhi is a mass of gardens where mosques and palaces and mausoleums stand. It was balm to escape from the city's dusty streets to well-watered lawns of the Red Palace, to breathe the smell of new-mown grass after the acrid stink of the bazaars, to lie by flower-beds of purple and scarlet and yellow in the shade of ample trees and contemplate the cool, white marble of the buildings and the erect ranks of cypresses attending them.

Enclosed in bastions of red sandstone and outer courtyards of red buildings, the Palace, in its inner garden, is white as the kernel of a nut. Three-quarters of a century later than the Fort at Agra, it represents the efflorescence of Mogul architecture, and has all the refinement which Fatehpur Sikri lacks. Its buildings have an exquisite delicacy of decoration and design. Here are no slabs of mutton fat but marble fretted and moulded and chiselled to an airy lightness. This sequence of buildings is like the Courts of a Mohammedan heaven. Each one is a vista of open colonnades, with screens of marble trellis-work. Channels of water, paved with marble and precious stones, once ran through them, as you can see, and to one a waterfall brought rippling coolness. Tanks are carved with a lotus design and resemble ceilings placed upon the ground. Marble panels and arched embrasures are painted with Persian floral designs in faded gold or shades of blue and green; or they are inlaid with semi-precious stones. The panels of the durbar-balcony are jewelled with gaily plumaged birds against a background of black by a renegade French jeweller, Austin de Bordeaux. There is a tiny, pearl-white mosque; there are kiosks and summer-houses of exquisite marble fretwork; there are baths where not only the walls but the floors are inlaid with precious stones. When great scarlet awnings were placed across the colonnades, when the Emperor sat on the peacock throne amid a setting of richly embroidered stuffs this palace must have been wonderful to see. As it is to-day it gives a grateful impression of coolness and luxury.

Opposite the red walls is the great mosque, the Jama Masjid, where the Mogul emperors went to worship. Standing on a mighty plinth of steps, where traders spread their wares, its courtyard astonishes you by its size. There would be no room in any European city for so huge a cloister. In the centre is a square tank of water, where Moslems perform their ablutions. On each of three sides a gateway, three storeys high, breaks the open colonnade. On the fourth is the mosque itself, an utterly harmonious union of sandstone and marble in delicate stripes of red and white. Bulbous as they are, the three great domes (white marble ribbed with black) and their soaring minarets have a wonderful lightness and grace.

It was not until I had been several days in Delhi, enjoying its shade and spaciousness and the beauty of its buildings, that I penetrated beyond the Jama Masjid into the native quarter of the city. Before visiting India I had been inclined to ascribe the average Englishman's antipathy to the Indian to his disproportionate nasal fastidiousness. Outside our own country we are, as a race, ridiculously sensitive to smells, an abnormality which goes far to account for our dislike of foreign and, especially, native races. This had always seemed to me an exaggerated foible, due to the Englishman's tendency to find the unfamiliar unpleasant. I had never found that Arabs or negroes smelt nasty. They smelt different to ourselves; that was all.

But the native quarter of Delhi was to prove a violent exception. An Arab or a negro town would be pure and spotless compared with it. There was something particularly venomous and malignant about its smell: an acrid stink of burning excreta, of rotting food, filthy humanity, drains, refuse and decay. It pierced me like a needle in the back of the nostrils, and set going some nerve which induced blind rage. I felt savage. I wanted to hit out right and left, at everything and everybody. Humanity had no right to descend to such depths of filth. It was an outrage on the rest of the human race.

Squatting on the foul pavements were lank, inhuman skeletons with shaven heads, protruding crania, hollow cheeks, mad eyes, low foreheads. Lean and spiky, they scratched their diseased bodies, they hitched up stinking garments, grey with dirt, they trailed their shirt-tails in the dust and the mud and the rubbish. Indifferent to the squalor, indifferent to the disease and madness and deformity which flourished in their hideous streets, they sat like things inhuman, they moved but did not live, their chatter was a perpetual death rattle.

I was stifled, assailed with claustrophobia, I became frantic to escape from this living hell. I emerged as if from a nightmare, and it was long before I could breathe freely, could get that suffocating, piercing, screaming stink out of my nostrils.

My reaction, superficial maybe and hysterical, yet seemed to explain a lot. Henceforward, though I might not defend, I could at least sympathize with the exasperation which is so apt to poison the Englishman's relationship with the Indian. I understood why his nerves are set aflame, why his voice so often rises to a scream of shrill rage, why mere contact can provoke his intolerance. I had found myself irritated by the incompetence, the dishonesty, the cringing servility of the low-caste Hindu. I had observed (if superficially) the inhuman

Delhi: New and Old
Above: Council House *Below:* Eighteenth Century Observatory

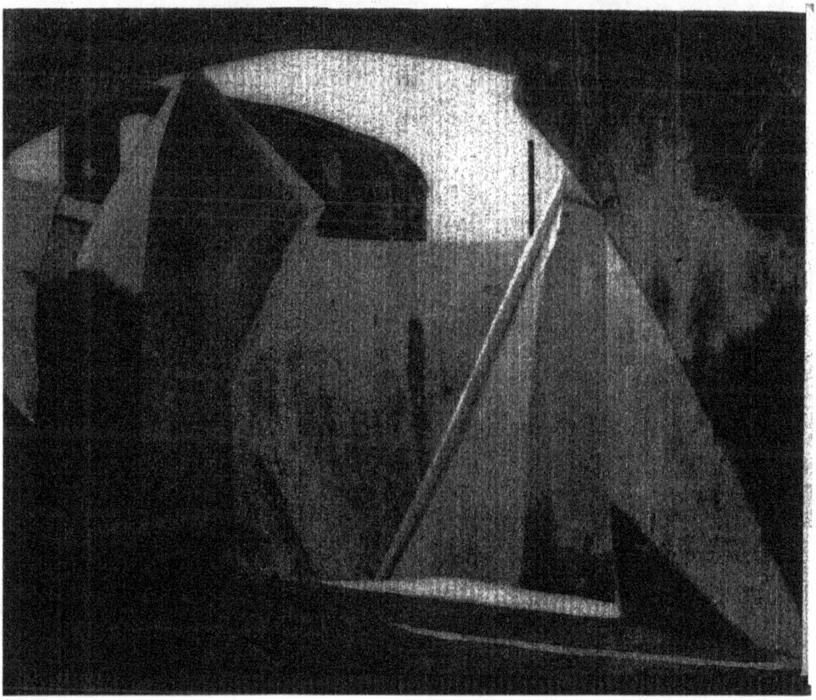

Observatory, Delhi

influences of his religion. But it is his filth, his total disregard for any semblance of physical decency and cleanliness, the degradation of his standard of life which, more than his moral and religious outlook, give rise to racial prejudice. Many a European woman, in particular, never gets beyond the savagery of that smell in the native quarter.

It was a relief to turn towards buildings, dignified and aloof. The landscape for miles around Delhi is dotted with the dark stone domes of mosques and tombs which loom through the haze of the flat, park-like landscape. Alone as I was in Delhi, I found them strangely companionable. Architecture is often better company than humanity, and these domed, solitary monuments, each enshrining the mortal remains and breathing still the spirit of someone forgotten, have a personal atmosphere of their own.

Every building, moreover, has a personality unconnected with its history or its purpose, unconnected too with its associations as set forth in the palaver of guide-books or with its technical qualities as set forth by the architectural expert. Buildings have many of the characteristics of human beings: they can be honest, generous, kind, haughty, sympathetic, arch, skittish, eccentric. Above all they have gender. Though the French distinction between *la* maison and *le* château hardly implies a recognition of sex principle in architecture, it has a certain appositeness: a castle is always masculine, a house more often feminine. Generally speaking gender goes according to periods: Tudor is feminine, Jacobean masculine; Queen Anne is feminine, later Georgian is masculine, but the Regency, once more, is feminine. Modern architecture is sexless. Gothic varies: Notre Dame is masculine, so is Chartres. But Bourges, I think, and Salisbury are feminine. Modern Gothic is neither: it is effeminate, like other styles and other buildings, mannish or hermaphrodite, which fall betwixt and between. The Taj Mahal is effeminate too. The Jama Masjid, on the other hand, has all the grace and lightness of a woman in her prime: it is womanly.

These early tombs which rise from the scrub around the cities of Delhi are for the most part masculine in gender. Rugged they are, of rough stone, and often battlemented so as to be more like fortresses than tombs. Among my favourite was a group some miles from the road, known as the Tin

Burj: a family of three tombs standing in ploughed fields. One is large and strong, with three storeys of filled-in arches: the second, though rough, is decorated with lace plasterwork and a necklace of turquoise: the third, which is small, looks like the child of the other two. Beyond, in a primitive village, is the earliest octagonal tomb in Delhi. Women in yellow sarees, unaccustomed to visitors, were walking about the village unveiled, but hastily covered their faces as I approached. Better known are the Lodi tombs and mosque, dating from the fifteenth century. Moss-grown, they stand in a scattered thicket of thorn-trees and are built of rough yellow stone, with an occasional ornament of red sandstone and the remains of turquoise tiling on their kiosks. The interior of the mosque, with its gallery resembling a triforium, is not unlike that of an English Norman church. Two of the tombs are of an octagonal design. One stands in a cloistered courtyard, now overgrown with rank hay and populated with parrots. It is moving to watch through these early tombs the spark of artistic sensibility in a rough and rugged race develop slowly into a flame.

Prominent among the architectural forms which bespatter the empty landscape are to one side Humayun's Tomb, towering vivid red and white above the rest; to the other in the distance the slim, high chimney of the Kutb Minar; and in the centre the long bastions of the Purana Qila, the early Mogul capital—each representing a different age and city, each worthy to be classed as Delhi's finest monument.

The Kutb Minar and its surrounding group of buildings are among Delhi's earliest structures, yet oddly enough they are among the most ornate, the richest in decoration, for here the pre-Mohammedan Hindu influence still prevailed. The pillars of the cloister surrounding the mosque are pure Hindu in ornament, and survived from an ancient Brahmin temple. All that remains of the mosque itself is a screen of lofty arches which at first sight might almost be Gothic. They are of red sandstone, built as a first Mohammedan protest against the surrounding Hindu architecture, exquisitely carved nevertheless by Hindu workmen with Arabic writing from the Koran and conventionalized floral decoration. The union of Hindu and Mohammedan in these early buildings combines the best of both styles—Hindu vitality of carving with Mohammedan simplicity of design—more extensively and successfully than in Akbar's buildings, three hundred years later, at Fatehpur Sikri.

Rising from their midst is the gigantic Kutb itself, a fluted thirteenth-century tower eighty *yards* high. Narrowing to a point, broken by three balconies at regular intervals, it is wonderfully built, perfectly preserved, exquisitely decorated with bands of carving from the Koran. Here in the Delhi Plain where domes predominate and minarets are rare, the Kutb is especially striking.

But even more impressive is the pillar of solid iron which stands beside it. Fluted at the top like the pillars in front of the Nepalese temples, it is sixteen hundred years old, dating from long before the Mohammedan Conquest, and is said to have been cast in honour of Vishnu. Once a garuda may have been perched on top.

The succeeding dynasty of the Tuglaqs, whose romantic capital of Tuglaqabad still survives in the shape of a huge, fortified circuit of wall, turned its face steadfastly against Hinduism and reverted to a stern simplicity of décor. This influence, though modified, is apparent in the Lodi and most of the other tombs in the plain. But when we come to the Purana Qila, the sixteenth-century capital of Humayun and Sher Shah, we find in Sher Shah's mosque a combination of this rugged simplicity of design with the elegance of colour and decoration which prevailed in later Mogul buildings. It is a strangely moving work of architecture, a masculine building by comparison with the feminine grace of the younger Jama Masjid, like a strong man who is also sensitive to art and beauty. The dome is flat and of dark stone. The roof is slightly battlemented. The back is of rough stone, broken by turrets and balconies of red sandstone in Hindu design. The rectangular front is equally simple, but each of the five archways is flanked and supported by perpendicular layers of different-coloured stone, alternate strips of rough grey and smooth red sandstone, white marble and blue slate. Above the central gateway are mosaics in red and white, broken by a small window and balcony, while a close-carved pattern of arabesques and Arabic writing relieves the plain stone. But the carving is not the essence of its decoration; its beauty lies in the masterly combination of the various materials. In later buildings this combination is apt to be garish. Here it is utterly satisfying.

From the Purana Qila it is a logical step to Humayun's Tomb, towering through the trees a couple of miles away. This building represents in architecture the bloom of Mogul civilization. It is infinitely finer than the Taj Mahal, and must rank with the greatest Mohammedan buildings of the world. Huge and of perfect proportions, it has shed the ruggedness of its predecessors to emerge smooth and polished and elegant. The rough stone of the earlier tombs is gone. Standing broad, square and dignified on a noble plinth of sixty-eight arches, it is a balanced, harmonious blend of marble, red sandstone and slate, fitted together with the neatness of marquetry. But the pattern is bold, not fussy, and its elaborateness of colour in no way detracts from the restrained effect of the building. Each front has a tall central arch with a smaller arch on either side, while in between, in the bays and at the corners, are two storeys of small arches. The marble dome is the finest I have ever seen. It has no trace of the effeminate, waisted effect of the Taj's dome, but rises broad and confident and perfectly rounded above the kiosks which act as its satellites. The interior of the tomb is simple, but has some interesting plaster decoration, like delicate lace mats on a red ground.

I used to look for hours at this building. It has all the attributes. It is graceful yet masculine, elaborate yet austere, smooth yet strong; it is mathematically and artistically perfect. I can think of no Christian church so flawless, so complete.

There are many curiosities in Delhi's architectural landscape, but none more curious than the observatory of Rajah Jai Singh of Jaipur. When, by accident, I walked into its gardens I found myself in the centre of a cubist's dream. Here was cubism, not merely on canvas or in the imagination of Zadkine, but solid, three-dimensional and many times life-size. These grotesque bits of masonry, this jumble of solids, of cubes, cylinders, globes, hemispheres and spirals, shooting at abrupt angles from one another, some in shadow, some lit by the sun into brilliant relief, were once astronomical instruments. Two hundred years ago they were at home in a world of higher mathematics, of equinoxes and eclipses of the heavenly bodies, trained to the measurement of altitude and azimuth, taught to reduce the wonders of sunrise and sunset to algebraical terms. To-day they stand derelict, their original functions forgotten, pointless but fantastic, the only really modern buildings in the world, the reductio ad absurdum of present-day architecture.

There is a tall, straight staircase, leading nowhere at all but to the sky. There are curved staircases like slices of melon, finishing abruptly in mid-air, equally barren of destination. There is a kind of maze in masonry, propped up at a slant to show its tortuous inside, like the model of a tube station in section. There are two colosseums, each with a sawn-off pole in the centre, stone spokes radiating to the sides, and a bewildering network of shadows cast by the sun. There are two hemispheres, sliced inside with a very sharp knife into a series of truncated spirals, recalling from above the fretwork design of some modernistic "Silver Bullet" puzzle, and from below, when you enter them, the bewildering nightmare world of a surréaliste film. His science, we are told, died with the Rajah, his wives and his concubines on his funeral pyre, in 1743.

A few miles beyond, the newest of Delhi's cities rises from the plain. It is no good pretending that New Delhi is anything but a muddle. It has one good building, Sir Edwin Lutyens's Viceroy's House. But it is one of the tragedies of modern India that its dome and façade, except, it is true, at the end of a two-mile vista from the War Memorial Gate, are hidden by a steep slope in the ground until you are within a few yards of them, and only Sir Herbert Baker's inferior Secretariat buildings are to be seen. Lutyens's designs were based on the verbal understanding that the slope in question was to be levelled. But this, by some blunder, was never done; nor was the mistake discovered until too late. Imagine the Champs Elysées with no more than the top of the Arc de Triomphe protruding above the roadway at the end. That gives the measure of the New Delhi tragedy.

In the Viceroy's House Sir Edwin has made full use of Delhi's different-coloured stones, and its colour is perhaps the most satisfying part of the building. The greater part is of yellow sandstone, with a strip of red along the top and a broad band of it at the base. The dome is a masterly combination of blue slate, white marble and red sandstone, and at each corner is an effective device of the architect's own: a kind of open bowl resting on a plinth of steps. Inside, you come into the entrance hall with its great staircase. You look upwards to a rich blue ceiling and discover, to your astonishment, that it is the sky. The rooms are large and imperial, and the circular Durbar Hall, with its floor of polished black marble, is reminiscent of a Roman bath. But in furnishing we have lost the taste for the palatial. Comfort rather than splendour is the keynote here. Sofas, as in a country club, prevail where gilt and Chippendale would once have shone.

Ceilings, panels and furniture were being painted in the Indian style by an Italian, by name Colonello, who was discovered by Lady Willingdon and given a six years' contract. The garden is architectural, in the Mogul style, with many steps and intersecting canals and fountains like low pyramids of plates in red sandstone. There is a circular garden, like an amphitheatre, with tiers of stone-edged flower-beds and creepers round the walls: clinging convolvuli, of blue and yellow and white, liquid red bougainvillea dropping like blood over a white surface. These are the flowers which symbolize India.

The rest of New Delhi is weak. The circular, colonnaded Council House is good in conception but inadequate in execution. Sir Herbert Baker's domes and his attempt to imitate Indian decoration in the detail of the Secretariat are lamentable. The building, yellow sandstone above, red beneath its spindly columns, is thin in its effect. Instead of standing firmly on the ground it fades into it like a person in a long red dressing-gown.

New Delhi is more extensive than the other cities. It covers so big an area of ground that its life is scattered and it gives an impression of emptiness. Its miles of intersecting avenues give its inhabitants ample gardens, but one and all complain that their houses have been skimped for the sake of the central buildings. Here you dine night after night in identical houses on identical chairs at identical tables, surrounded by identical Government furniture. Your neighbour criticizes its arrangement with an eagle and expert eye, and says to you: "Lady Tattle has managed to squeeze in ten at this table, but most of us have discovered by now that it isn't comfortable with more than eight."

From the end of one avenue the Purana Qila, from the end of the other the fort of Shah Jahan, from the distance the Kutb keep a weather eye on the new capital. Cities of

Afghan, Mogul and Turk, they wonder sceptically how long this English city will last.

"In eight hundred years," says the Kutb, "I have seen eight different Delhis. Yet they talk about India governing herself."

"That new-fangled capital," says the Purana Qila, "will make a poor ruin compared to me or the city of the Tuglaqs."

"What next, I wonder?" speculate the walls of the Red Palace, predecessor of Lutyens's Viceregal mansion.

A Russian Corbusier Delhi? A Delhi of Japanese pagodas?

If it follows the architectural standard of its predecessors it will not be a negligible city. Imperial Delhi is as rich in buildings as Rome. I left it with many regrets.

I spent Christmas with Army friends. The British officer is the most charming and probably also the most contented man in India. At the best of times he is more satisfied with his profession than most people, and that profession is in itself more human than commerce or stockbroking. A man usually becomes a soldier, not because he has military instincts, but because he likes life, and the Army in peace-time offers him an easy one. It gives him leisure and the opportunity to employ it in certain ways. In India it affords him the attractions of polo, pigsticking and big-game shooting at moderate cost.

No British Army officer is a permanency in India, and this is a mixed blessing. It is an advantage because he has not time to acquire the civilian's embittered resignation, his narrow intolerance or his proprietary snobbery. It is a disadvantage because he has not time to make himself a home. The private quarters of the Army are mean and drab compared with those of the civilians. Their bungalows have no gardens: it is not worth while planting flower-beds for the next comer to enjoy. They are poorly furnished because it is not worth while getting furniture out from home.

Outside my hostess's bungalow a pair of oxen were laboriously walking down into a sort of grave, disappearing from view as if in search of the centre of the earth. But up they came, and down again; up and down, all day long, turning the wheel which drew the water. Otherwise the derelict environment of the bungalow afforded no distraction to the eye. This was one of the superior residences. Elsewhere they stood in rows, like suburban villas devoid of seclusion, with poky rooms and tin roofs which made them almost uninhabitable in the hot weather. Since people live mainly on their verandahs there can be little privacy, and neighbours, besides, are "dropping in" all day long.

At the club, remembering my Kipling, I asked brightly for a chota peg.

A major winced as though he had been struck.

"Please," he said, "*please!* Can't you call it a whisky-and-soda ?"

I apologized humbly.

"You never say chota peg," my friend explained.

"Unless," said the major, "you're a perishing infantryman."

Yet later, amid the shrieks of her high-spirited child, I heard his wife instruct a servant, "Go and tell Mohammed to wash his hands and come and play with chota sahib."

The linguistic aspect of Anglo-India's social distinctions is a mystery indeed.

I watched a game of hockey in which bearded players wore their hair tied up in buns behind, and rank upon rank of natives cheered with enthusiasm. I attended a sergeants' dance of decorous demeanour and danced the Paul Jones in a room festooned with paper decorations. I enjoyed delightfully English dinners where the conversation began flippant, slowly grew serious, dealt exclusively with politics over the port ("after-dinner stories" are rarely told after dinner), and became utterly infantile in the subsequent presence of the ladies.

Conversation, at these meals, dealt largely with India and the Indians: with the absurdly high wages of the I.C.S. compared with those of the Army, but with their proportionately harder work; with the natives' unlimited capacity for graft and the fortunes that (supposing such a being existed) a dishonest A.D.C. could make from bribes; with the fantastic superstitions of the Hindu religion.

"I was talking to one of the more educated fellows the other day," said the brigadier. "He's a damned good scientist and mathematician and told me a lot of interesting scientific facts about astronomy. Then at the end he said, 'But I still believe a dog swallows the moon every night, and what is more I teach my children so.' "

The major, who had been instructing native troops in English, said he had asked his pupils to write what they would do if they inherited a fortune. The results were interesting. Many said that without money they had no preconceived wants, but that with money the wants would undoubtedly grow. The majority would devote the greater part of their fortunes to religious purposes, and next, to their children, of whom they were very fond.

Later the conversation drifted to "shop", to the imminent departure for camp, over which the brigadier had some control. Hitherto he had been slapped on the back and addressed by his christian name; now by an abrupt and curious transition, he was addressed respectfully over the port as "sir".

On Christmas Day the natives presented us with posies and decked the cars with garlands. It was the sahibs' religious festival, whose economic possibilities must on no account be neglected. Early in the morning the sound of native drums mingled incongruously with that of the police pipe band and the bugles and brass of the troops, and later they beat from bungalow to bungalow. It was curious, on the twenty-fifth of December, to sit in a church with its sides flung open and sunlight pouring in from a hot, dry landscape. It was curious, in the afternoon, to play a sixsome at golf on ground as hard as iron, where each of us had two caddies (one to mark the ball, one to carry the clubs) but the ground was brown and the greens (called "browns") were grey. It was curious, at six o'clock on Christmas evening, when the half-moon had just risen and crickets chattered in the scented trees, to sit out of doors beneath a banyan-tree and drink cocktails of gin, brandy, vermouth, Benedictine, Grand Marnier and lemon-juice mixed.

But even in the evening the Indian landscape is unyielding, grudging of beauty. The colour which is drained from it soon after dawn never flows back with the twilight. Whether they are sensitive to scenery or not, the monotony of the country must affect its inhabitants. The slightest undulation, the merest strip of colour would be a psychological tonic. But here there is neither. How can a race be human to which nature is so niggardly ? The sea once covered this part of India. The dead landscape and its native inhabitants still recall it.

CALCUTTA

I reached Calcutta in time for the New Year, travelling in the company of a Eurasian who had walked from India to England, "under the patronage", he said, "of the Commander-in-Chief and the Viceroy, Sir Malcolm Hailey" (sic). He talked loudly and incessantly of his adventures. In a curious form of broken English ("picturesque" he pronounced as a word of two syllables, "admirably" with two r's and the accent on the i). The cities of Kidderminster and Ostend had impressed him above all other marvels (he was particularly taken with a giant clock let into the ground at Ostend), and he preferred Birmingham to London or Baghdad. He distributed pamphlets describing his tour and read them to himself throughout the journey. I envied him the faculty of being amused for so long by his own writings.

Calcutta is like Liverpool, except that the Lancashire cabbies do not pull their own cabs; a naked man, smeared with ashes, could hardly parade the Liverpool streets without attracting attention; while a white cotton skirt, looped through the crutch, with the usual uniform of felt hat, jacket, collar and tie, umbrella, shoes and socks (with clocks), would there be considered an inadequate substitute for trousers. Calcutta is a thoroughly commercial city. Imposing blocks of offices surround the central square (which I thought was "de lousy square" until I saw it spelt Dalhousie). But Government House is copied from Kedleston, eighteenth-century church towers beckon to you from the end of sordid streets, and, as in Liverpool, many of the business houses have an honourable and ancient tradition.

But after a bit I began to see that Calcutta was also like Paris. It was "the season", which rages for a fortnight in the year, throughout the Viceroy's residence at Belvedere, and the parties had a Parisian atmosphere. The high-caste Indian women, lovelier than any Parisienne in their classical sarees, were as sophisticated in their manner, as chic in their maquillage and their exquisite jewels. Here was no imitation of the English but real cosmopolitanism. The smart cars, speeding across the huge Maidan to the racecourse, had the air of cars in the Bois. The racecourse itself—an expensive racecourse where the minimum tote bet is fifteen shillings

—was an Asiatic Auteuil. The sporting Indian is far more like the "sportif" Frenchman than the sporty Englishman. Sport, for him, is "Le Sport", where elegance prevails over the flavour of heartiness.

The polo in Calcutta is probably the best in the world and, though a purely aristocratic sport, the Bengali crowd watches it with the enthusiasm of an English crowd watching football. The Maharaja of Jaipur was their hero, a superb youth like a young English "blood" of the eighteenth century. Dressed, like his team, in an apple-green silk vest and white breeches, discarding a blazer embroidered with his arms, surrounded by retainers in coloured puggarees, by rows of magnificent ponies, he radiated glamour; and when his team won the cup the crowd surged across the ground and carried him shoulder high to his apple-green and silver Rolls-Royce.

I explored the native streets and bazaars. I bought silks for next to nothing in the fine modern market and took them to a native tailor to make into shirts and pyjamas. I bought shoes at fifteen shillings a pair from the Chinese shoemakers. I bought a tropical suit, made to measure, for eighteen shillings.

I explored Calcutta's eighteenth-century churchyards and cemeteries, with their many beautiful tombs and monuments and inscriptions, indicating how few of the early servants of the East India Company lived, in this climate, to be more than forty, how many died in the twenties.

I wandered through the hideous marble Victoria Memorial in the middle of the Maidan, built on such a scale that it has been difficult to find enough to fill it, eked out with inferior Victorian relics, but containing a good collection of Daniells and Zoffanys.

I was hospitably entertained to meals. I went to a *cocktail dansant* on a committee evening at Calcutta's most exclusive club, where the women were hatless, in teagowns, and discussed the band. Here social and commercial life are so closely intertwined that a firm had recently given one of its subordinates the sack because he was blackballed for the club. This was the provinces again, not Paris; Firpo's, Calcutta's one and only restaurant, is a mixture of the two, a cross between Ciro's and a Corner House; but on New Year's Eve you could not have told it apart from Liverpool on the night of the Grand National.

It was not for this sort of life that I had come to Asia. A naval friend offered me a passage to Penang in a man-of-war. I accepted his invitation with alacrity, and two days later was steaming down the Hooghly towards the Indian Ocean.

CHAPTER VI

THE ANDAMAN ISLANDS

IN the middle of the night I was awoken by a siren, and I looked out of my porthole. Our engines slowed down. The sea was dead calm and the moon was bright. Through the darkness ahead I saw a great white yacht. Ships that meet in the night, like animals meeting in the jungle, regard one another, at first, with suspicion: then they communicate, recognize one another, exchange civilities. A boat splashed alongside, beneath my cabin; a gangway was lowered, a man got into the boat and was rowed across to the yacht, which swayed gently like a white cradle in the glimmering darkness. Our engines started up and we were off again, incredibly swiftly, into the night. To pilots who know not land year in, year out, but only the currents of the Hooghly, this yacht is a home, now calm and secure, but in the monsoons leaping frenziedly in the swirling waters of the sea. It is India's farthest outpost. As it faded from view my spirit was freed from India's weight, like a bubble rising to the surface.

It is pleasant to be a passenger in a warship; I was soothed by the ordered routine, the atmosphere of efficiency to which I need not contribute, the swift inevitability of our course, the civilized silence at breakfast, the comfort of the wardroom, the pouring tropical heat in which I wallowed in an afternoon coma, the coolness and ritual of dinner at night on the quarter-deck, when the band sometimes played and we drank the King's health, seated over our port.

On the fourth day we reached the Andaman Islands. The Andamans since the Indian Mutiny have been a penal settlement for Indian, and now Burmese, convicts. Trained to lurid tales of Devil's Islands and so forth, I was prepared to find a few slabs of baked sand, where a pitiless sun beat down on grim prison barracks. The Bengal terrorists, for whose reception the place is now primarily intended, have lost no opportunity to spread propaganda about its barbaric conditions. Since the Islands are difficult of access and contain no sort of accommodation for law-abiding visitors (short of the hospitality of European officials) this propaganda is apt to remain uncontested, and not long ago a Calcutta newspaper played into the hands of the agitators by publishing in attempted refutation a series of photographs of the prison taken some twenty-five years ago, when it had little of that "dernier confort" which it boasts to-day.

I had expected a desert: I found a terrestrial paradise where coconut-palms inclined their plumes over coral lagoons and the Indian Ocean was unbelievably blue. To the southeast of our anchorage was Port Blair; to the north-west was, oddly enough, Aberdeen. Port Blair is on Ross Island, the small civil station. It must be not unlike the West Indies. Bungalows stand among pleasant lawns, where hibiscus and poinsettia flare scarlet out of the prevailing green. The palms sway gently in the breeze, and the surf breaks on a white beach at their roots, where you can find mother-of-pearl and other shells and precious stones. Jutting out into the sea, which surrounds it on two sides, is the club, with a bathing-pool protected from the sharks, and an ample bar, panelled in modernistic style with plain, polished slabs of the Islands' numerous woods. Here you can sit in the shade of big trees and relish the oysters and turtle steak (like a tender luscious beef steak, melting in the mouth) which are the Andaman specialities. Opposite, on the South Andaman, a golf-course with fresh, green turf fringes the ocean.

Inland, from marshes thick with lotus where water buffalo, epicures of the sensual, wallow up to the neck in cool water, the country rises to rolling grassland spattered with low thickets as on English downs. Peasants inhabit neat villages of huts, and cultivate rice in the fields. Palms with feathers for leaves, conventional in shape but unconventional in attitude, never stand upright but curve away from the road and cast a fern-like pattern of shadows. Profuse jungle looms beyond, providing a variety of rare timber: marble or zebra wood, gurjan, satinwood, silver-grey koko and red pedauk, immune from the ravages of white ants, and throwing out buttresses so big that from a single slab you can make a dinner-table to seat twenty. "Their woods", said Marco

Polo, "are all of noble and valuable kinds of trees." In the creeks which fret the coast you can fish for mermaids (dugong, with breasts like a woman's). There is unrivalled big-game fishing, and birds' nests of finer quality than the Chinese can boast in their own waters.

The climate is equable: it was hot, but there was a breeze. But weather, in the East, is no absolute factor; it is in the eye of the beholder. It is commonly supposed that men's spirits vary in ratio to the climate: more often it is the climate which varies in ratio to their spirits. Thus a young man, cheerful and rosy-cheeked, described the climate of the Andamans to me as "Good all round, except for two months of the year"; while an older colleague, hankering after the greater social amenities of the parched United Provinces of India, referred to the "seven terrible monsoon months". Both agreed that here you do not get in the cold weather that sharp nip that you get in India; and this, as, thinking still in terms of Europe, I did not at first grasp, was held to be to the disadvantage, not the advantage, of the place.

Be that as it may the Andaman Islands, equidistant from Calcutta, Rangoon, Madras and Penang might, had fortune and the Government decreed otherwise, have become an idyllic leave-station for harassed officials themselves, instead of an internment station for their insubordinate subjects.

As it is, apart from a number of officials, I found only a planter or two, languishing in poverty; for while ten years ago coconuts fetched ten rupees a hundred, to-day the price was Rs4.8, and Rs5.8 was the cost of production. Most remarkable of all European characters was Max Bonington, shipwrecked here as a German ship's carpenter, thirty-eight years ago. He remained on the island, took up forestry, and was ultimately appointed to the Indian Forestry Service. After his retirement he went into timber from the business end and made a fortune. A year ago he returned to Europe with an O.B.E. Timber is a staple industry, and there is a factory which supplies the wood for Swedish matches and matchboxes.

But the European population is small, and the enjoyment of the amenities of the Andamans is left to its prisoners. For all these jolly peasants, lounging about the villages and working in the fields, are convicts. The man who cooks your turtle soup, the Madrassi servant in smart red jacket and puggaree who mixes your drinks, the chauffeur who drives you about the island, the traders in the bazaars who sell you native tortoiseshell cigarette-cases and shoe-horns—each, in all probability, has a perfectly good homicide to his name.

The population of the Andamans is about twenty-seven thousand, of which twenty-three thousand are convicts. But at the time of our visit no more than two and a half per cent of these were in gaol. The ordinary prisoner spends only the first three months of his sentence behind prison walls. Then he is loosed to work on the soil like an ordinary peasant, at first under supervision and sleeping in barracks, but, after a specified period, on his own bit of land ; while later still he is allowed to have his wife and children over from the mainland. At the end of his sentence the prisoner is free either to go home or remain, and a large number choose to remain or, at least, return. This, when you compare the richness of Andaman soil with the barrenness of the Indian continent, is hardly surprising.

Some, of course, marry among themselves ; but since women prisoners are no longer sent to the islands they are limited in choice. At one time there was a marriage parade in the gaol every Friday, when the woman prisoner was at liberty to select a husband (a selection which the lucky man was equally at liberty to veto). But the women prisoners gave far too much trouble, and the settlement is now confined to men.

In the event of misbehaviour convicts may be sentenced to a further term of incarceration ; but I found only one hundred and twenty-four of these temporary prisoners in the gaol, a proportion of the population small enough to do credit even to a non-penal community. Executions take place in a small building like a lavatory, with room for three, a beam to which the rope is attached, a lever to open up the floor when ready, and a mortuary chamber below, where the bodies are cut down. But they are rare. So too is flogging. I saw the rack, a grim-looking easel of iron, to which prisoners are manacled for this punishment. But there had only been two floggings in the past few months. One was in the case of a Sikh who tried to knife a family foe and announced that he would do so again if he got the chance. He took his thirty strokes with the cane without a murmur. The other was a Burman who cut his wife's nose off. He was sent back to goal for two years and in the meantime plastic surgery gave his wife a new nose. No sooner was he released than he cut that off too. He was sentenced to another two years and a flogging. There is an occasional murder on the Islands, due as a rule to jealousy. Otherwise they harbour a singularly law-abiding convict community.

The gaol is a thoroughly modern establishment on a point commanding fine views over the Indian Ocean. It is built in the form of a star, with a high watch-tower in the centre and four long, flat roofs where warders parade and survey the prison courtyards. Some fifty of the warders are themselves convicts. Of the other inmates the greater proportion are Bengal terrorists. As a rule ordinary convicts, except at their own special request, are no longer sent to the Andamans, which have reached their population limit, and the immigration is confined to political prisoners. Their treatment, for obvious reasons, is more rigorous than that of the rest in that they serve the whole of their "time" in gaol and are at no time released to work on the Islands. About two hundred and fifty of them were serving life-sentences (in practice sentences of fifteen to twenty years) when I was taken round.

My previous though innocent acquaintanceship with the interior of gaols had always led me to compare them favourably in the matter of amenities and routine with the average public school. At least, in prison, you have a cell to yourself, and privacy, far from being discouraged, is enforced. The Andaman Islands proved no exception to the rule. I found an industrious community of men contented and well fed, the political poison successfully drained from their fangs. In up-to-date workshops they were extracting every imaginable product (oil, cattle-cake, soap, rope, sweetmeats) from that astonishingly versatile fruit, the coconut. They wove textiles and carpets; they carved wood, ivory, tortoiseshell and so forth into fetching curios. There was printing and book-binding, carpentering, leatherwork, potteries, metal-foundries and departments for the setting of precious stones. The ringleader of the Chittagong riots was the Governor's own highly efficient typist and personal secretary. The Bengali who fired at a Calcutta editor some years back was now presiding genius of a soapworks, and excelled in the magical transformation of coconuts into shaving-soap and other toilet necessities.

The terrorists give little trouble; for, coupled with Oriental resignation is the knowledge that incitement to mutiny would be fruitless: the rest, being but temporary prisoners, have everything to lose by insubordination. They have an eight-hour working day, from six till ten and from twelve till four, with leisure to sleep or take exercise or peruse a library of ten thousand books. They awake to early-morning tea, a square meal follows at ten, high tea at four, with eggs and whatnot, and another square meal in the evening, with meat once a day and ample vegetables. Their diet, in fact, is not only superior to that of the average public school but infinitely superior to that of the less-fortunate Indian at liberty.

At the hour of the siesta, with dark brown gentlemen lounging on shady lawns about the quadrangles, I could almost have imagined myself in Balliol College, Oxford—except for the roar of the surf beyond the walls and the palm-trees nodding over the battlements against an aquamarine sky. As I contemplated the island, with its lush green vegetation, I had a contrasting mental picture of that awful bleak fortress amid the fog-ridden spaces of Dartmoor, and reflected that the Asiatic convict has all the luck.

But would such a system work with the European? The hardened criminal of Dartmoor is a rarity in the Andamans. The Indian prisoners for the most part have been sentenced with a crowd for complicity in some riot; in the case of the Burmese it is more often a question of murder in the heat of the moment, resulting from the fact that knives are always carried; vendetta also provides a prominent motive. The average prisoner here has no fundamental criminal instinct, and as a rule settles down after a single aberration to a peaceful and unblemished life. It is a melancholy fact that deliberate and cold-blooded crime is a prerogative of the West.

Besides the prisoners and the Europeans there are a few thousand free Indian and Burmese inhabitants of the islands, some of them freed prisoners, others ordinary traders. But these by no means account for the whole population, of which there is another and far more interesting section. The evening of our arrival I was strolling along the shore of

Ross Island when two canoes appeared round the point. They were narrow, pointed, built of bark and propelled, as I thought, by black children. The children landed, and struggled up the jetty, chattering shrilly beneath the weight of two enormous turtles, which they flung into a tank. Then I learnt that they were not children but full-grown aboriginal inhabitants of the Islands, who had been spearing turtle to make soup for the Commissioner's dinner-party. (Even aborigines can be useful citizens of the British Raj.)

Marco Polo says of the Andamanese that they

have heads like dogs, and teeth and eyes likewise; in fact, in the face they are all just like big mastiff dogs . . . they are a most cruel generation, and eat everybody that they can catch, if not of their own race. They live on flesh and rice and milk, and have fruits different from any of ours.

He must have been gulled by travellers' tales! There is no evidence of cannibalism at any time among these people, nor, oddly enough, do they resemble dogs. Averaging four foot ten in height, their bodies are well formed and their features, of the negro type, are in no way grotesque or exaggerated. Their hair is thick and black and curly, and on the whole they are well proportioned. They reminded me of the little nigger boys of the nursery rhyme, more especially as they are not brown but coal black, as negroes seldom are except in pictures. The men wore a string for a loincloth, while the women, in the interests of modesty, wore a leaf in front, attached to a belt of plaited straw, and sometimes strands of straw hanging in the form of an exiguous kilt. Some were tattooed on the body, their skin cut with flakes of quartz or glass in zigzag patterns. Otherwise they had no form of ornament.

Of Negrito origin they are held by some to represent the oldest type of man surviving in the world. In any case they are thoroughly primitive. Various tales of them were told me by the Europeans on the island—that they use poisoned darts, that they kill their widows in the interests of public morality, that they sleep in trees, and so forth. These are fantasies. It is a fact, however, that they do not know how to make fire but carry about an accidental conflagration (of sacred origin) by land or sea, wherever they go, in terror lest it should go out. It is a fact, too, that they have never learnt to cultivate the soil; so that Marco Polo was equally wrong to include rice in their menu. Apart from fruit and roots they live entirely by hunting, harpooning pig and fish. For the former they have an ingenious type of spear, with a detachable barb which comes loose when it enters the pig; the shaft drags behind by a string until it gets caught in a bush or tree, impeding the animal's progress; thus they are enabled to catch and kill it. To harpoon fish or turtles they jump into the water with the spear in their hand, adding their own momentum to its weight, and kill the turtle subsequently by driving a spike through its eyes into the brain. Their agility and accuracy of aim is fascinating to watch.

There are three main races in the Islands: the Andamanese, the Onge, and the Jarawa, so distinct that, until the arrival of the English, they had no intercourse with one another and could not understand each others' language. The first two are harmless, but the Jarawas are still savage and it is dangerous to penetrate their jungles. The Andamanese have by various means in the past been brought into contact with the convicts and the Europeans, but they are now left more to themselves, and appear less frequently in the civilized parts of the islands. The reason of this policy is the harm done to the aboriginals by contact with the more civilized diseases and particularly with opium.

For the "healthy savage" is a myth. Primitive man is a puny creature as a rule, accustomed to gratify every sensation as it arises, hence ill-equipped to endure fatigue, discomfort, hunger or thirst. Andamanese vitality is low. Native marriages in the Andamans, for instance, are singularly infertile, often producing no children at all. Resistance to disease is weak, and the aboriginals die quickly from infection or injury. The European has greater stamina to withstand the diseases of the tropics than the savage to withstand the diseases of the West, and (apart from his indigenous malaria, sunstroke, rheumatism and catarrh) contact with pneumonia, syphilis, influenza and measles, gifts of civilized man to the savage, have all proved fatal to the Andamanese. The clearing of the jungle and consequent exposure to sun and wind, over-clothing, European food, and the use of tobacco, are equally responsible for their gradual decay.

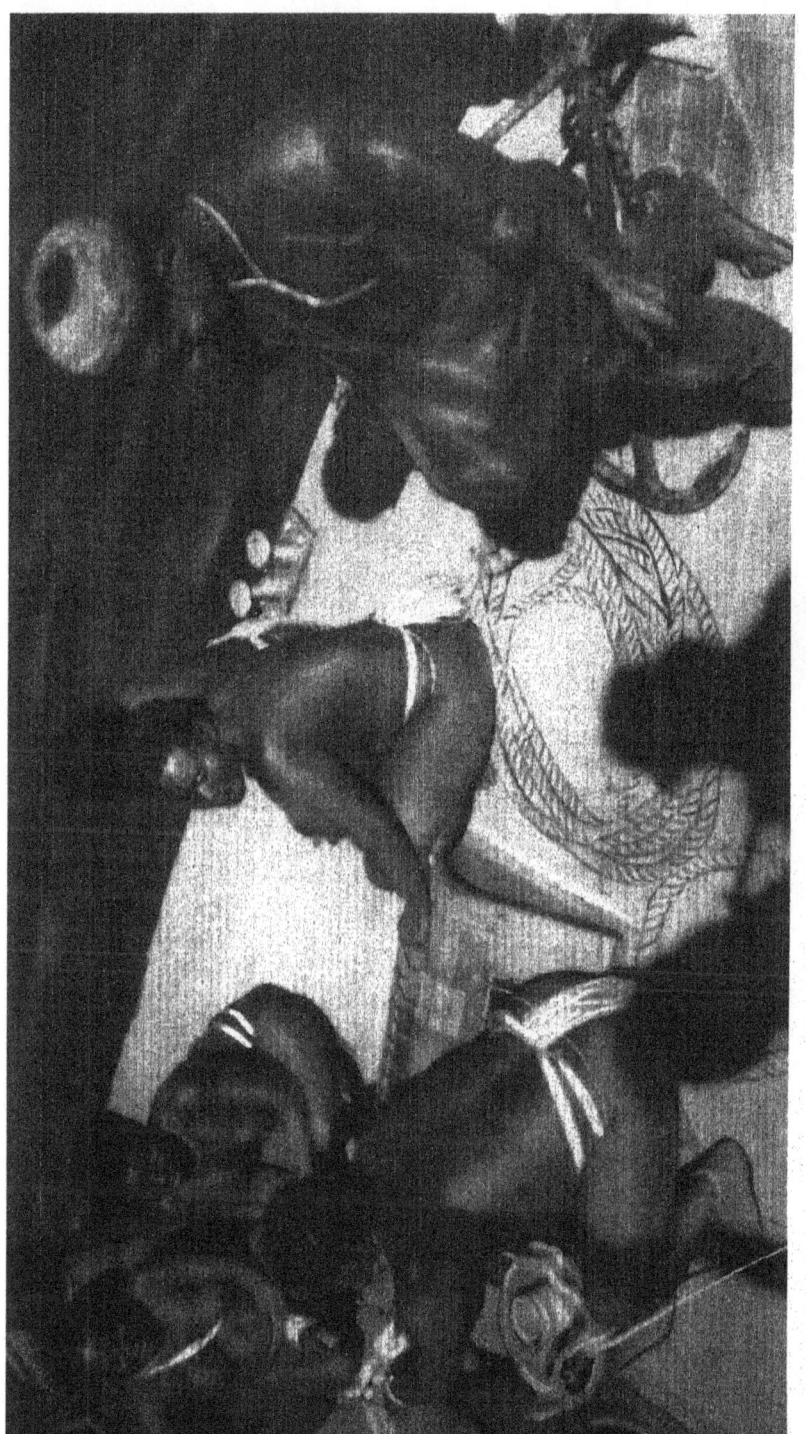

Aboriginal Women, Andaman Islands

Above: Cockfighting in Malaya   *Below:* On the Kelantan Coast

The Jarawas, being wilder and virtually unexposed to civilized influences, are in consequence a healthier tribe than the Andamanese. They could easily, if necessary, be exterminated by rifle fire, as were so many of the aboriginals of Australia and Tasmania. But as a danger they are negligible. Occasionally they will raid a European forestry camp and kill a convict, but only in the most cowardly manner: stalking their victim from behind a rock and shooting at point-blank range when his back is turned. On such occasions a punitive force of British officers and convict troops is sent out into the jungle against the Jarawas, a number of whom are killed by way of reprisal. Accustomed to an eye for an eye they are reputed only to resent the retaliation when the number of casualties exceeds that of their own victims. The Jarawas sometimes use trunk armour consisting of bark.

On one such expedition a Jarawa woman was captured and brought back to Port Blair. She remained for some time among the English, who attempted to educate and civilize her and to obtain information as to the manners and customs of her tribe. But she was difficult to pump, as she simply repeated, parrot-like, what was said to her, volunteering nothing in return. Finally she was sent back and, it is believed, murdered by her own people as a reward for the excursion. I saw a collection of trophies brought back from this expedition: vessels made of tree bark or bamboo, a variety of arrows and spears—some simply of sharpened wood, others with iron heads—well-made baskets and an old "Flit" tin bound with fibre!

The Andamanese languages bear no relation to any other known roots. They have very little syntax, are purely colloquial, and depend largely on mimic action for lucidity. The native religion is animistic, but without ceremony or manifestations of worship. The sun is believed to be the wife of the moon, while the stars are their children. Animals and birds are held to be on a level with the Andamanese themselves; thus when he murders a convict the Jarawa will put a stone on the body and stones leading along the path by which he escapes. This is to warn the birds not to tell the English of the murder or to divulge the murderer's whereabouts. There is a pleasant custom by which relatives, on meeting, sit in one another's laps for a considerable time, first in silence and subsequently in floods of tears. Dancing is popular, but uninteresting. It consists of bending and straightening the knees and kicking the buttocks with the flat of the foot, and is accompanied by clapping, monotonous singing, and drumming with the feet on a sounding-board. Leap-frog, blind man's buff, hide-and-seek, ducks and drakes and mock funerals are among the more innocent aboriginal amusements.

After death the widow breaks up her husband's bones and wears them as ornaments, while his skull is tied round her neck. Marriage is arranged by the parents but is to some extent a matter of choice on the part of both boy and girl. A hut is built and the bride is put in it. The bridegroom coyly runs away into the jungle but is eventually caught, brought to the hut, and made to sit on her knee; after which they are held to be duly married. Infidelity is punishable by the death of both adulterers, but free sexual intercourse between the unmarried is customary. Though the woman is held to be inferior to the man she is not markedly so, and she has some status and influence. The degradation of woman came only with civilization: the cave-woman, we may assume, was relatively free.

The British Raj provides many contrasts. Waiting for a boat at the jetty one night, watching the tropical sunset and the aboriginals skimming over the water in their canoes I saw a filthy launch come in, containing a European lady in a pink lace evening dress. She was evidently coming over from the island of the convicts and the Jarawas for the Commissioner's dinner-party on Ross Island, and she was looking suitably dignified. But she had a harassed expression; this was clearly the dreaded moment of the evening, for it was not easy, in a heavy swell, to climb up from the launch in white high-heeled shoes on to the steep and slippery jetty. If she fell, and tore her dress, all was over. Nor did the accompanying convict crew make any effort to assist her. I gave her an arm, which she grasped, too flurried and concerned with her precarious footsteps to express a word of thanks. She reached land without mishap, her anxious expression relaxed, and she hurried to the waiting rickshaw. But to my surprise, before stepping in, she changed her white high-heeled shoes for a pair of black ones.

A change of shoes was one thing; but plimsolls or goloshes

with evening dress, to facilitate the intricate manœuvre of stepping from the launch, would be unheard of, even in the Andaman Islands. The British Raj must stay on its high heels.

We sailed for Penang next morning.

CHAPTER VII

MALAYA

PENANG looked over a silken sea to a gentle outline of Malayan hills. Save for the mangrove swamps in the foreground they might have been the hills of Gairloch seen on a summer day from Skye; for the scene was painted in opalescent colours of blue and grey and silver. The harbour was stacked with ships. Indian gondoliers plied their sampans, each painted with a gigantic watchful eye, between the jetties and the steamers in the roads. Motor-launches chugged like sewing-machines through the silk. In the distance the huge brown sails of the junks were like bats' wings made of bark; but when you saw them closer they were quilted as in some Victorian material.

Early in the morning I went ashore and stepped into heat like a bath: a chemical bath with a queer and pleasant smell derived from the mud. A Chinese coolie pulled me through the streets in a rickshaw, and the muscles of his bent shoulders rippled from side to side with the exertion. It was curious to drive so fast and yet so silently, for he was barefoot and the tyres were of noiseless rubber. The girls in the streets wore pigtails and bright-coloured silk pyjamas, tight at the neck.

In the afternoon we drove outside the city, through groves of coconut-palms and gardens wonderfully green, to swim in a blue bay and sip drinks on the verandah of a comfortable club. In the evening the sunset was amber and gold against a sky still blue as day. At night, among lawns descending to a moonlit, phosphorescent sea, the Penang Club entertained us to a dance and with true hospitality instructed its members to leave their girl-friends to the Navy for the occasion. Here I met people who lived in Penang, as one might live on the Mediterranean, for no other reason but that they liked it.

It was the first time since leaving Europe that I had found a place where Europeans lived from choice. The idea of anyone *choosing* to live in India would be grotesque. But Penang, by virtue of its climate, its scenery, its inhabitants, its many amenities, is livable and human. In the same breath I saw its charm and decided to leave it next morning.

An India in Calcutta had said to me: "It is impossible for me to visit the West without seeing Western life. It is equally impossible for you to visit the East and see Eastern life."

Within the orbit of a European journey one would choose to spend some time in a place like Penang, and do so with pleasure and profit. But in so doing I should see very little of the East. The average Englishman in such a station is like a stamp superimposed on a letter, having no idea of its contents.

Next morning I wired to a cousin up-country and caught the bi-weekly international express from the mainland. "PRAI-BANGKOK" was printed on its elegant wagon-lit coaches, and this, more than anything, gave me a feeling of the East. It might have been "Shanghai Express". I travelled second-class, among a pleasant crowd of Malays, Chinamen, Siamese and Japs, so clean that even a puling infant was less offensive than a baby in an English train would have been. There was a corridor down the middle of the coach and the seats, covered in rattan, stretched out longwise, to make beds, with another row of bunks above. Many of the passengers cooked their own meals of rice and chicken on little spirit-lamps. At one station a young bride got in, exquisitely dressed, like a wedding cake in pink icing. Her silk gown was embroidered, a veil framed but did not hide her face, which was white and solemn like a delicate mask, and a wreath of tuberoses surrounded her head. She sat unreal and fragile and impassive, awaiting her fate at some wayside place.

My feelings warmed to the attractive people around me. They wore bright-coloured sarongs (or skirts), bare legs, bare chests, singlets or bajus (pyjama jackets). They were human and carefree, gay and good-looking, untroubled in this luscious, lethargic country by the grim superstitions of the Hindu. The freshness of the landscape was a joy after the colourless Indian plains. Marsh and jungle, rice-fields, rubber-trees, undulating forest and distant hills were an endless panorama of delicious green, with the plumes of the palm-trees dipped in silver. The hot-house smell of the country was balm, and I felt that I had emerged from a nightmare into the gentle ease of reality, from the country of the dead into the land of the living.

Lunching in the dining-car I discovered that the Straits dollar (2/4) has about the same purchasing power as the rupee in India (1/6) and the shilling in England. It was odd to see King George's effigy on a dollar note. At two o'clock I alighted at Padang Besar, the Siamese frontier, and slept through the hot afternoon in a pleasant, thatched rest-house. A Malay boy brought me tea; I lay in a chair on the verandah and looked over fields and a stretch of water towards some curious finger-shaped hills of stone, steep as buildings, which rose uncomfortably from the jungle. Slowly the evening closed in, the landscape grew cosier, the birds wheeled low and the crickets chattered; I breathed the smell of my first Malayan night.

Next day I had a long day's journey in a halting, Siamese train (very different from the elegant Bangkok express), drinking still the green of the landscape as though I had been starved. But its tropical profusion did not astonish me. It seemed quite natural to see huge, hot-house palms growing in the open air, and plants in station gardens which I had never before seen outside a conservatory. Surveying these palms and ferns and exotic plants in their hot-houses at home one imagines the country of their origin as something utterly fantastic. To see it must therefore be a disillusionment. The fault lies in the limitations of our imagination, which pictures the unfamiliar in relation only to familiar environment. The effect of a coconut-palm growing in an English hedgerow would indeed be bizarre. But in their native context, where all the vegetation is homogeneous and to scale, the effect of tropical plants, though novel, is no more startling than that of a hawthorn tree in the English landscape. In an orchid-house you imagine a country of orchids; you expect to see a continual blaze of them, isolated as if the whole tropical landscape were a kind of vast, exotic herbaceous border. But nature unaided does not run to such riots of colour (in fact an English herbaceous border is probably the brightest stretch of growing colour to be found anywhere in the world). The flowers in a tropical jungle, rich as they may be to the eye individually, are no more vivid in proportion than the celandines in an English wood : they bear the same relation to their own landscape as English wild flowers do to theirs.

Occasionally a dead tree stuck up oddly from the jungle, like a bit of cardboard scenery planted in natural surroundings. The villages were thatched or built of planks. Shops and cafés were square, like stage-sets open to the street, showing various tableaux. At a junction truckloads of live elephants were attached to a passenger train. I ordered lunch from the native cook on the train and waited an interminable time. When it came it consisted of four dishes, served simultaneously —eggs and bacon, fried fish, chip potatoes, and beefsteak. Presumably he expected the Englishman, like the Oriental, to heap all his dishes into one. I crossed the frontier back into Malaya, and Nigel met me. That night he killed a fatted calf (which is to say, in the East, that he opened a tin of *pâté de faisan truffé* from Fortnum's) in Tumpat, for travellers rarely come to this out-of-the-way spot.

Kelantan and Trengganu, on the east coast of the Peninsula, are the remotest states of British Malaya. Until 1909 they belonged to Siam, but they were ceded to the British in return for our abandonment of other extra-territorial rights and a loan of four million sterling to finance the Siamese railways. They are, however, native states, outside the F.M.S., each governed by an independent sultan under the advice, but not the regency, of a British representative. Hence their European population is small. In Tumpat, which is the port of Kelantan, I found only five Europeans : a railway official and his wife, and three representatives of Boustead & Co., the British trading firm, of whom Nigel was one. But their scanty numbers did not hinder them from having a club with two billiard-tables.

It is a tranquil spot. In its sandy main street are cafés and Chinese shops, selling a variety of European and Eastern junk, and its side-streets peter out into coconut groves, where the poorer Malays inhabit dwellings of plaited straw, on piles. Curiously enough, though thousands live in coconut groves, cases of natives being killed by falling coconuts are exceedingly rare. The Malays say that this is because the coconuts have eyes, and never drop until a passer-by is out of their radius.

At one end of the street, as in all Malayan villages, is a small covered platform, known as a wakaf, which is intended for the sole and estimable purpose of gossiping and was the rendezvous of all the town.

The rest-house, where I stayed, overlooks a wide rectangular bay, fringed with coconut-palms, and a jetty provides the inhabitants with their favourite evening promenade. But the bay is too shallow for shipping and lighters have to go two miles out, beyond the bar, to meet such boats as come; sometimes it is too rough to reach them and ships toss inaccessibly out at sea for days, awaiting calm weather to take in their cargo. Few passengers travel this way, but a line of small cargo steamers plies up and down the coast between Singapore and Bangkok. It has innumerable ports of call but at most of them the ship does not stop unless hailed, like a bus, by means of a red sarong hung on a tree. The rains were not yet over and the sea was the colour of sand, while beyond the bar the monsoon churned the waves into a long strip of foam. It rained a little every day, so that the climate was never unendurably hot.

The rain, at its worst, can be terrible. Mrs. Prentice found it so. She came out from England to marry Prentice in Penang, and he brought her to Kelantan immediately after the wedding. They arrived in a downpour and it continued to rain, without respite, for twenty-nine days on end, so that Mrs. Prentice could not move from her bungalow. Even for Kelantan this was a record rainfall; but it was hardly an auspicious beginning to a marriage nor an encouraging first sight of the East to a young bride. All her trousseau was mildewed. She grew more and more hysterical. One rainy day she discovered that their Chinese servant was living with a woman who was not his wife. Fresh from England, she was filled with righteous Protestant indignation, and ordered the Chinese boy to leave her service immediately. Prentice protested; you couldn't take up that sort of line with Chinamen; there was a battle; finally Prentice gave in and the boy departed. But it was Mrs. Prentice's one and only victory. Ever since, Prentice has had his own way. Before they married those who knew them prophesied that Mrs. Prentice would dominate her husband. Her personality was the stronger. But those twenty-nine days of Kelantan rain destroyed her spirit: she never altogether recovered. It is said by some

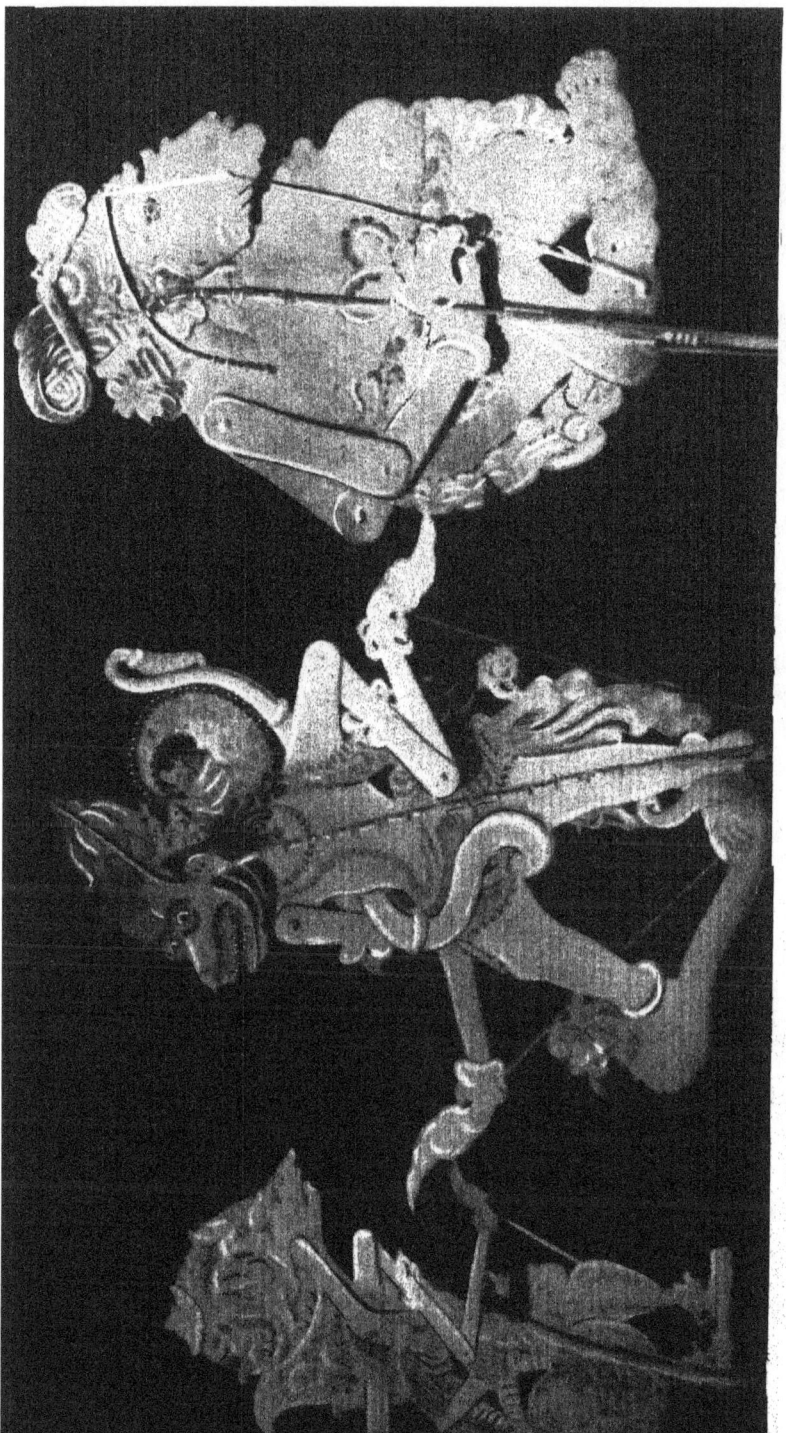

Kalantan Shadow-Play

Rama, the Hero-King, Hanuman, the Monkey God, and a Sacred Clown

Casuarina Trees at Singora

that Prentice arranged on purpose to be married at the beginning of the rains. Even so, he could hardly have foreseen that a record rainfall would play so neatly into his hands.

There was pleasantly little to do in Tumpat. Nigel and Bill shared a well-built house, where we would recline in baju and sarong in the evenings, drinking stengahs (whisky-and-sodas), talking and watching the chick-chack lizards stalk the flies on the ceiling. The natives say that these little creatures, which inhabit Malayan bungalows in hundreds, are the crocodile's younger brother. If a Malay is wounded by a crocodile he will not sleep in a house until the wound is healed, because he knows that the chick-chacks, following up their brother's murderous attempt, will unite in their hundreds to finish him off.

With Nigel I would visit the Chinese shopkeepers. He told one of them that I was going round the world.

"He is eating the air of various countries," he said in Malay.

"Velly good, see world. See Kelantan, no good."

Then we would go down to the copra sheds, where the river spreads itself all over the landscape in a last-minute panic that it will not be allowed to reach the sea ; for a long sandbank bars its progress, turning it into a lagoon. The copra sheds stand among coconut and nipa or oil-palms. There would be a curious chemical smell of mud and stagnant water, mingled with the thick, sickly-sweet smell of coconuts in various stages of desiccation. Scantily clad Malays were piling the husks in heaps to the ceiling, putting them in the sun to dry, on plaited stretchers, packing and weighing them for export in sacks. One or two native growers had come from up-country to sell their copra. Nigel cracked jokes with them and bargained. Each knew exactly what he would get for his stuff but bargained for more as a matter of form. When paid his due he pronounced himself grievously ill-used, but was perfectly content.

Nigel kept an aviary in his garden, together with a samba deer and an otter which he used to lead about on a chain, like a dog. There were innumerable birds, some big, some small, some rare, some common. There was a pair of hornbills*

---

* Now in the London Zoo.

which used to hop about the house. One invariably perched on my shoulder to read what I was writing (I think it must really have been a secretary bird) and tried to take my pen in his prodigious beak, which was hooked and streamlined like the bonnet of a Renault car. There were haughty Argus pheasants,* one of which would occasionally spread out its magnificent tail like a fire-back. Very few of the birds were brightly coloured, and many were simply starlings, thrushes, sparrows and pigeons of a Malayan variety, slightly more vivid than their European namesakes. The rarest was a gentleman of the stork tribe, who used to pick his way about the lawn in the most delicate, finicky fashion and was very stand-offish. There was a kind of bittern, which honked and shot out a magnificent crest when annoyed. When, later on, Nigel took his collection back to England, to present to the Zoo, he put the bittern in a cage with twenty small birds. One morning, in the Suez Canal, he went the round of the cages and found to his horror that only one of these small birds was left. The bittern had eaten all the other nineteen, feathers and all. But this gruesome story had a not unsatisfactory ending; for the Zoo declared that the bird was an excessively rare variety of which they had never before had a specimen. If it had not given way to cannibal impulses it would almost certainly have died and been lost to ornithology.

Animal fights are popular with the Kelantan Malay. Tumpat has a regular season of bullfights. These are between bull and bull, or more often between two water buffaloes. The fight does not usually last more than four or five minutes because one of the animals always (and with admirable sense) runs away. But fights have been known to last an hour. The bulls rarely gore each other: they wrestle and butt and one will sometimes throw the other right over his back, as in jiu-jitsu. Sometimes they charge straight for one another from the start and their heads meet with a report like a cannon. Once, after such a charge, a bull ran wild round the town for an hour, chased by its adversary, and when it finally collapsed its head was found to be smashed to pulp. Sometimes, if the bull does not at first catch sight of his opponent, he singles out someone in the crowd instead and chases him round and round the ring.

Once a fight was staged between a water buffalo and

---

* Now in the London Zoo.

a black panther. But on seeing the buffalo the panther turned and fled. It then looked around, caught sight of its keeper, and killed him. The general European opinion (which is against such gladiatorial shows) held that it served him right.

Fish-fights, where the fishes tear one another to pieces in bottles are popular, though forbidden by law. But the favourite sport of the Kelantan Malay is cockfighting, at which he gambles frenziedly and enormous sums change hands. Though it was not yet the season a special cockfight was staged for us for a purse of $1.50. The birds fought as scientifically as two boxers, with none of the wild disorder that one might expect from animals. Heads down, they watched each other warily, then closed; broke apart, watched, closed again. Most of the hitting was done with the feet, the beak being used primarily to get a purchase on the other cock's neck. When tired one would put its head under the other's wing and take a rest—like boxers clinching. The rounds lasted twenty minutes each. In the interval the owners bathed their combatants like seconds do, put feathers down their throats to clear them, sewed up their wounds, lifted their eyelids and so forth. One, obviously the weaker, was a sorry spectacle, much exhausted, but fought gamely when the next round began, resting a good deal beneath its adversary's wing, but scoring a few shrewd hits. Finally it ran away: the greater stamina of the other cock had told. A fight nearly always ends in this way and cocks are rarely killed.

Another Tumpat amusement was the opera. It was given in a kind of tent by a touring-company from Malacca. The orchestra was a family affair, composed almost entirely of children. A very small boy beat away at the drums and cymbals when he felt inclined, but got a bit listless at times. Another small boy, whose feet hardly touched the ground, played a violin almost as big as himself with remarkable confidence and skill. He looked as a grown man would look if he played the 'cello like a violin, holding it to his neck. He too stopped whenever he felt like it. Two other children played the saxophone and the second violin respectively, and the father of the party thumped what notes he could persuade to sound on the piano. Perhaps because it was tuned a semitone higher than the other instruments, he played it quite independently of them, as though in a different orchestra altogether. Between them they produced an astonishing and cacophonous mixture of American hot jazz and Oriental wailings; a singularly infelicitous union of East and West.

The show was a melodrama interspersed with musical turns. It seemed to be largely impromptu, like a children's charade, the actors talking whenever they felt like it and losing all interest when they did not. Like a children's performance, too, it lacked all sense of time or dramatic effect. A bewildering series of languid abductions, secret assignations, clandestine marriages and revolutions followed one another in lethargic and desultory sequence, the big revolutionary scene being performed to a speeded-up and almost unrecognizable version of *The Man Who Broke the Bank at Monte Carlo*. The cast was all female except for the comedian. His principal joke was to have a football for a tummy, to which the ladies of the chorus pointed now and then, giving it an occasional tap. He had various English phrases which he interchanged indiscriminately: "I say!" "My God!" "All right!" became "I right!" "All God!" "My say!" "I God!" "My right!" "All say!"; and sometimes he strung them all together.

There was a chorus of houris, made up pink and white in European style, who sang in shrill, monotonous voices like schoolchildren chanting a "piece". Each number was interminable, as every member of the chorus had a verse to sing, and it was a long verse. The leitmotiv was a dreary tune, half Eastern, half Western, whose name, apparently, was *Amy Johnson*. There was no attempt at dancing: the chorus shuffled back and forward in listless steps, continuously, with an occasional apology for a chassé. Two of their numbers were more sophisticated, the ladies appearing dressed in turn as sailors and as jockeys, and wailing in Malay to the tune of *He's a Jolly Good Fellow! I'm For Ever Blowing Bubbles* was another success, but the principal boy could not quite manage the top notes and descended to a lower register when they came.

We left after the first two hours. The show was then half-way through. The audience displayed as little enthusiasm over it as the actors, but still it went on and still they sat.

On the Feast of Hari Raya, which ends the fast of Ramadan, I was invited to breakfast by the Sultan of Kelantan.

My invitation was worded as follows:

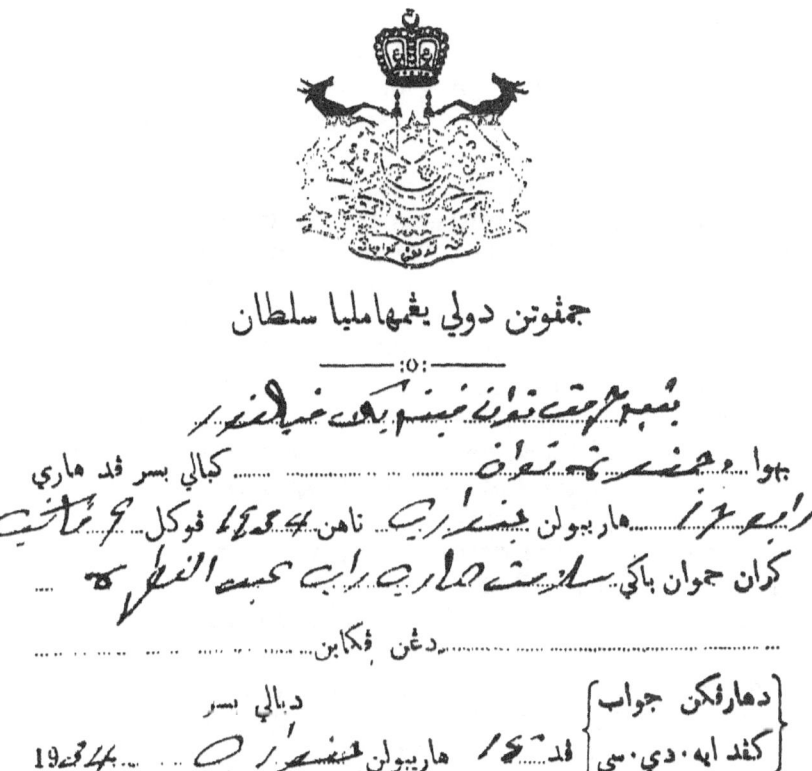

The Sultan's palace is in Kota Bharu, the capital, which is not far from Tumpat but cut off from it by the river. Either you take the train two stations down the line or a car, for a dollar, carries you along six miles of sometimes impassable road; then a ferry takes you across a river dotted with square-sailed fishing-boats. Some of the native motor-launches are very insecure, and when I was there an overloaded one capsized, drowning fourteen people. A native woman was on her way, by the river, to a wedding in Kota Bharu with four hundred dollars and a good deal of jewellery. Two men sat opposite, eyeing her, awaiting their chance to grab. The launch hit a log, and heeled over slightly; taking advantage of the mishap the two men leapt for the woman and their movement was enough to capsize the boat. The woman, jewels and money went to the bottom of the river; the villains escaped.

About twenty Europeans inhabit Kota Bharu, which is a nondescript but tree-shaded town with a few streets of shops, the British Adviser's residence overlooking the river, and other European bungalows in pleasant gardens a mile away. There is usually a cheap auction going on outside one of the Japanese shops, trying to capture the Chinaman's trade. To-day, for the feast, the town was gay with colour, for the Malays invariably wear new clothes for the occasion. Both men and women wore vivid multicoloured sarongs, while underneath the better-dressed men had Chinese trousers and bajus of black, white, brown, crimson or apple-green silk, with a little round velvet cap on the head. The children were dressed up like dolls, in every colour of the rainbow. The Sultan's Palace is a wooden villa with windows of frosted glass. The adjoining balai, where he entertains, is always open to the public, and here, on the Feast of the Hari Raya, he is bound to give audience to any of his subjects who crave it. In the evening it is turned into a public gambling-den for which the Sultan gives the Chinese a concession and a share in the profits. It is a large room, not unlike the booking-hall of a railway-station, with one side open to the roadway. Here breakfast was laid for a hundred and the Sultan, a thin, emasculate figure in white silk pyjamas and a gorgeous yellow sarong, attended by beautiful Raj Malays in purple silk, shyly received his guests. We then proceeded to a somewhat silent meal of cold curry and warm ginger ale.

A large proportion of the Europeans appeared to be Scotsmen, who formed, I am convinced, the aboriginal population of the Malay Peninsula. But odd things happen to the Scotsman in the East. His repressions break down. He does not invariably remain the reliable, strong, silent man. Here a Scottish nationality is no evidence of uncompromising sanity, and the respectable Presbyterian Scots housewife gets to enjoy her gin as much as most.

By far the most imposing figure at the ceremony was the Captain, who commanded the Sultan's bodyguard in their white and scarlet uniforms, followed by a regiment of police in neat little khaki shorts to match their complexions. The Captain himself, an enormous genial figure with a pink face and a white moustache, wore a uniform of his own design: white, with a lot of gold braid, and a plumed hat like a field-marshal's. The Captain was an Australian in the Sultan's service, and more or less created the Kelantan Police Force, which was the apple of his eye. Whether or not they were adept at the detection of crime I would hesitate to say, but a smarter lot of Malays it would be hard to imagine; they would have done credit to the Life Guards, and their band was the pride of the Captain's heart. The history of this band is a wonderful example of Imperial endurance. The Malays have no idea of Western music, and the Captain used to strum out a melody on an old piano for days and days until they got it into their heads. Thus bit by bit, very slowly and laboriously, a band with a repertoire of several tunes was evolved. Then a Malay was found who could transcribe European music into his own language, and the Captain did not have to strum on the piano any more. A bandstand was erected in a coconut grove outside Kota Bharu and here, each evening, we would hear the band practising away to its heart's content.

The Captain's main concern was with the military demeanour of his force. He considered the position of a warder to be an ignominious one, because he had no opportunity to display a uniform, and often, by way of punishment, would degrade a policeman to his level. Provided his policemen looked smart, marched nicely, and presented arms on every suitable occasion he was satisfied. They were apt to carry the latter ceremony to uncomfortable lengths. Once the garrison presented arms at the British Adviser as he was negotiating a tricky putt on the last green. The British Adviser missed the putt and was not best pleased. There is a similar story, belonging to another part of the country, of a prominent official who was slinking back to his bungalow scantily clad, under somewhat compromising circumstances, at dead of night. The sergeant of police saw him as he tiptoed past the station, and promptly turned out the guard to present arms.

The Captain had his uniforms and those of his force made to his own design by the best London tailors. He even sent his boots back to London to be repaired. (But in this he was beaten by a certain Scotsman in the F.M.S. who sends all his shirts home to be washed in Glasgow.) Yet oddly enough the Captain had never been in London. He was on his way there, during the war, but was abruptly recalled from Colombo, owing to trouble which had broken out in Kelantan. Part of the British Navy had been called out to suppress a native rising, but was making little headway owing to the fact that its shells burst in the middle of virgin jungle, miles from the insurgents. The story (for whose complete accuracy I cannot vouch) goes that the Captain arrived on the scene, exclaimed: "The Navy indeed! What's all this nonsense about?" marched into the field of battle, got hold of the two native ringleaders (whom he knew intimately), knocked their heads together, gave them each a kick in the pants, told them to go home and not to be so foolish; the rising was over, and the Navy steamed rather shamefacedly away.

The Captain, though a man of unfailing friendliness and a generous host, was renowned in his official capacity for his somewhat summary methods. On one occasion a detachment of the Chinese Army, escaping from a revolution, found its way across the sea to Kelantan and anchored off Tumpat. The British medical authorities ordered that all the passengers should come ashore to be inoculated against plague. When some of the Chinese demurred the Captain stood no nonsense. It is said that he took them by the scruff of the neck and hurled them one by one down the luggage chute, into boats. Later it turned out that some of those whom he had ejected so ignominiously were important Chinese generals and consular officials, and there was nearly a diplomatic "incident" as a result.

The Captain was a great stickler for etiquette and an epicure. Even when alone he invariably dressed for dinner every night, and sat down to a table laden with polished silver, indulging, despite the tropical heat, in half a bottle of burgundy and a glass or two of vintage port. On one occasion he is reputed to have sent one of his servants to prison for twenty-four hours for confusing claret and burgundy at a luncheon. From time to time the Captain would make a royal tour of his police-stations; he rarely travelled without a case of burgundy and when he had to spend a night in some far-off station an army of policemen would be sent ahead with canteens of silver and glass, hampers of linen, beds and other furniture, not to mention an ample cellar, to ensure his comfort.

Punctuality, with the Captain, was a mania. Once he was kept waiting by a prominent Chinese trader (equivalent in importance to a Gordon Selfridge) who was bringing some goods ashore for his inspection. The Chinaman was promptly clapped into gaol for a night.

It would be hard to imagine a more unique and enchanting personality than the Captain.

After the Sultan's breakfast we repaired to the Kota Bharu club. There was a record attendance as all the planters and officials and private residents had come in from the ulu (up-country) for the Hari Raya. There was a great deal of gossip and exchange of drinks : gin pahits mostly (gin and bitters) or stengahs ; people played billiards or bridge, and the women sat in basket-chairs in a screened part of the room and read the new batch of illustrated papers which had just arrived. Later I played a round of golf on fresh green turf. It was a well-kept course, devoid of rough as a cricket field, but with one prominent hazard in the shape of a lunatic asylum. The lunatics stood behind their bars and watched the golfers, shaking their heads meaningly at each other, and pointing to their foreheads as they watched the crazy club-swinging. The English doctor had written in his recent report : "It is a pity that there is no accommodation for European lunatics."

There was a certain amount of discussion in the club about the Sultan's swans. The British Adviser had brought him a present of two white swans from England, for the lake in the grounds of his new country palace. The Sultan was delighted and said he would like some black swans as well, for which he was prepared to pay. So, under the Captain's auspices, a pair of black swans was procured from Australia. But by the time they arrived the Sultan had lost interest in the swans. He contended, in fact, that they were not swans at all but geese : they would not sit on his ornamental lake, but frequented only the drains. What was to be done with the black swans, and who was to pay for them, was the principal topic of the hour.

One of the native princes in Malaya was the traditional wicked ogre of the fairy-tales, of whose treatment of animals gruesome stories were told. Once he coveted a retriever belonging to an Englishman in his state, but the owner firmly refused to sell it, even for five hundred dollars. One night he was awakened by piteous groans and howls from the dog. He turned on the light. There was the animal lying by his bed with its ears cut off and its beautiful tail cut short. On another occasion the same charming gentleman returned a dog to its owner castrated.

One of the chief European celebrities in Kelantan was Monty. Monty was a leisured dandy of the Edwardian era whose financial fortunes met with a sudden reverse. He started to go round the world, but his funds ran out when he reached Malaya. He had business acumen, however, as well as his social gifts. He got a job on a rubber estate, then went in for coconut planting and found his way up to Kelantan, where he has remained ever since. Very occasionally he goes to Europe, but a fortnight is the utmost period he will spend there, returning immediately when it is over. He speculated very successfully in land, at a time when the country was almost undeveloped, became also a building contractor, amassed again a considerable fortune, and was recently awarded the O.B.E. He built himself a splendid bungalow on an estate outside Kota Bharu, with ample panelled rooms, club fenders, deep armchairs, and every sort of luxury: a marvel to behold in such a remote and primitive country. Here we would sometimes be honoured by an invitation to luncheon or dinner; and it was an honour indeed, for Monty, despite the smallness of the European community, contrived to remain very exclusive.

I remember a superb curry tiffin with twenty-nine different side dishes; but it was Monty's dinners which were truly memorable. Some ceremony attended these functions, for Monty, as befitted an Edwardian, set store by etiquette and made an art of entertaining. Anyone who arrived a few minutes late was in disgrace for the rest of the evening; but such a solecism was rarely committed. Real cocktails took the place of the inevitable gin pahits, and the staple drink was invariably the best champagne. No one who dared to ask for a whisky-and-soda would ever be invited again. Name-cards indicated where each guest was to sit, old silver and crystal gleamed on a lace tablecloth, and a meal fit for gourmets was served by good-looking Malays in liveries of purple silk. Here one would sample all the gastronomic specialities of the country: delicious little crabs, served hot, prawns as big as écrevisses, mock whitebait, cut from Malay salmon, lamb, gamebirds, mushrooms, but above all umbut, one of the rarest delicacies in the East. It is the kernel of the coconut-tree, taken from where the branches spread out, and can only be obtained by the extravagant process of cutting down an entire tree. On one dreadful occasion the umbut was forgotten. "Send out at once," roared Monty, "and cut down a coconut-tree." And the servants went out to do so by the light of flickering candles. Umbut certainly lived up to its reputation. Eaten raw, like celery, its taste was a heavenly blend of all that is best in a fruit, a vegetable and a nut. Afterwards there would be vintage port and Napoleon brandy. Monty was a brilliant and outrageous talker, and his dinners sparkled, but he made a rule of turning his guests out at ten o'clock, in case their conversation should begin to flag.

A fortnight after the Hari Raya there was a Hindu ceremony in Tumpat among the imported Tamil inhabitants. It was full moon and the sea, for the first time since my arrival, was calm. The streets were crowded : nobody, not even the children, had gone to bed, and pedlars did a good trade. There was that air of suppressed animation, fulfilment combined with expectancy, which the full moon brings. From the jetty I saw fires burning behind the palisade of coconut-trees which hid a native kampong, and there were sounds of drums and Chinese crackers in the distance. Outside a Tamil shop a makeshift porch of branches and banners had been erected, and crowds of children, from the windows opposite, were waiting for something to happen. I followed the noise towards the station, and saw the procession coming in a blaze of torches beneath the trees. Two huge and grotesque papier-mâché figures danced about desultorily on pins of human legs. Some beat gongs and drums and blew on reedy instruments. Tamils, straining at a shaft, attempted to drag along an enormous kiosk of tinsel, festooned with paper flowers and crowned with a cheap umbrella. Beneath it was an idol like something from a confectioner's shop, with bananas at its feet, a few children sitting back to back and several petrol-tins. The whole contraption was most insecure, mounted in front on a beer-barrel and a pair of low, thick wheels, behind on two large and spindly wheels of wire. It was top-heavy and kept going crooked, so that the procession had to stop every few yards, and made very slow progress. Sometimes the vehicle proceeded at an alarming rush for as much as a hundred yards, but always, obstinately, strayed from the road again. Frenzied directions were shouted above the noise of the gongs : there was more straining at the shafts, and the car jerked forward another few yards.

The Malays watched the pantomime with good-natured amusement. They have none of the Indian Mohammedan's intolerance.

Chapter VIII

MALAYA (*continued*)

THE Malays have virtually no art or culture. But they are a pleasant people to live among because of their curious beauty and elegance, their simple loyalty and good humour. The men are extraordinarily young in appearance : what you take to be a boy of sixteen will turn out to be a man of twenty-eight who has been married three times and has a growing family. After thirty, on the other hand, they are apt to age very quickly and look fifty. They are fastidious and elegant in dress, to the point of extravagance, choosing only the best available silks. Nigel's servant Ibrahim wore bajus and trousers of silk far dearer than I could afford and real gold studs. They are prodigal of money, easily led astray by gambling, and no more honest than any Oriental. Bribery flourishes. A retainer of Nigel's came to ask him for five dollars. A relative, he said, was appearing in court on a burglary charge and he wanted to pay his fine to keep him from gaol. Nigel told him to wait until he *was* fined : then it would be time enough to give him the five dollars. The man was embarrassed, hummed and hawed and finally blurted out that he really needed the five dollars to bribe the witnesses in the case.

The Malay is lazy. Nevertheless, despite such shortcomings he makes an excellent servant. He is exceedingly devoted, with a respect and love for the tuan who respects him in return. He has a genuine feudal spirit, and Nigel had a whole host of unpaid retainers who came unasked to help with the work of his house. But if a Malay does not like a certain European nothing on earth will induce him to work for him, and if offended he will walk straight out, not deigning to ask for his wages. He is proud. It is no good raging at a Malay if he does wrong : anger simply makes him smile. But ridicule him and he bursts into tears, like a child : that is the punishment he understands, for it touches his pride. But he appreciates the tuan who displays his superiority. A Malay foreman one day pointed out to a companion of mine that he was wrong about some point. He turned on him: "And what the hell's the good of my being a tuan if I can't be wrong?" The man understood and acquiesced without more argument.

It is difficult to say what qualities the Malay admires most in a European. Bravery means nothing to him in his elegant, lethargic existence. Generosity he appreciates but despises. Of all peoples he is among the most elusive. The number of tuans in the peninsula whom the Malays would follow to their deaths could be counted on the fingers of two hands, and it is impossible to diagnose or define the particular magnetism which creates this gift.

Malays have a loyal family spirit and no man can starve as long as he has relatives, for, however poor, they will invariably take him in until he finds work. Ibrahim was supporting several of his relations. This is a habit of the Mohammedan religion from which many Christians might profit: only in Europe do men cast off their children.

Malay religion is simple, as befits a simple people. A friend of mine had an argument with two or three educated Malays who maintained that the world was flat. When he declared that on the contrary, it was round, they merely smiled as at a quaint superstition. Riled, he determined to convince them, and delivered an astronomical lecture, concluding, "I left my home and followed the sunset; I came here. If I were to leave here and still follow the sunset I would reach my home again."

The Malays were silent for a moment. Then one of them said slowly: "If I thought that was true I should lose my faith entirely."

Mohammedanism is six centuries younger than Christianity. Far less than six hundred years ago Christendom was just as primitive in its beliefs: people took Genesis literally just as the Mohammedan takes the Koran literally. We are only just beginning to evolve beyond beliefs and superstitions quite as primitive as those which the Mohammedan still holds. It is not for us to mock at his simplicity, but rather to envy him the relative purity of his religion. (With Hinduism it is different, for this, by comparison, is a decadent religion which has reverted to the primitive extreme.) With regard to language and social customs, as well as religion, one is living here in a past age; as for instance with the flowery conventions of language and the exaggerated formalities of correspondence, abandoned by us not a hundred years ago but here still flourishing as in our eighteenth century.

In regard to their royal marriage ceremonies the Malays have a custom more sensible than our indiscriminate present-giving. Each invited guest has to contribute a certain sum of money, proportionate in value to his rank or office. The Crown Prince, for instance, will be called upon to pay a hundred dollars, the Chief Minister seventy, other chiefs fifty, wealthy merchants twenty-five, and so forth. The sums are fixed by the host, and the more a guest is asked to pay the more does he esteem it a compliment. Some such scale might well be adapted to our own marriages, though it would have to be calculated according to means rather than rank. Couples would get far better value from the resulting cash than from the hundred lamps and early-morning tea-sets which are showered on them as it is. The snobbish nouveau riche could always be assessed on his invitation at £100; but whether or not he would take it as a disinterested compliment is open to question.

Mohammedan as the country is there are still traces of pre-existent Hinduism in Kelantan and more especially in Trengganu. There the children wear little gold fig-leaves, as only the Tamil children do elsewhere, and in their marriage and puberty ceremonies, their worship and fear of spirits, there is much in Trengganu that is neither Mohammedan nor animistic but decidedly Hindu. Hindu deities appear in Kelantanese mythology, notably the garuda. Pusat Tasek is the centre of the ocean, where a giant coconut-palm represents heaven, and beneath its roots is a whirlpool: the boiling-pot of hell. There are two accountants, one in heaven and one in hell, recording the good and bad deeds of the world, and the accountant of hell is kept so busy that sometimes he flings his pen on the ground in a temper and exclaims (in literal translation), "This is *too* much!" The garuda lives at the top of the coconut-palm. There is a highly confused legend that Raja Iskandar (Alexander the Great) went to China to marry the Emperor's daughter. But King Solomon disapproved of a Moslem (sic) prince marrying an infidel and told the garuda to prevent it. The garuda duly wrecked the Raja's ship, drowning all his suite, but carried off Iskandar himself to Pusat

Tasek, put him in a box, and flung him into a whirlpool. Unfortunately, instead of disappearing below, the box was carried off by the current and landed on the coast of China, where Iskandar married the Emperor's daughter after all. King Solomon was furious at the garuda's incompetence and condemned him to remain for ever on a mountain at the end of the world (in the Caucasus).

This is one of the scenes enacted in the Wayang Kulit, the Kelantan puppet shadow play, which is a complete survival from Hindu times. Though more primitive in technique, it resembles the puppet shows of Java. The figures are made of leather, beautifully stencilled and painted, and are mounted on sticks like Japanese fans.

Nearly all of them represent Hindu deities and mythological characters. The Wayang Kulit performance which I attended was a simple affair in a sort of yard, surrounded by trees. The yard was also used, in season, as a cockpit, and in the background were fighting cocks in large basket cages, their women and children roosting on the top, for in the families of fighting cocks it is the male who is petted and pandered. The stage was a rough, thatched erection, with a white screen, as in a cinema, and a large audience of Malays, many of them children, squatted round it on the ground in the moonlight, watching, chattering, applauding. Behind the screen a lamp flickered; gongs and drums of different notes and a clarinet made rhythmical music; a voice chanted continuously in Malay, often changing its tone in dialogue like that of a Punch and Judy man, as a sequence of silhouetted figures, grotesque and semi-human, performed various gyrations on the screen.

The show, partly owing to its imperfections, was remarkably beautiful. The flickering light elongated the shadows and continually threw the figures out of focus, so that they swelled, receded, became blurred and grew sharp again in a continuous concertina of motion. As a rule they were only sharp and realistic at a central point, beyond which they grew eerily large and ghostlike, disappearing into great banks of shadow. They moved on and off the screen with a swiftness of motion such as only the arm can achieve, rushing into focus and out again with a series of startling, impressionistic effects, such as the most modern of film-directors would envy. It was impossible to follow the story, and I was content to watch the kaleidoscope of shadows, blown like leaves about the screen by a tornado of music. Sometimes they looked like fish in an aquarium, looming suddenly to the front, then fading away. It was the "fade-out" technique of the film, but more effective because at some time a fade-out must end in a "click", and here the rhythm was unbroken. The best scenes were the fights, where figures followed each other on and off with abrupt rapidity, subject to none of the delayed action of human beings and creating a vivid impression of action and violence.

Later we went behind to see the "performers". One man, seated cross-legged in the centre, was responsible for the whole show : brandishing his figures in a frenzy, chanting and shouting incessantly. The puppets were massed on a board in front of him, stuck in by their points. He looked like some extraordinary dervish in the flickering light. The band beat madly around him ; boys striking drums and gongs with the flat of their hands, working themselves up into such a paroxysm of rhythmical excitement that it seemed as though they would never be able to stop. The scene had a weird and thrilling beauty.

The Wayang Kulit is probably one of the oldest entertainments in the world. It is strange that in effect it should have so much in common with the newest. It certainly has lessons to give in film technique.

Next day I went to call upon the Tengku (or Prince) who had arranged the performance. The front courtyard of his palace was a sort of farmyard where a number of Malays were camped in huts, cooking their dinner. We drank ginger ale and exchanged courtesies round a table in his balai, where people wandered in and out as in a café. Then the Tengku asked if I would like to see the harem. Sensible of the honour, I accepted graciously. He took me through a drab muslin curtain into a bare, wooden room, with a raised platform at one end. There were mats on the ground and a pair of common chairs and tables against the wall. A cheap mirror sat on each table, which was covered with a dirty white tablecloth. They were like the makeshift dressing-tables arranged in the cloak-room of an English town hall for a hunt ball or some other unaccustomed function. At the opposite end of the room a grubby muslin curtain hid a large and rusty iron bedstead covered with mosquito-netting, its linen very much rumpled. Otherwise the place was unfurnished but for a couple of bookcases stuffed with German glass and other junk. From behind other and dirtier curtains came sounds of a child squalling and women's voices whispering hoarsely, while now and then a woman's khaki face peered furtively from behind a doorpost to take a peep at the white man. The Tengku tapped the carved woodwork proudly and said, "Fifty years old". There were no luxurious divans, no embroidered hangings, no exquisite houris languishing on cushions, none, in fact, of the paraphernalia you might expect to see in the harem of an Oriental prince.

Later I was taken to call on another Tengku who had the grandest house in Kota Bharu. Built in the European classical style, it was furnished in the elegant manner of the Tottenham Court Road, and as scrupulously tidy as a shop window. The Tengku was a polite little fellow in smart grey flannel trousers and patent leather pumps. He spoke English with a strong Glasgow accent and looked about nineteen. Actually he was a good thirty-five and chief magistrate of Kelantan, with three wives and a large family of children who could be heard in the background. He presented me with two knives, each curved like a sickle. Lest their gift be interpreted as a hostile gesture I gave him one cent in return, according to the custom of the country.

Manfred joined me from Bombay, via Singapore, when I had been in Kelantan a fortnight, and we made some expeditions round Kota Bharu. We went to bathe at Farrar's Falls, some twenty miles from the town. They are named after a former British Adviser called Farrar who died in tragic circumstances. At a function in his honour some Chinese fireworks, of a type which he himself had prohibited on the grounds of danger, were produced for his entertainment. In truly English fashion, instead of embarrassing his hosts by vetoing the fireworks he said he would light them himself. The first one killed him.

We drove through the liquid shade of woods, where the sarongs and parasols of the natives made drops of colour on the road. We came out into rice-fields, glistening with water, seldom rectangular but curving like emerald rivers between banks of palms. We passed native schools by the roadside, no more than roofed platforms, thatched on top. The attention of every child, not to mention their teacher, strayed from his task as our car went by. Each school was surrounded by plots of cultivated garden, for it is our enlightened policy to concentrate on the cultivation of the soil rather than on book learning in our education of the Malay. We passed the Government agricultural station where, for the sake of instruction and experiment, rice is cultivated in the right way, the wrong way and every way conceivable, providing a remarkable mixture of crops in various stages of growth. We passed a cart full of pigs, each packed in a tight little basket which can be slung on a pole between shoulders. Frequently, on the Kelantan coastal steamers, you are kept awake all night by the squealing of a pig, unable to move though its neighbour is gnawing its leg through the basket—much as if a human passenger were to start gnawing the ankle of the man in the upper berth. After a time blue hills appeared to our right and we turned down a sandy track through bush of arbutus and rhododendron, European in character. Soon it grew into forest and we heard the roar of the falls. We bathed in a green pellucid pool, with branches and creepers forming a roof, and a rich scent, thicker than thyme, filled the air. It might have been any woodland stream instead of the centre of a tiger-infested tropical jungle, impassable beyond the point we had reached. The sun did not reach us but the air was soft and chill-less. In this absence of chill is the magic of a tropical bathe; for however hot the European sun you can never elude a momentary shiver on emerging from the water.

The coast of Kelantan is an unbroken stretch of magnificent beach, fringed with coconuts, where the breakers of the China Sea pound the white sand and cloud the air with a mist of spray. Now and again the mouth of a river (a kuala) breaks the line, spreading into an inland lagoon before it reaches the sea, and a spit of sand shoots out as if to hinder its exit. The trunks of the palms form palisades to hide the native kampongs. Here, where the tropical air is thick and soupy, Malays, of soupy complexion, live in a few straw hives, on stilts. On a remote part of the beach, cheek by jowl, live Johnson and Thompson (which are not their names). Their bungalows are the only European habitations within twenty miles, and within a stone's throw of each other (which doubtless both have put to a practical test), but five years ago they had a difference of opinion over some land, since when they have cut each other dead.

One day the Customs Superintendent in Kota Bharu took us to call on this curious pair. The Customs officer of Kelantan is six other things as well, and in each capacity spends most of his time writing letters to himself and answering them. Sometimes he and himself have differences of opinion and the letters stiffen in their tone. He is deputed by himself to audit his own accounts and writes to himself the result of the audit. In the event of his committing a misdemeanour he would have, as public prosecutor, to issue the warrant for his own arrest. On this occasion he was on his way to inspect some native post offices in his capacity as Postmaster, but before we left he showed us a haul he had just made in his capacity as Customs Superintendent. To all appearances it was an ordinary coconut, and it had been found in a cargo of other ordinary coconuts; but on closer inspection a sinister black pigment oozed from the top; it was full of opium.

Our journey was slow, because ahead of us was the scarlet car of the Captain, and the Captain will never exceed the majestic speed of fifteen miles per hour. To pass him would have been lèse-majesté and might have involved a night in gaol for speeding. Besides, the Customs officer's sister, who accompanied us, was in the Captain's bad books. She had just mislaid a couple of his prisoners. They had been requisitioned to work in her garden, and, owing to some relaxation of vigilance, had walked quietly away. The warder deputed to guard them was in a great state about it, and in hourly anticipation of being imprisoned himself.

Prisoners, in Kelantan, have an easy time on the whole. When working outside the gaol, as they do, they are supposed to wear leg-irons; but in fact they usually take them off during the daytime and clamp them on again at night. Many of them work all day in the fields, and use the gaol simply as a kind of hotel to sleep in. A certain prisoner once got into the habit of coming in late at nights. First it was seven-thirty, which gradually extended itself to eight o'clock, and even eight-thirty. One night he did not appear until nearly nine. This was going a bit too far, and the gaoler was roused to severity. "Look here," he threatened, "if you go on staying out as late as this you'll find yourself locked out altogether, one of these nights." There is a characteristic photograph in Kota Bharu of a couple of prisoners in the floods of 1931. One is carrying a warder, pick-a-back, and the other his rifle.

In a village opposite the police-station, the Captain's car drew to a majestic standstill. The police guard presented arms.

Minions in smart uniforms leapt from the back of the car and held the door open. The Captain emerged, a noble figure in shorts, red tabs and an enormous topee, with silver buttons on his tunic and the crown and stars of a major-general. An attendant handed him his gold-knobbed stick, which he waved at us cheerily, disappearing into the police-station. Meanwhile the red and blue flag which had been fluttering from the bonnet of his car was changed over to that of a battered hireling, in which he was to continue his journey over inferior roads. The Customs officer inspected his post office, to the jibbering terror of the Malay in charge, and we drove on. We reached a river, piled our lunch-baskets into a rickety sampan and were paddled across. Through a stretch of grass-grown sand-dunes, peppered with bushes and nipa-palms, with the roar of the China Sea beckoning us ahead, we proceeded to Johnson's bungalow.

When Johnson first came to Kelantan he was a man of means, and bought a third share in a rubber estate. All went well for a bit and might have continued well had it not been for feminine interference. But each of the three partners had a native female cook and each of the servants spent her time in sowing dissension, in pitting the one master against the other. The partnership crashed. The third man was bought out by the first for forty-five thousand dollars, but Johnson, for some reason, was less fortunate, perhaps because less clever. He lost his share in the partnership and his money into the bargain. With a few dollars saved from the wreck he bought himself a bit of notoriously barren land, where he has been trying to grow coconuts ever since. But what he lives on is a mystery. Johnson, however, is a man not easily daunted, refusing to admit that he is unlikely ever to see his much loved native land again; and I hope that some day he may be rewarded. He survives on very little and contrives to remain an optimist. The pride of Johnson's life is his flagstaff, by virtue of which he has become a familiar figure to every steamer that passes up and down the coast, earning for himself the nickname of "the Ancient Mariner". A mariner in fact, before he took to rubber planting, Johnson has a whole set of flags with which he signals to the ships: "Hope you are having a nice trip"; "Could you let me have a little ice?"; "My indigestion is a little better, thank you." He spends many hours glued to his telescope and can identify any ship, however far away, with the naked eye.

Before lunch we bathed from the Ancient Mariner's beach. The beaches along this stretch of coast must be among the finest in the world, rivalling those of Sydney and Honolulu, but unknown to all save the few Europeans who inhabit Kelantan. But in the tropics there is always some sort of snag about bathing. Here, if not sharks, it is sea-snakes or poisonous little fish which live beneath the sand and pierce you with a spike like a periscope if you walk barefoot. Fortunately it was now too rough for the sharks to come close to the shore, and the Ancient Mariner has bathed here twice a day, year in year out, without setting eyes on a sea-snake. The breakers were terrific and beneath the monsoon the China Sea was a cauldron in strips of elephant grey, eau de nil, olive green, khaki and brown. Close, but inaccessible, was the misty outline of the Perhentian Isles, a haven of coral and blue lagoons when the weather is calm. We unpacked our lunch in Johnson's bungalow and he shared it with us. He pressed us to sample a blancmange, prepared by the Siamese woman who looks after him, he eats sparingly because of his indigestion.

When there are no ships to watch and nothing to do to his coconuts the Ancient Mariner, always busy-minded, spends his time studying the habits of the innumerable insects with which he shares his dusty bungalow. Whenever in course of conversation one of us mentioned a word which he did not know he jumped for the dictionary, read out its definition, and mentally added it to his small store of knowledge. He was continually saying in answer to one of our remarks, as when Manfred criticized the routine of a P. & O. boat, "You should write in about that." "Writing in" was clearly one of his favourite pastimes, and I imagine that, when he can afford the stamps, the Ancient Mariner's outgoing mail is a heavy one. He "wrote in" to the Empire Marketing Board to complain that only Chinese tea was sold in the neighbouring kampong. He had got "a man who was then in the Cabinet" interested, and now, after three and a half years of "writing in", it was his proud boast that a single packet of Lipton's Indian tea was on sale in the wattle hut of the local Malay merchant.

When you mentioned Thompson to Johnson he affected a certain vagueness, as if he *had* heard that there was another Englishman living along the beach, but had never actually verified the fact. When you mentioned Johnson to Thompson he took the line of a Mayfair inhabitant who professes an airy ignorance of his next-door neighbour's identity. Johnson would have been rather offended to know that we were leaving his bungalow to call upon Thompson, so we expressed a desire for a walk along the beach, left him to his afternoon siesta, and walked the twenty yards to Thompson's house.

Thompson is as different from Johnson as a polo pony from a cab-horse. Quick-witted, brilliant, cultured, he was one of the outstanding brains of his time at Balliol and swiftly rose to a position of importance in the Malayan Civil Service. He was marked out as a man who would go far in his career, even as a possible Governor of the Colony. In the days when few white women came to such outlandish parts he lived with a Tamil woman who bore him children; one fine day the Colonial Office started a morality drive, deplored "concubinage" of their Civil Servants with native women, and issued a circular which amounted to a veto on such practices. Thompson regarded this as an unwarranted interference with his personal liberty and, being an obstinate man, promptly (and perhaps quixotically) married his Tamil as if to say to the powers that be: "There now! Do what you please. She's my wife." Naturally this put a brake on his career: he rose as high in the Service as was compatible with the possession of a native wife, but the "plums" were barred to him. His wife subsequently died, leaving him two children. He retired at the proper age, and built himself a bungalow on the edge of the China Sea.

A lively little figure in baju and sarong, he received us enthusiastically, gave us tea, asked all manner of questions about his old college, chattered briskly of Jowett, of "Ponners" and "Graggers" and the Devorguilla and Gordule. He sparkled with literary allusions, darted about, showed us his bungalow and the refrigerator which produces ice by the heating of an oil-lamp beneath; spoke of his daughter in Singapore and laughed at his experiments with coconuts.

"See these photographs. Same tree's to be photographed in a year's time. See if it's any different. Won't be, of course. Or d'you think it will? Lots of ideas about coconuts. Great fun. Bore you to hear about them. See my casuarina-trees? Good spot for old age, isn't it? Fancy you being at Balliol. Bless my soul. Arnold still going strong? And Ponners and Graggers and all? Eccentric place, Kelantan. B.A. in my day always wore hat at tiffin. Afraid the white mice would get out.

Used to walk up and down the streets in baju and sarong, casting a fishing-line. Mad as a hatter. Have some more tea. Comic things, coconuts. Got to go ? Come again. See if the coconuts are any different. Bet they won't be. You never know. Farewell."

CHAPTER IX

MALAYA (*continued*)

ONE day Bill and I took the train into the ulu : an hour or two down the line to Kuala Krai. The railway provides the only route to Singapore, since there is no through road from Kelantan in any direction. Hence a train journey in Malaya is never dull, for the Malays use the track as a road and a continual procession of people walks along the line, getting out of the way of the train when it comes. It is a single line, and once two trains met on it, face to face. After a heated argument one of the two was forced to return; but it was fortunate that neither was travelling fast. Once, in the early days of the railway, an elephant charged a train, head-on, to protect its young, and was reduced to pulp. The arrival of the weekly Singapore express is a great event. Everybody knows everybody on board, and there is a luxurious observation-car where you sit and have drinks. To-day we had it to ourselves but for a rubber planter, who was off on a few days' leave to Kuala Lumpur for the sake of his health. He came from a remote estate, and said that when he relieved his predecessor he found him making patterns on the wall with a revolver. But in fact none of these outlying posts are as far from European contacts as I had imagined. The furthest is a day's sampan journey by river from the nearest town, and even that can be reduced to a couple of hours by motor-launch.

Kuala Krai is a town which grew up during the building of the railway, but having now no raison d'être has decayed. In its principal street are a few overstocked Chinese shops, an abandoned branch of the Mercantile Bank of India, boarded up and falling down, and an empty building opposite bearing the sign, in English, Chinese and Arabic : "Eton School. Kuala Krai. Kelantan." We sat drinking beer and smoking cigarettes in Tye Phong's shop, the central meeting-place of the town; but no Europeans were about. We saw only a lugubrious trio: a seedy-looking white man in a creased white suit, carrying a garish cushion, a wife in European dress but of pronounced half-caste appearance, and a son whose Malay features left no doubt as to his mother's origin. Nobody knew who they were or anything about them except that they were looking for a car, but it was assumed that they were prospectors for gold or tin.

In the afternoon we walked a mile or two along the river to the Doctor's house, where we were to spend a night. It was raining, and we slithered helplessly through yellow mud. During the flood of 1926 the Doctor was marooned in his upper storey. The flood carried off the doors and windows and most of the walls of his ground floor; but he did not bother to have it repaired or repainted, and we found him sitting amid the wreckage of eight years ago at an enormous desk. He rose to greet us, a formidable bulky figure, like some prehistoric creature, in baju and sarong, hook-nosed, with a truly magnificent belly like a Buddha's. He started to talk at once and did so without drawing breath for the next five hours; but it was not a dull five hours.

The Doctor was an independent practitioner with a retaining fee from the Government. He was an Irishman, but had not seen Europe since before the war. Unlike an Irishman, he was extremely conscientious over his job, and when not going his medical rounds on the rubber estates, spent his time writing prodigious minutes and reports. From his bungalow I gathered that he was as prolific a reader as a talker. Books were everywhere. The bookcases had long since overflowed and pile upon pile of books towered from the floor and from tables; medical periodicals stacked in heaps, scientific works, the classics, "books of the month" and the latest works of biography and fiction: all sorts of volumes, part-eaten by white ants, colourless and worn as books in the tropics invariably become.

His talk varied from the reminiscent to the speculative, with a preponderance to the former and a tendency to interminable parenthesis, so that it would sometimes be an hour before he finished an anecdote, sandwiching as it did some two dozen others between its beginning and end. Medical reminiscence predominated, with stories of all the great surgeons in their youth, proceeding to notes on the hypothetical importation of yellow fever from West Africa to the East by means of aeroplanes. The Doctor would invariably translate England into Malayan terms, referring to the "kampong of London" and the "ulu of Surrey" or to his native "ulu of Galway". There were endless stories of Kelantan, displaying a phenomenal memory for dates. No story was undated : "It was on November the eighth in nineteen hundred and six that I came up from Penang to Kuala Krai. My young friend O'Reilly came up two days later from Singapore, walking in here round about six thirty-five in the evening." Alternatively he was fond of referring to things that happened to him "a thousand years ago". ("I keep telling the D.O. he'll have to hurry up and build a workhouse or there'll be nowhere for me to die".) One's attention would wander and return to find him discoursing on theology . . . "that the Hindu religion was every bit as good as the Christian. But my young friend O'Reilly said, 'We'd better hurry up and introduce dancing-girls into our cathedrals.' "

He showed us his garden, of which he was proud. There were some good hibiscus : double ones and pink ones varying the inevitable scarlet ; ixoras from the jungle, begonias, hydrangeas, betel-palms, thinner and more graceful than the coconuts, oil-palms, many creepers on pergolas, a moonlight flower which comes out only at sunset, a complementary flower which blooms only in the daytime—and a shamrock from the Vale of Avoca. The Doctor's garden was the best I saw in Malaya, yet compared with any European garden, its lack of colour surprised me. It amounted to little more than a few drops of blood-red amid the cave-like green darkness of the vegetation.

At the bottom of the garden the Kelantan River crawled like a sluggish monster through the forest, reinforced by a brother, the Lebir, which joined it a hundred yards above. There is a legend that in the flood of 1926 a mountain in Ulu Kelantan opened its gate and a giant dragon with scales of gold plunged into the Kelantan River. At Kuala Pergau it collided with another, with scales of silver, and the two merged into one. Here, at Kuala Lebir, it collided with a third, whose scales were of steel. Then the dragon was carried out into the ocean to reinforce its brother at Pusat Tasek as a guardian of the Gates of Hell ; for the work there in the flood time was heavy.

Stengahs were brought, the Doctor scratched his prehistoric belly and went on talking. Towards seven o'clock an old gentleman appeared in shabby white shorts : he wore thick spectacles and a straggling discoloured moustache, and looked like some myopic professor. "Ah," said the Doctor, "here comes my young friend O'Reilly. Young O'Reilly here is our chemistry expert. You should hear the debates we have when we get together of an evening with the books on the table."

Thenceforward "young O'Reilly", though his stream was thin by comparison, contributed to the Doctor's flood of talk as the dragon of the Pergau had merged with that of the Kelantan River.

O'Reilly was a rubber planter in chronic difficulties. He was the survivor of the Ancient Mariner's famous partnership, but now almost as broke as the Mariner himself. "I've made and lost fortunes two or three times over," he quavered, in his intellectual voice, "but I've always had the sense to split them. Last time I left £20,000 for my wife and came out here with the other £20,000 to lose it in rubber. I live on £3 a month from writing on chemistry for papers and publishers at home. But it's a good life. I haven't had a day's illness since I was fourteen and I can drink any amount without getting a thick head." In reality I gathered that young O'Reilly's affairs were much more complicated. He was always engaged in incomprehensible transactions to retrieve his fortunes and at the moment, as far as I could see, this involved the sale of his own estate to himself, at a loss.

But there was always the prospect of gold. It is curious how men by nature thoroughly sane and sensible will be beckoned into the paths of fantastic speculation by the beacon of gold. Such a man was the Doctor. That there is gold in Kelantan nobody doubts ; but nobody has yet succeeded in working it. Fortunes have been flung away in the attempt and chunks of the Doctor's capital, otherwise so carefully administered, had gone that way. Yet still he remained optimistic. His hopes were now pinned to the researches of the German. The German was a mining engineer, the third member of this curious trio, as it might be the third dragon, from the Lebir, joining the united forces of the other two. The three of them would sit for hours round the Doctor's table, pooling their knowledge, debating far into the night on science and chemistry (for O'Reilly added the latest chemical journals to the Doctor's medical literature) and performing experiments. But now it was the topic of gold which monopolized their symposium. The German had recently reappeared in the ulu after a long absence. Thirty years before he had dredged for gold for the Duff Company, which first exploited Kelantan. No one knew more of the country's gold resources than he: for thirty years he had kept certain things to himself; now he had returned to put his knowledge to account.

I imagine the trio debating into eternity round that table, the Doctor scratches his Buddha-like belly, O'Reilly wipes his watery spectacles, the German booms authoritatively, while the piles of books grow higher, the palms grow thicker round the bungalow, and the Kelantan River crawls muddily on to the gates of hell. Perhaps the composite dragon will indeed turn back from steel to gold. I hope so. But I know that the flood of its talk will not be stemmed nor its optimism dimmed.

We left next morning at about ten o'clock, but not before we had eaten two substantial meals. In the Ulu Kelantan early-morning tea is a meal in itself. We sat down to tea and piles of fruit, round a table, while O'Reilly and the Doctor talked. We bathed, and as we were dressing the servant brought gin-slings, recommended by the Doctor "as a mouth-wash". We sat down again to piles of fish and eggs and bacon, with coffee, jams, and a large selection of Crosse and Blackwell delicacies, while O'Reilly and the Doctor talked. We thanked the Doctor for his hospitality and returned along the bank to Kuala Krai.

There is a man in Kelantan who, when you walk with him in a certain dense and savage part of the jungle, will assume a concentrated expression, as though searching for something.

"What," you ask him, "are you looking for?"

"The post office."

You become alarmed. Sunstroke? Fever? Kelantan madness?

"This is the racecourse," he says. He points into a dense black wall of undergrowth and tangled trees. "Through there, over the crest and a five-furlong gallop round the other side of the hill. A good little course, but I always said it was a pity you couldn't see the far side from the grandstand."

In triumph he pounces on a peg, driven deep in the undergrowth. He brandishes it above his head.

"The grandstand!"

Not sunstroke: the Duff Company.

The Duff Company has become almost a legend in Kelantan. This was the scene of one of its most grandiose schemes. Plans were made for vast cities in the jungle, with every modern amenity, and sites were actually pegged out. It was nearly forty years ago that Duff, then a police officer, first set foot in Kelantan and became the pioneer of the English settlers. With Sir Hugh Clifford he led an expedition to suppress a rising in Pahang. The expedition penetrated as far as Kelantan, which was then Siamese. The expedition returned, but Duff, seeing the possibilities of this undeveloped country, obtained huge concessions, amounting to nearly half the State, from the Sultan. The Duff Company was formed, with an ambitious programme involving hundreds of square miles of rubber and coconut plantations, of gold and tin mines and I do not know what all.

Kelantan rings with stories of those early days; of the lavish scale on which the Duff Company worked, of the prodigious salaries paid to experts and general managers and of their fantastic exploits. The Company's fortunes fluctuated; many of its schemes proved impracticable; but though its practical interests in Kelantan are not what they were it is still a flourishing concern financially. On three occasions compensatory sums running into six figures have found their way into its coffers. When Siam conceded Kelantan to England in 1909 the Government bought up a large proportion of the Company's interests for £250,000. Part of the conditions of sale stipulated that the Government should extend the railway northward and that Duff should extend the road southward to a certain point where they should meet. But the railway was not extended as agreed, the Duff Company claimed compensation, and after many years of litigation was awarded £300,000. A few years later Duff came out to Kelantan, found that railway-stations had been built on his land, that a lot of it had been parcelled up among the natives, that, in short, his rights had not been respected. He started proceedings again, but settled out of court—for £150,000.

My Scottish host at Manek Urai, one of the Company's original employees, related the Duff saga to me throughout an entire evening, and a fascinating saga it was. He himself, after twenty-five years in Kelantan (his wife was the first European woman to set foot there), went home, supposedly for good.

But they were both back within a year. They became so ill in Scotland that the Doctor advised them to return immediately to the tropics or die. They built themselves a house in an isolated spot, high up in the jungle, nowhere near a road, and separated from the railway by the Kelantan River. Perched as in an eyrie among tall trees, on an almost inaccessible slope, it has the finest view in all Kelantan. Here I spent a homely and comfortable two days, showered with curry and hospitality. Impenetrable virgin jungle stretched away from the verandah and we heard tigers howling at night. When the monkeys began to chatter in the trees it was a sign that a tiger was near: tigers only recently had taken two of my hostess's dogs, and a cobra had taken a third. In the cool of the evening we sat in the garden, amid hibiscus, mauve jacaranda and flame of the forest—a fern-tree, with horizontal branches like those of a cedar, but of brilliant scarlet. Directly below us, seen as if from an aeroplane, was the river, and from a kampong on the opposite bank the minute figures of villagers came down for their evening bathe. One night there was great commotion from the kampong, for each house was surrounded by Malays chanting an incantation a thousand times over, to ward off cholera. The river shone dully like a stretch of brown gelatine, as if you could walk across it. An occasional sampan appeared on its surface, and only by the slowness of its progress upstream could you guess at the strength of the surging current beneath. It would have been a grand and terrifying spectacle to watch from the safety of this height the great flood of 1926, when the river rose seventy feet to become a floating shambles and whole villages, lights still burning, careered along on the gigantic stream.

At sundown the river turned to dull, white metal. Huge bats came out, insects as large as birds, the racquet-tailed drongo bird, followed by two black blobs beyond the end of its tail, like an aeroplane towing a target. The landscape became a landscape of sound, above which we had to raise our voices to be heard. Insects, noisier than beasts or birds, let loose a pandemonium of metallic din. The "six-o'clock beetle" deafened us with its two alternating notes, like the klaxon of a police car in an American gangster film. Factories of crickets chiselled and throbbed at full pressure, or rang in our ears like a burglar alarm. Other insects let off steam, whistled their sirens, honked their horns and shrieked like a hundred sawmills.

Colourless as metal, the night hummed with the incessant clamour of machinery, and the scrape of the bull-frog, the intermittent chop of the nightjar on his anvil were as melody to the insect dynamo's untiring scream. If the din of a tropical night were to be reproduced in the London streets outraged and sleepless householders would write to *The Times* in their hundreds.

Somewhere in these jungles live the Sakai, aboriginal inhabitants of Malaya, and the Semang, more primitive still, who are believed to be kinsmen of the Andamanese. Few Europeans penetrate their forest strongholds, not because they are hostile, but through fear of disease, and those who venture there on foot come out as a rule on a litter. (The Sakai, through superstition, will not allow a white man to die on their hands.) Once a party of them was brought down to Kota Bharu. It was the first time they had ever left the jungle, and their primary reaction was one of disgust. They formed a low opinion of the cinema, and refused to pay it a second visit. They enjoyed a drive in a motor-car and appreciated the sea, asking where all the water went to, but found no pleasure at all in sea-bathing. Tigers and elephants had few terrors for them, but the pet dogs of the European residents scared them into fits. What they missed most of all was hunting at night, and after a very few days they were off to their native jungle again, armed with cooking-pots, knives, fishing-nets and cloth, but with no regrets for the other amenities of civilization.

The Sakai use blow-pipes, as long as billiard cues, from which they shoot poisoned darts. For fire they have a patent lighter of their own, which works by compressed air, on the principle of the latest Diesel engine.

TRENGGANU

Before leaving Malaya Manfred and I spent a few days in Trengganu. Though as big as Kelantan it is virtually undeveloped. Kuala Trengganu, the capital, is a hundred miles from a railhead and a hundred miles from Kota Bharu by road, and gets all its mails (at very irregular intervals) by sea from Singapore. No other road connects it with the outside world and in the wet weather this one is often washed away. Some day Trengganu may be connected by road with the F.M.S. in

Pahang, which would give her a direct line of communication with Singapore. But that day is still far off, and Trengganu remains a distant paradise with no more than a dozen European inhabitants.

The last of the Captain's boys saluted us at the Kelantan frontier and two hundred yards on a sharp little policeman in a less elegant uniform ushered us into Trengganu. The landscape changed at once. The road was a rich apricot in colour. We ferried a river of luminous dark green jade, whose sandy bottom was a contrast to the muddy Kelantan monsters. Then the country opened into spreading, luxuriant scrub, with a range of blue hills in the distance.

We lunched with Childe, a tall, friendly young man who at once communicated to us his enthusiasm for the place. It was the first time I had heard anyone up-country express anything but a conventional distaste for his lot and surroundings, but it was not the last, for everyone in Trengganu considers himself lucky to be stationed there. Those who have seen them have always a nostalgia for these Eastern States of Malaya. Childe had been sent straight out from England to Pahang. As a cadet, he had an easy time, lazing up and down the rivers in a launch. Then he was transferred to Kuala Lumpur, which plunged him in gloom, and he hankered to escape from the sultry mangrove swamps of its coast to the open beaches of the East. He had his way in the end. Here he was, back in the East, monarch of a large district at an exceptionally early age, too absorbed in his work and the beauty of the country to be lonely. The shooting was wonderful, and he had it all to himself. The country was so open that it was always easy to find the birds. "And you have no idea," he said, "what a sight that plain is in the early morning, as you motor across it towards the mountains."

The jungles above the plain were infested with tigers, and it was the D.O.'s job to shoot them. But tiger-shooting in such places is a very different affair from the secure and highly organized shikar: it is more of a necessity than a sport. Tigers *must* be shot because of the danger to villagers and their flocks: one, in the Ulu Trengganu, had killed twenty natives in two years, and no one could get near him. The jungle is so dense that the pursuit of a tiger is a risky business. When a kill is reported you set out about five o'clock in the evening and conceal yourself in a tree. Owing to the thickness of the vegetation you get no more than the merest glimpse of the beast when it appears. You fire, but as often as not you cannot see the result of your shot. You remain in your tree for a bit, but, short of staying there all night, you come down sooner or later, cautiously, gingerly, for you do not know whether you have killed, wounded or missed. You may find the headlamps of an enraged and wounded beast awaiting you at the foot of the tree in the darkness; you may find nothing, in which case you have a nervous walk back through the jungle, lest the animal intercept you in your path. I learnt for the first time the doubtless elementary fact that a man-eating tiger is no particular breed but as a rule an ordinary beast that is maimed or too aged and infirm to kill wild game for itself and has recourse to easier, human game. One specimen, recently killed, was found to have an abscess in its head, so that its sense of smell had gone.

Malaya rang with tiger stories, but the one which appealed to me most, whether accurate or not, was that of the playful tiger. A man was fishing by a stream when a tiger came up behind him. It had no hostile intent, but was fascinated by the regular movement of his casting, following the line with its eyes like a kitten, up and down, up and down. And then, like a kitten, it jumped playfully on to the fisherman's back. His body was found with the claw-marks in his flesh, but otherwise untouched, and the tiger never returned to its kill. "Accidentally killed by a tiger" would be an unusual verdict at an inquest! (I do not expect anyone to believe this story, but I like to think that it is true.)

The Sakai have a complete mythology of tiger legends. The home of the tigers is Kandang Balok, said to be in the south of Trengganu, where the beasts take human form and are ruled by a grey-haired chief. He lives in a palace built of human bones, whose roof is thatched with human hair. When leaving their home to hunt the tigers pass through a bamboo tunnel under the White River, where they assume animal shape until their return.

Five Europeans sat down to lunch at Childe's bungalow for the first time in years—perhaps the first time ever, for it is remote and white men are few and far between. But it so happened that two P.W.D. officials from Kuala Trengganu coincided with Manfred and myself. Childe was a refreshing host. Before we went he said that he was going up into the ulu for ten days, to do the rounds of his territory.

"Look here, why don't you both come with me? It would be grand!"

I thought it would be grand, too; but we must think it over.

"Well, come to tiffin here on your way back, and if you decide to come we can make the arrangements."

In the afternoon our road to Kuala Trengganu took us into the jungle. A narrow, orange ribbon fringed by tall grasses, it wound through a forest of lofty trees and dense undergrowth. For the first time we were in the real tropical jungle. It was exciting, but somehow disillusioning. Unreasonably one has formed since childhood images of tropical jungle so fantastic as to transcend ordinary experience, as though it were fashioned from some unknown element, shaped in some fabulous, more animal than vegetable form. But this jungle, though vast and tortuous and impressive, was yet still related to English woodland as a giant is related to a pygmy. Though a monster, its derivation was from the familiar world. A tree remains a tree, a bush remains a bush whether in Surrey or the tropics. These trees grew to a prodigious height, but their trunks were thin, and a beech in Savernake Forest is finer. As in the social state parasites hampered their freedom: ferns and creepers sprouted from their trunks, strangled them in an evil embrace; but the trees stood mute and unprotesting. resigned to an inevitable nuisance. From the road the jungle appeared dense and impenetrable, but in the interior it was freer, where the sun never penetrated and the undergrowth languished. When we stopped our car the home of beasts was silent as an English churchyard.

But when I think of tropical jungle now I still see the fabulous world of my childhood's fancy. However far you travel the mental fantasies which you weaved at home will still prevail over the realities which you have seen.

After fifty miles the country opened out and grew more populous. Then we came to the great Trengganu River, wide as a lake, fringed with coconuts and scattered with islands. As we ferried across it sailing-boats swarmed around us, with parallelograms of Victorian patchwork for sails.

Kuala Trengganu lived up to the promise of its hinterland.

Were it not for its remoteness it could become one of the finest seaside resorts in the world. Half a dozen European bungalows overlook a stretch of sand-dunes and natural turf of which the golfer would be inspired to make a second St. Andrews. Beyond it ranks of surf break on a flat yellow beach which goes on for ever, mile upon mile unbroken. To the north is the estuary of the Trengganu River, to the south the beach opens into another wide Kuala, with lagoons and a headland beyond. Seaward are islands, landward a distant range of blue mountains. As we walked along the beach thousands of tiny crabs popped in and out of the sand, blown like beads towards the sea. We saw fishermen throwing their lead-weighted nets like lassos. A rough boat, tapering to a graceful point at either end, had just come in with a catch, and Malays in lampshade hats were hauling it ashore. They carried away baskets of silver fish balanced on a pole from their shoulders, like a pair of scales. At sunset the casuarina-trees were outlined like very tall grasses against a sky of metallic green, with rose and amethyst clouds.

The inhabitants of Trengganu were charming. There was our host, the amusing young Assistant Adviser, who had that sportsman's and geographer's love of his countryside which is so much akin to the aesthetic. He was for ever planning enterprising walks across the mountains: pioneer walks through jungle towards the other side of the peninsula. There was his young superior and Cornish wife, living in a delightful bungalow on the beach, who entertained us to a regal dinner and five kinds of bitters with our pahits. There was a vigorous Scotch doctor and a dreamy Irish policeman.

The Scotsman vowed that he would never have a wife out here. A wife is apt to be a hindrance to efficiency in such jobs as his; for where a bachelor can go off for weeks at a time into the ulu, as a doctor should, a married man will stay at home and slack.

"Then you will never marry?"

"Certainly I shall. When I leave here I shall travel all over the world, for two years. Then I will settle down, marry, and take a practice at home, probably in Wolverhampton."

"Wolverhampton will be gloomy after Trengganu."

"No. Wolverhampton won't be so bad when I've had my fill of travelling."

The Irishman complained that he was being pestered by

the League of Nations with memoranda on the subject of whales. There are no whales within five thousand miles of Trengganu. Unlike the Captain he got his uniforms from Singapore instead of Savile Row and was instructing his policemen in English : creating a fantastic situation in court when the constable could read the depositions and the judge could not.

The Irishman was full of ambitious schemes for walking home, through China or Siberia or Tibet or South America. He was fortunate to have no ties. A young man who is stationed in the Colonies often sees less of the world than a young man at home, who can at least travel about Europe. He is lucky if he can go home in leisurely fashion each leave, exploring the world on the way. More often an exigent family at home demands his exclusive company throughout his leave ; and when he gets older and his home ties diminish he has lost the energy to travel.

At midnight we went down to the sea with surf-boards to bathe. (At Trengganu, for some reason, there are neither sharks nor sea-snakes.) The sea was colourless as death when we first plunged in. Then the moon came out from behind fleeced clouds. Each wave caught the silver moonlight as it turned and broke, like a woman flinging aside a silver lamé cloak to disclose billows of foamy white chiffon. We strode far out and came in on the crest of a wave on our surf-boards, at exhilarating speed.

Next morning we drove towards the mountains of Kuala Bran, at the end of the short road which leads inland. Here a lovely view met us, soft and gentle as one rarely sees in the tropics. At our feet a wide, blue river flowed in a majestic bend to the blue mountains behind it. A spit of fresh sand pointed towards marshy flats which are covered by floods in the rainy season but had just been released. The inevitable band of coconut-palms divided the water from the wooded hills, which showed in silhouette as though they were bare.

The landscape which one welcomes most, in the tropics, is always the least tropical in character. The freshness of this scene, relieved from the opaque and smoky pall of tropical haze, might almost have belonged to the Scottish highlands. The poets talk about "England's green and pleasant land" ; but England to tropical eyes is every colour in the world besides green. The green of the tropics is unrelieved : nowhere do you find anything to approach that rich variety of colour which makes the plains of Provence or the Western Islands of Scotland a joy to the eye. Tropical scenery is vastly overrated. The thick, green hirsute growth of nature covers the earth as a beard will mask the outline and changing complexion of a face. Vegetation, like a great python, will swallow a neglected clearing in a month: rice-fields are only wrested from the jungle's grip by force: the struggle to keep it at bay can never be allowed to relax. There can be no true colour, in landscape, without form, without light and shade. But here the form, the bone-structure of the country is obscured, like the figure of an over-dressed woman. The perpendicular jungle trees throw out no ample horizontal branches to cast a pattern of shade on the land. The joy of European scenery is in the racing shadows of cloud on bare grass, in the shadows of the earth itself where it undulates like a human body, falls into curves and hollows, runs away into a little cupped dell or climbs a gentle slope. All such shadows the tropical forest greedily absorbs, like a sponge.

We rejoiced in the wide Trengganu River because it was fresh and clear, not sluggish with mud as tropical rivers can be. A fisherman sitting cross-legged like Jeremy Fisher on his leaf floated down the current as though he had no boat beneath him. We called him to the bank: his tiny craft was no more than a scooped-out branch. His rod was a bamboo, his line of pineapple fibre, his bait a green leaf, and hé held up two silver fish with flame-coloured fins, which we bought.

We returned to tiffin: a perfect Malay curry, far kinder than the Indian variety, with a delicious Trengganu dish, Iteh Goleh. This is a duck, stuffed with herbs and roasted on a sweet spit of sugar cane. As a sweet we had Gula Malacca: a sauce of melted sugar (like maple sugar) from a palm-tree, poured over an ice-cold creamy mould of sago.

We said good-bye to our Trengganu hosts next day with regret. They were a delightful and hospitable group, and one of their most distinctive features was that they needed no club. But if the East is unchanging its European masters change all too often. Next year Trengganu may harbour a completely different community. An official rarely spends more than three years in one spot. After each leave he is appointed to a different part of the country. Though this arrangement may avoid the dangers of stagnation, its impermanence can only be bad for the colony as a whole; for just as a man is beginning to master his district and to know his people he is whisked away, possibly before he has had time to make his influence deeply felt. In Trengganu, for instance, the police are thrown into confusion every few years by the arrival of a new commissioner with entirely different ideas from his predecessor. Such permanent residents as Monty and the Captain (whose intention it was to settle down in Kelantan after his retirement) do far more good to Malaya as a whole than the movable officials.

We had decided to accept Childe's invitation to explore the ulu, and stopped to lunch with him on our way back to Tumpat. But Childe's manner seemed to have changed. He was less cordial than before, abrupt, almost rude in his remarks, and discussed the possibility of our accompanying him with a dull lack of enthusiasm. Clearly he was trying to put us off, but was at a loss how to do so gracefully.

It is an error to suppose that men who live alone in the wilds of the tropics are lonely, hankering after human company. For the most part they are contented in their way of life, enjoying their solitude, too busy to need distractions and put uncomfortably out of their stride by the invasion of extraneous elements. Though always hospitable to visitors they would just as soon be left alone. (With their wives, perhaps, it is different: women crave for human society and a change of faces.) Childe, in a warm and impulsive moment, had asked us to come with him into the ulu. But in the cold light of reason he had seen that we would be an encumbrance. Solitude, when a man has acquired its habit, becomes a possession to be treasured beneath lock and key. We said to Childe that, on reflection, we had not the time for his expedition. He beamed with ill-concealed relief, begged us to stay for dinner, for the night, for as long as we liked until his departure. But we said good-bye.

Next morning we left before dawn for Siam.

CHAPTER X

SIAM

SINGORA, BANGKOK

I HAD never thought highly of the casuarina-tree, despite its romantic name and reputation. It had seemed to me a scraggy creature, a cross between an overgrown tamarisk and an untidy larch, without either the rakish fantasy of the one or the airy dignity of the other. But at Singora, on the coast of Southern Siam, a wood of casuarinas, immensely tall and delicate, stretches to the point of the peninsula, and walking in this wood I began to feel the beauty of their ghost-green gossamer forms.

The casuarina strikes a gentle, faded note against the enamelled glaze of the other jungle trees. It is a touch of Corot in a Gauguin landscape; it has the wistful distinction of a grey old lady amid the polish of exotic sophistication. The slim trunks rose from a smooth turf carpet, flecked with shadows, slippery with pine (or rather casuarina) needles, broken by an occasional fairy pool, and the wood had the evanescence of a magic wood. Where its flank was exposed to the sea the sensitive trees turned their faces away from the wind and hunched their shoulders, wrapping their veils around them in protection. In front and on either side of me was water: to my left a great lagoon, to my right rank upon rank of slim white waves running swiftly to the shore. The waves did not pound the beach with solemn majesty: they ran, like traffic for ever in a hurry, towards the white sand. The sea was still a water-colour wash of elephant-grey and brown; when the monsoon died vivid colours would be painted on top—blue, jade green, perhaps crimson; but now it was a subdued accompaniment to the soft grey-green of the casuarinas. On the point the trees dwindled to rough bushes and the air was scented by red and white flowers which had at last found an open space to bloom in. The air was hot and the wind was strong and the white foam of the China Sea broke from two directions on the point, each side racing to see which could first strike the shore.

In the twilight you could hardly believe that the casuarina trees were real : they were wraiths, which ended in diaphanous smoke.

Singora was more alert than the towns of Malaya. Siamese boys flew kites on the beach, sped by on bicycles, with tennis-rackets under their arms, sparred with boxing-gloves in a garden, in eau-de-nil Chinese trousers. Here, evidently, was an energetic and sporting race.

We climbed up the moss-grown steps to the top of a steep, wooded hill, where a Buddhist temple rose above the tops of the trees. There was no one there, but Siamese names were carved all over the walls (the habit of defacing monuments is not confined to Europeans) and on one piece of wall was scrawled in childish pencil, "I meet you on hill this hill in 6 o'clock I love me to-day. Because you are very platy I love very much." From the ground I picked up a scrap of newspaper which informed me incongruously, in English, that "Mrs. Edward James (Miss Tilly Losch, the dancer) was injured in a taxicab crash in Grosvenor Square, W., yesterday. She was taken to her home in Culross Street, Park Lane, W., in an ambulance, suffering from bruises and slight concussion."

The rest-house at Singora stands in a magnificent position on top of a steep hill. The Visitors' Book testified to the prevalence of airmen among the guests, and contained besides an entertaining variety of comments : "Turkish bath excellent" ; "Diseased rabbit should be fricasséd" ; "The absence of a Dutch wife is very much felt by a widower"; "Food B. Awful" ; "Food fine" ; "Le serviteur de cet hôtel est très bien, il est très fidèle, très poli, très respectueux. Mais sa sœur est très malpropre. Elle est un peu folle."

A Mr. Shakespeare from China maintained that the place was "a fair dinkum possis ! A spot to return to if only on the wings of memory." In the opinion of an Italian, "every think" was "wonthefull". An Englishman made the laconic remark, "Mosquitoes." A Hungarian countess, on her way from Penang to France, wrote, "Petit coin idéal pour une lune de miel"; directly beneath, Mr. Clarence Oft, of the

U.S.A., added: "Just what I think—and here we are"; on the next page three Italians and a Swiss "cordially agree with la Comtesse Hongroise of the previous page".

It seemed a very decent rest-house.

Next day we caught the Bangkok Express and, after a night in the train, awoke to find ourselves in a different season, for the monsoon here ends sooner than in Malaya. The rice was harvested and the fields were brown and the bamboos were fading to almost autumnal shades. Nature would grow more and more withered and dusty until, eight months ahead, the rains came again to freshen her. The landscape was flat, jungle had given place to bush, the houses had high-pitched roofs, pointed at either end like boats, and the voices of the Siamese on the train were like saxophones imitating the wail of a baby. A man at a wayside station tried to sell me a tiger cub for five pounds, but I mistrusted its precocious snarl.

The moment I set foot in Bangkok I was conscious of the transition from a colony to an independent country. Siam has never been colonized and is never likely to be, and the effects of this are at once discernible in the demeanour of the Siamese race. It was refreshing to be among a people without racial inferiority or colour-consciousness, to be again, as in Europe, on terms of equality with the man in the street. I was no longer a sahib or a tuan or even a white man: I was just a human being like everybody else. The people were charming and helpful and good-mannered but it would never have occurred to them to kowtow to me in any degree.

In so far as it is European the atmosphere of Bangkok is cosmopolitan. English, French, Danes, Germans and Dutch live side by side, and though English is the European language of the country no one race predominates in prestige over the rest. The Siamese are staunchly pro-English. Almost the whole of their aristocracy is educated at English public schools; in fact one young prince who recently returned to Bangkok after ten years' education in England found that he had forgotten every word of his native language and had to learn it laboriously all over again. Most of the shop assistants and even the conductors on the trains speak English, which is taught everywhere in the schools.

But the Englishman does not send his daughter to be

"finished" in Paris from a conviction that the French, as a race, are superior to the English. Nor is it from any belief in the racial superiority of the Englishman that the Siamese educates his son in England. Western influence is never allowed to undermine his national character. He contrives to borrow from the West without aping it. He has taken what is best in Western civilization and grafted it on to his own, but without in any sense weakening his pride of race. Thus Siam has achieved the perfect compromise between East and West.

Bangkok is not an ancient city: it dates in importance only from the latter part of the eighteenth century. Hence its up-to-date commercialism is in no way alien to its original character and creates no jarring impression. Until comparatively recent times it had no streets, but only waterways. The buildings of the big banks and business houses still give on to the Menam River, approachable only by narrow streets from the central highway of the city. They have lawns and gardens stretching down to the water's edge, and when you go to cash a cheque at the bank you can pick a bud from its magnolia-tree to put in your buttonhole. The greater part of the population still knows only the water. Their streets are a network of klongs (or canals) where they live and keep shops in floating houses, and an immense variety of dug-outs, sampans, motor-boats and river steamers take the place of bicycles, buses, taxi-cabs and delivery vans. It was thrilling to steam up the congested river at sunset, when the water, as if the two elements had become confused, turned red as fire.

Because of its canals Bangkok has inevitably been labelled "the Venice of the East". It would be hard to imagine a city less like Venice. Actually, if you like to label towns with neat phrases, it would be a degree less apposite, though still too flattering, to describe it as "the Hamburg of the East". Its water traffic, its atmosphere of busy efficiency, its several examples of modern architecture, its up-to-date dance-halls and restaurants and cinemas have, if anything, a German flavour, and there is an enormous new building, with a different restaurant on every floor and a dance-band on the roof, after the style of the *Haus Vaterland* in Berlin. One night, when I was there, a convivial party of Germans, Danes and Dutchmen broke into vigorous community singing over their beer to complete the illusion. It was an amusing place with an up-to-date band and attractive Siamese dancing partners.

But commercially Bangkok is Chinese. The Siamese were for long too proud to go into trade, and are still reluctant to take up any occupation more menial than that of a taxi-driver. Thus, as in Singapore, the Chinaman has made the city his own. It is not a beautiful town: featureless, with long, jangling streets intersecting at right angles and a web of wires and tramlines. But it has atmosphere. Chinese life has a strong fascination. It was a nuisance to be unable, owing to climate, convention and the complete absence of pavement space, to wander freely about the streets, for only in this way can one catch the true feel of a town and the hang of its geography. But I was conscious, as I drove about, of a network of alleys spread with a mass of varied merchandise; of lithe humanity with smooth, bare yellow torsos, in black Chinese trousers or little white shorts; of Chinese lettering in picturesque confusion; of that inevitable, but still not unpleasant Chinese smell. In this surging life I sensed some of that feeling of the East for which men hanker who have tasted it. The fascination of Chinese life is akin to that of the stage, where the fourth wall is demolished to enable you to pry into private lives. The East is without gêne: the Oriental has none of the Westerner's desire for privacy. Our semi-detached residences with their closed front doors and their discreet lace curtains would astonish him. There is far more mystery in an English suburban street than anywhere in the "mysterious East". The Chinaman lives as in a doll's house in section, for all the world to see, giving to the European the faintly prurient thrill of seeing what he should not. His house, like his shop, is open to street or river. You can watch whole families eating, sleeping, gossiping, busying themselves with the housework, fulfilling all their accustomed daily functions. If you lingered long enough in their streets you would see their dramas too: their passions, the loves and hates which impel them to fight and kill. Life here is lived frankly and openly, and if so be you had the instincts of a voyeur I believe that you could even watch the intimacies of the marriage chamber.

The Chinese restaurants in Bangkok are supposed to be even better than in China, and our friends of the Borneo

Company entertained us one night to a superlative Chinese meal. The menu was as follows:

>Shark's-fin soup with crabs' eggs
>Fried prawns in sweet sauce
>Crab-meat and asparagus with mushrooms
>Duck's skin with unleavened bread
>Cold duck
>Bird's-nest soup
>Fried Pomfret
>Pilau with sweet ginger sauce

At the beginning and end steaming hot towels were brought, as after shaving, which we put over our faces and round our necks to refresh ourselves. Each dish was placed in the middle of the table, and we filled our bowls from it, adding a selection from the innumerable liquid sauces which accompanied it. Chopsticks were provided but I soon gave them up in despair, in favour of a porcelain spoon. The roast duck's skin, with a sour-sweet sauce, was particularly crisp and delicious, but the bird's-nest soup was slightly disappointing. It contained too much chicken and tasted of chicken broth.

Afterwards we went to the cinema which is the most modern building in Bangkok and boasts an up-to-date system of air-cooling. The latest American films were fascinating to watch, regarded anthropologically as an illustration of "how the other half lives". They portrayed a mode of life which from this distance seemed as fantastic and unreal as a fairy story, as indeed a film of Oriental life would seem in a London cinema.

One night we went to a Siamese theatre, which provided a similar entertainment to our Malay opera, but on a grander scale. It was still hard to believe that the play had been rehearsed, as the Siamese actresses sat and chattered aimlessly away in their raucous, monotonous voices. But the Siamese are a musical race, and the melodious orchestra of drums and gongs and xylophones was agreeable to listen to. The principal comic turn was borrowed straight from Will Hay: the English schoolmaster (pipe, top-hat, horn-rimmed spectacles, bow tie, blue coat and black trousers) with his two pupils, one bright and cheeky, the other a dunce. It aroused great amusement from the audience which, in the stalls, was largely composed of women with withered complexions, spectacles, and close-cropped grey hair standing on end in freakish fashion.

The social centre of Bangkok is the Sports Club, which is frequented by Europeans and Siamese alike. Even the half-caste is admitted here, for Siam is probably the only Oriental country where no stigma attaches to him. This is one of the finest clubs in the East, with tennis-courts, squash-courts, a swimming-pool, a golf-course and even a race-course of its own in front of the club buildings, much as if the R.A.C. were to be situated in the position of the Epsom grandstand. The young Siamese princes use the club a lot, and we had some high-spirited times with them, talking and laughing and dicing for drinks. Except for their clothes (tunics buttoned up to the neck, sarongs looped between the legs so as to look like trousers, white silk stockings and ordinary shoes) they were entirely European in their manners, their humour and their tastes, and took a great deal of interest in sport. But their names were incomprehensible because never pronounced as spelt. "Karagachingr", for instance, became "Kuntchit", "Kambaeng Bejra" was "Kampen Pet", "Gadadharabhodi", inconceivable as it may seem, was "Katatawn".

The Siamese princesses, some of whom I met at a European party, were equally friendly and self-assured, and one of them was as lovely and as chic in her European clothes as any girl I have seen in a London ballroom.

Race-meetings are a continuous event and business firms have a half-holiday on race-days. (They do well in this matter of holidays, for what with the various religious festivals, Christian and Buddhist, the Siamese New Year, the Chinese New Year, the European New Year, the French "Quatorze Juillet", the Siamese national anniversaries and the usual English Bank Holidays, there are over twenty non-working days, besides Sundays, in the year.) The jockeys were often mere children, with shrill, treble voices, who had some difficulty in controlling their enormous steeds. It took them a good twenty minutes to line up for the start. The horses kicked each other and threw their riders again and again in the process, and one would not have been in the least surprised to see one or two of them start off in the opposite direction.

For sheer fantasy the religious architecture of Bangkok must be unequalled anywhere in the world. The city contains innumerable wats, or groups of Buddhist temples, so extraordinary in shape and colour and material that they leave Western eyes entirely bewildered. At first I could make neither head nor tail of their eccentricities. It was clearly impossible (with a few exceptions) to apply normal architectural standards to these buildings, any more than to stage scenery or the contorted fantasies of a Luna Park. But judged as an extravaganza, as the Alice in Wonderland world of a child's imagination, their charm began to grow upon me.

The first I visited was Wat Po. Here huge spiral towers, like the cream horns of the confectioner, surrounded the temple buildings, whose great expanses of roof sloped steeply upwards to an enormous height in a sequence of overlapping planes. Each roof was tiled, in red or green or yellow, and ended at either side in a gilded flourish as of flowery handwriting. The buildings stood in a paved garden among magnolia-trees, where a variety of grottoes, kiosks and other grotesqueries were dotted about. The place had a faded air of inconsequence, like the lumber-room of some scene-painter, filled with objects whose use and purpose has long been forgotten. Porcelain cocks and hens, giants and goblins and other such toys might have been designed for the entertainment of children, and in a corner, in fact, was a child's school. Two little boys who were playing among the pagodas attached themselves to us and showed us round.

In one of the buildings they showed us a gigantic, reclining Buddha of gold, fifty yards long and fifty yards high, so neglected that its gilt was peeling off to disclose the plaster. There were shrines where quantities of Buddhas sat in different attitudes. Various offerings had been laid at their feet : a couple of watches, a collection of cigarette cards, little parcels tied up with string, like the Christmas presents of a child. In the central temple a lot of old women squatted in ranks before the Buddha on a carpeted floor, raucously chanting. The party had the air of an afternoon outing, the Oriental equivalent of a mothers' meeting or tea-fight. The hags had come along with a picnic meal and settled down for an hour or two, surrounded by teapots, glasses, spittoons for their betel-nut and a variety of odd little possessions. When they saw us they took a few minutes' rest, regarded us with friendly curiosity and went on with their hideous carolling, which nevertheless provided as good a way for old wives to spend an afternoon as in backbiting and gossip. Floral posies and plates of fruit lay before the Buddha, and in a corner a priest lay asleep, lulled into Nirvana by the scent of flowers and incense.

At the far end of the temple precincts were shacks, where people lived. Women, apparently toothless from the stain of betel-nut, were putting sugar-cane through a mangle in one of the arcades. Encamped about the cloisters were a few poor people, cooking their meals or weaving, their possessions spread around them. Boys worked at their books in quiet corners, but were only too ready to be interrupted and chat to us. A toothless old priest played with a patent cigarette-lighter, and cackled with rich laughter at our comments; while shaven novices, draped in yellow and carrying black umbrellas, wandered aimlessly about. The place was peaceful, the home as it were of a toy religion, simple and unexacting.

Wat Benjamopitr, of more recent (nineteenth-century) origin, was smarter than Wat Po. Its gilt and scarlet decoration was fresh and new, contrasting vividly with the white of the buildings, and the innumerable roofs were of a dull orange tiling. The white marble courtyard, spotlessly swept and garnished, provided a cool relief from the glare of the sun, and a haven of absolute quiet. Round the cloister were hundreds of black marble Buddhas, imitating the art of different races (Khmer, Burmese, Siamese, Chinese, Japanese, Cambodian, Lao), and in one of the temples a large gilt Buddha sat beneath an artificial fig-tree. Yellow-robed novices bathed in a stone-paved canal and lazed on its steps, for a monastery is attached to the wat. These boys seem to have an agreeably easy life, with no cares or responsibilities and their food provided each day in their begging-bowls. They have little to do but the somewhat negative occupation of avoiding deadly sin and preserving that vacancy of mind into which alone the divine light can penetrate. It is an inexpensive life and many go into the priesthood for a year or two as in Europe their contemporaries do military service.

Nearby is the Golden Mount, an artificial hill of masonry,

like the stylized mountains in the background of a primitive painting. It is covered with shrines and grottoes, some of them almost inaccessible owing to the steepness of the artificial rock. Beyond is Wat Suthat, with its enormous swing, a hundred feet high. Here, once a year, men swing for money bags perched on bamboos, which they attempt to grasp with their teeth. This is a ceremony of Hindu origin, whose result is intimately connected with the weather prospects of the coming season, like our own little games round the maypole.

But the quintessence of architectural fantasy is contained within the walls of the Grand Palace. Here is the hobgoblin city of the Children's Hour, the dream-world of every child's imaginings, the splendours of heaven and pantomime come to life. No doubt the Grand Palace (a city in itself) is gaudy, exaggerated, grotesque in the lavishness of its colour and the profusion of its designs. But it is fascinating, because utterly unreal.

Before you reach its ultimate courtyard of extravagances you are confronted by the audience hall. This is the best piece of architecture in Bangkok. Somewhat Gothic in effect, it is a T-shaped building whose high white walls are broken only at the base, by a row of pointed black windows. Above, three-tiered gables, curling at the end like the prows of ships, pile up until they meet in the centre to culminate in a long and slender spire. A rectangular lawn is stretched at the building's feet, bounded on one side by the palace and on the other by the throne hall, and the surrounding terrace is broken by curious Chinese trees. Their leaves are trained to grow in massed circular balls so that they have the air of those old-fashioned genealogical trees which have circles for the names.

The royal throne is raised so high at the end of its great hall that it almost touches the ceiling. But it is usually reserved for the Buddha and the king sits in a gilt throne beneath it. From the ceiling hang countless chandeliers, many of wax flowers, replicas of the real Chinese floral candelabra. It is a relief to find in this room none of the Western bad taste which mars Oriental palaces nearer to Europe. Such bad taste as there is is exclusively Oriental.

The courtyard of the Emerald Buddha contains a galaxy of brilliantly coloured and fantastic buildings, shaped like cactus-plants and wedding-cakes and conchological freaks.

Curious towers taper to a pinnacle through an extraordinary variety of spiral decoration. There is a temple which looks as though it were of cloth of gold. There are giant pieces of porcelain, forty feet high. There are spires inlaid with coloured glass. There are huge painted ogres, guarding the gates. There is a solid golden obelisk. The temple of the Emerald Buddha, with its high portico of columns and its carved teak doors is of such a height that the image inside, perched on a towering dais, is hard to distinguish. Hundreds of gifts are arranged on each tier beneath it: groups of wax or tinsel flowers, Japanese gardens, quaint scenes, intricately portrayed in tinfoil and a variety of stuffs—all beneath domes to delight the Victorianist; while one step is covered entirely with offerings of horn. Many of these are birthday presents, for in Siam, on your birthday, it is held to be more blessed to give than to receive, in gratitude for the years you have been spared.

I had hoped to see white elephants in Siam. But the white elephant is a fraud. It is pink; and seldom pink all over, at that.

Before leaving Bangkok I visited the snake farm at the Pasteur Institute and watched the keepers taking the serum of poisonous snakes. Sometimes they are bitten, but it does them no harm since an injection is immediately made, to counteract the poison. The dangers of snake-bite in the tropics are very much smaller than I had supposed. The average snake is terrified of human beings and will invariably run away unless trodden on or otherwise surprised. Moreover his striking power is less swift and his orbit more narrow than one might imagine. Doubtless the cobras at the Pasteur Institute were weakened by the monthly extraction of their poison, but the keeper seemed to find it childishly easy to keep out of their radius. First he routed them out of their little stone blockhouses with sticks: coiled masses of black, hissing, wriggling intestines. Then, for the benefit of the crowd, he started to show off, picking them up by the tail and throwing them nonchalantly about, slapping their faces and so forth. Though angry, they could do little to retaliate. The cobra can only strike downwards: it has to rear up into a vertical position before it can bite you. Thus it had to perform two movements to the keeper's one: the keeper stepped back as it rose, and when it struck was out of range, so that the snake had nothing to strike at but waved its hood foolishly in the air, hissing with mortification. It could not move forward while in a striking position, so that as long as the keeper stood a yard away he was safe.

To take the serum he held the cobra's head down on the ground with a forked stick and picked it up by the scruff of the neck, while another man forced a round glass disc into its mouth and a greyish fluid oozed from its fangs. The banded kraits, lovely creatures striped horizontal black and yellow, were easier game. The keeper grasped them out of their cages with his hands, and when he picked each one up to take the serum he did so casually, by the head, and with no thought of caution.

Even if you are bitten by a poisonous snake and are carrying no serum, you can often eliminate danger by means of a tourniquet and a slash at the wound with a knife, to cut it right out.

All the same I was not sorry to avoid encountering a single snake in the East.

Chapter XI

SIAM (*continued*)

UP-COUNTRY

SIAM has skipped an era in transport: she has virtually no roads. Even Bangkok is unapproachable except by rail or sea, and such roads as exist up-country are only in the nature of short feeders to the railways. Since the State has the railway monopoly this system is easy to understand, for roads would provide embarrassing competition. But the comfort of the Siamese railways, with their modern Diesel engines, is such that one could not wish to travel by any other means.

A single road *is* under construction. It will link Bangkok with its aerodrome, twelve miles off. When this aerodrome has been adequately protected from flooding Bangkok will be the great air junction of the East. As it is she boasts three air services a week (British, French and Dutch) to Europe. More or less equidistant from Calcutta, Singapore and Hongkong she forms the essential link between them, and when (as can only be a question of time) the air service is extended via French Indo-China to China itself, Bangkok will hold a key position among the air stations of the world.

As I left by train one Sunday morning for Ayuthia and Lopburi, both ancient capitals of Siam, I felt as though I were engaged on a Sunday expedition to Potsdam or Versailles, for the outskirts of Bangkok, with its modern suburban boulevards, looked more European than Oriental. Manfred and Simon, after a late party at the *Alliance Française* the night before, had both overslept: so I was alone.

I stopped at Bang-Pa-In, to have a look at the king's summer palace. The station was on the river, and I was propelled in a sampan to the palace grounds. I found a hotch-potch of buildings flung incongruously together by royalty's wayward caprice amid a haphazard garden of waterways. There was a Chinese pavilion with panels and beams of carved teak. For the sake of coolness the partition walls stopped short of the ceiling, but the gap was sometimes filled by an elaborate trellis-work. Around it was a Chinese garden, with grottoes and miniature trees. There was a wooden villa, like any Swiss châlet, but furnished and decorated in the Empire style. There was a classical trianon of stucco, with an incongruous mixture of French and English furniture, the fruit of royal visits to Europe. These intimate dwellings had the wistful charm of places that desire to be inhabited and, unlike great palaces, lose their raison d'être when they are empty.

Opposite the Chinese pavilion was a huge brick tower in the Ruskin manner, such as the Victorians used to build as a gesture of self-importance. Beyond, a classical gateway admitted, not an avenue, but a waterway to the main part of the garden, where in the centre of a rectangular tank stood an exquisite little Chinese temple, a thing of intricate beauty like a toy work of art. Nearby I found an imposing marble obelisk with the following inscription:

> TO THE BELOVED MEMORY OF HER LATE AND
>
> LAMENTED MAJESTY
>
> SUNADIDAKUMARIRATIR
>
> QUEEN CONSORT
>
> WHO WONT TO SPEND HER MOST PLEASANT AND HAPPIEST HOURS IN THIS GARDEN AMIDST THOSE LOVING ONES AND DEAREST TO HER
>
> THIS MEMORIAL IS ERECTED BY
>
> CHULALONKORN REX
>
> HER BELOVED HUSBAND WHOSE SUFFERING FROM SO CRUEL AN ENDURANCE THROUGH THOSE TRYING HOURS MADE DEATH SEEM SO NEAR AND YET PREFERABLE
>
> 1881

Audience Hall, Grand Palace, Bangkok

Wat Suthat, Bangkok
(note swing in centre background)

Temple Guardian in Grand Palace, Bangkok

At Chiengmai was still living the sixth of King Chulalonkorn's many widows, a shock-headed old lady with close-cropped hair and a cavernous mouth, red with the stain of betel-nut.

It was evident that Chulalonkorn had fallen under the sway of Victorian taste and sentiment in the course of his visit to England. Opposite the summer palace of Bang-Pa-In is a wat—and it is a Gothic wat. In the precincts golden Buddhas squat uncomfortably beneath canopies of the acutest Gothic Revival style, stuccoed white and beige. The temple itself, also in white and beige, is the usual English suburban eyesore, with steeple and bells complete. The interior is coloured in a horrid combination of pink, khaki and green plaster, with panes of crude stained glass (pink, green, amber and blue) in the windows, while a huge and elaborate Gothic reredos, of dark polished wood picked out in gold, houses inhospitably the Buddha. The devout English Protestant, accustomed to regard Gothic architecture as the exclusive preserve of the Christian religion, would be scandalized here at its sacrilegious adaptation to "heathen" uses. Certainly it was startling to find this grotesque monument of English provincial hideosity by a stream where sampans floated up and down, where half-naked Siamese lived on piles by the water's edge and water buffaloes wallowed luxuriously in the flooded rice-fields.

Manfred and Simon were not on the next train either, so, still alone, I proceeded to Ayuthia. It is hard to believe that this little town was the capital of Siam as recently as 150 years ago and, for centuries before, one of the most important cities of the East. Its destruction by the Burmese was thorough; but invasion apart, cities die quickly in the East if abandoned: their dwellings are always of an impermanent nature. Ayuthia's main street is the river. The houses are roofed, for the most part, with corrugated iron; but corrugated iron, adapted to the Siamese style, can look surprisingly attractive. Their high-pitched roofs shone silver in the sun, and they looked like Noah's Arks. Shop-fronts gave on the water. The smaller traders carried their wares from door to door in sampans and the housewives paddled along in their dug-outs to the larger provision stores. Though no more than the humdrum life of any street the scene had that air of carnival which always infects river traffic. The congested boats, the marketers in their huge straw hats and gay-coloured clothes had the light-headed look of a crowd in Boulter's Lock.

My gondolier landed me at a street where booths fluttered with bright cottons like flags in the river breeze. I took a car to the ruins of old Ayuthia. It was stiflingly hot inland, but the huge Khmer buildings looked the more impressive, looming out of the jungle through a haze of heat and dust. These great ruined cones and pylons were awe-inspiring rather than beautiful, like primeval monsters of architecture. One ragged tower, of incredible height, looked like a prodigy of nature, not of man, so long had it been at nature's mercy. Encircling creepers and roots had in places stripped the unreal monuments of their facing stone, so that piles of naked brick were all you saw. Occasionally a frieze of stone-carving had survived the stranglehold of plants, but for the most part no more than the bare bones of the buildings remained. A gigantic bronze Buddha glared out through jagged walls, intact though the vail of his temple had been rent in twain. Sitting untouched amid this wreckage of thunderbolts he had the awful majesty of a Jehovah contemplating the Sodom and Gomorrah which he has destroyed in wrath.

The ruins of Lopburi were very similar. Here hundreds of headless torsos and torso-less legs lay in heaps like a stone shambles as if some god, like a barbarous conqueror, had mutilated the bodies of those who had incurred his displeasure and turned them to stone.

Manfred was on the evening train and we arrived at Lopburi together. A fat little spectacled Siamese boy greeted us on the platform in pidgin English and welcomed us to "Lopbuli" (even to the extent of offering us "plostitutes"). He took us to his father's hotel: a primitive place, but homely and clean.

"My father, he cook dinner."

We explained our wants: Manfred had acquired a passion for a fruit called a papaia, a kind of melon, and demanded it on every occasion. He had at length mastered its name, just as we were leaving Malaya. But in Siam, as bad luck would have it, it had another name altogether and it was only after half an hour's complicated explanation that the boy contrived to identify it. Bicycles (of German make), ridden by small boys, plied for hire, and took us into the town in basket sidecars: a practical and comfortable means of transport. Here the Menam River was very low, and long mud banks stretched down to a dirty trickle from the houses marooned on their piles. Squatting in a shelter by the quay Chinese were gambling. They played a swift game with narrow cards which looked like a cross between rummy and mah-jongg. For dinner we had a mass of meat with vegetables, grilled pork, eggs, and a sickly-sweet kind of Chinese sausage.

Next morning our fat little dragoman took us to seek the ruins, which prepared us for what we were to see, on a finer scale, at Angkor. In the museum thousands of Khmer heads, some with an oddly Jewish expression, lay on shelves, like apples. We saw too the house of Faulkon, the Cephalonian adventurer who ingratiated himself with the King of Siam in the seventeenth century, and almost succeeded in selling the country to the French, on the pretence of converting the Siamese to Roman Catholicism.

The next two days we were to spend in the train, making for French Indo-China. Determined to avoid the ordinary and uninteresting route to Angkor, we had set off more or less into the blue, heading north-east from Bangkok and hoping to strike the Mekong River near the frontier. But since every Oriental country maintains a steadfast ignorance of its neighbour's ways, we had been unable to obtain information as to accommodation or means of transport beyond the French border.

The Siamese are a delightful people to travel with. They have more vitality than most Eastern races and little of the languid Oriental about them. They are full of life and fun, very much on the spot, and invariably amusing company. I know nowhere where you will find a friendlier atmosphere than on a Siamese train. We were travelling through a part of the country which Europeans rarely traverse, and so were the object of much amiable curiosity from the native passengers. I used to spend a lot of time in the third-class coaches, joking with them in an extraordinary sort of pidgin English. There was no servility about these people, no question of "losing one's dignity" or "impairing European prestige" by hobnobbing with them. I was not their superior. Just a funny fellow with different-coloured legs. The conversation was more or less limited to questions and answers, with gusts of laughter interspersed. Where had I come from? Where was I going? How old was I? Was I French?

How much did my shirt cost? And my camera? How often did I attack my wife? Had I lots of children? We patted each other to see if we were real, each said the other was "good man", or "funny man", vied with each other in feats of strength, and laughed immoderately. One of the conductors laughed so much that he was constrained to make me a present of a kidney, which we had cooked on the spot and shared all round.

The train was also a sort of travelling provision store, and at every station people swarmed on board to buy meat or fish or ice or groceries. When we felt hungry we would walk along to the larder, select some freshwater prawns, perhaps, or a duck, and superintend their cooking, with rice and tomatoes and various oddments. But we soon learnt that the cool-looking cucumbers burnt your mouth out and that unless you took steps to stop him the cook would chop up your bird into tiny pieces, bones and all, in the Chinese fashion, making it very difficult to eat. We drank pleasant Japanese beer and tea. Sometimes we would raid a train passing in the opposite direction, in case it had a superior store of delicacies.

The first night we spent at Korat. The rest-house was full. But a young Siamese doctor with whom we had talked on the train insisted on turning a friend out of his room that we might have it. Not many Europeans are as hospitable to foreigners at home. We had an excellent dinner of fresh fish and chicken. (Manfred had already forgotten the Siamese for papaia and had to go without.) Afterwards we took bicycle sidecars to explore the town. The Chinese shops sold bright-coloured stuffs and every sort of mixed merchandise. In their cookhouses were various and curious foods, including the feet of hens and the heads of fishes. There were many barbers, and through open doorways one saw men smoking opium in dark rooms. The silversmith sold silver belts and bracelets of linked medallions, tall little boxes to contain opium accessories and ingenious combined gadgets for picking the teeth, removing wax from the ears and hairs from the chin. The cinema was showing *A Farewell to Arms*, but as it was both invisible and inaudible we left and went to bed.

Next evening we arrived at Varindr, which is the terminus of the railway. Here an English-speaking railway clerk took us in charge and conducted us to a Chinese hotel. It was a primitive place which had come down in the world. "Once," he said, "you get much food here. European food, Siamese food, good food. Now too poor. No food, only tea." The kitchen certainly looked forlorn, with its empty shelves and a few rough tables, giving on to the street. We bought a chicken for elevenpence from a man in a cookhouse opposite and told him to cook it with rice and vegetables for our dinner. We bought potatoes from a neighbouring stall and a tin of lychees, and the entire meal cost us tenpence each.

The cinema, as in all these little towns, was the focal point of the night-life. The orchestra played outside, in confused and spirited fashion, until the show began. Tables and chairs were spread around and there were tea- and food-stalls. The cinema house was a spacious shed of corrugated iron, with an ample gallery. It was crowded: mothers had slung their babies in improvised hammocks between the benches, where they slept oblivious of the noise, and children even slept on the stage itself. The film, obscured by flickering black rain, was a Chinese version of the old-fashioned blood-and-thunder serial, intended for nightly instalments but run right through in an evening instead, thus eliminating all dramatic effect. Men were hurled head over heels down precipices, but no black-out followed: you didn't have to wait till to-morrow to see their fate: the film went straight on and the thrill was lost. Men were trussed up by bandits to be hanged, but rescued in the nick of time by friends galloping a hundred miles over mountain ranges (and then only because for some reason an hour and a half elapsed between the tying of the noose and the hoisting of the rope). But the suspense grew less and less agonizing as the identical sameness of each situation (forgotten under the serial system) became apparent. Chases and scuffles followed each other with unrelieved monotony. At what they took to be the dramatic moments there was complete pandemonium among the children, while the orchestra abandoned all semblance of tune to let itself go in a frenzy of drum-beating and trumpet-blowing. But the grown-ups were too sophisticated to fall for so tedious an entertainment. They came for half an hour and went away bored.

In the middle of the night we were awakened by a fusillade of machine-gun fire right under our windows. It was the beginning of the Chinese New Year—but a poor sort of Hogmanay which is celebrated only by a few Chinese crackers, all smoke and noise and no fire.

Meanwhile our plans were in some doubt. Our dragoman said that for forty dollars we could hire a car to Paksé, in French Indo-China, where I had an idea (based on an out-of-date time table) that we could catch a river steamer down the Mekong next morning. But forty dollars was exorbitant. The conductor on the train had thought we could get a boat to Pimouln, then a bus to Paksé. The dragoman also thought something of the kind. But he was vague about the hour of the boat's departure: it might be ten o'clock, on the other hand it might not. No, there was no way of finding out. It was Chinese New Year. We decided to trust to luck, and rose next morning at eight a.m. But the situation was complicated by the complete disappearance of our dragoman and sole interpreter. To make matters worse we ascertained by signs from the inhabitants that the steamer for Pimouln (or Paksé) left every morning at four a.m. However we piled our luggage into a bus and made for the river. A boat was sitting by the opposite bank at Ubon but no one knew where it was going or when.

"Pimouln?" we enquired. "Paksé?" "Pimouln," they repeated, "Paksé," and shrugged their shoulders. We crossed the river in a sampan and approached the boat. "Pimouln? Paksé?" The tone of the passengers was slightly more definite: they did not say no. "Pimouln?" we repeated to everybody we saw, "Paksé?"; and finally one of them nodded and pointed to the boat. A small Siamese child who had learnt English at school confirmed the fact that it did really go to Paksé (or Pimouln). But asked when, he knit his brows pathetically, concentrated hard, and then enunciated with effort, "I-do-not-no." There was nothing for it but to sit down on board and wait to see what happened. This we did, and two hours later the boat left. We were in luck. It might easily have been two days.

The boat was a two-decker barge towed by a steam tug and towing, in its turn, a smaller barge, full of rice, whose steersman slept throughout the voyage. Occasionally he awoke, let off a squib, and went to sleep again. We had a wide upper deck, with an awning, and straw mats to sit on. It spoke for the indolence of the East that the deck was not high enough for anyone to stand up on, far less walk about. Nobody wanted to do either. Why should they?

Gliding thus down a Siamese river seemed to me the nearest approach to Nirvana attainable. There was no possibility of action, no external stimulus to the thoughts or emotions. The monotony of our surroundings was unbroken. The river swept us inevitably on, never changing its course. No cloud relieved the sky. The high banks remained at a regular level, nor were they perceptibly inhabited. This was the East; this stream was like fate, which carries the Oriental along all effortless and unprotesting. The natives, their legs tattooed above the knee like patterned silk, squatted around us with their meagre belongings. Occasionally they took a stick of sugar-cane from a bundle and munched it; then they chattered or slept—mostly slept.

It would have been easy to see in their indolent vacancy an adequate solution of life. At least they were contented, demanding little, unruffled by care or strife. But it is dangerous to adopt the sentimental attitude towards lotus-eating. The East is not for us. We demand more; care and strife are life to us, and it is right that they should be so.

In the East there is no such thing as conscience: therein lies the essential distinction between East and West. Western man is tormented by two brands of conscience: regret for what he has done and regret for what he has not done. The former may be defined as moral conscience, of which the emancipated man, trusting to the rectitude of his instincts, knows little. It is fostered as a rule within the narrowness of religion. It amounts to a sense of guilt. But the second is a spiritual conscience. It is a sense not of guilt but of waste. It is the clamouring of man's neglected faculties for employment.

The East is free from both these brands of conscience from the first because the moral temptations most likely to assail the Oriental are legalized by his religion (hence for example the absence from the East of organized vice); from the second because the faculties of the Oriental are inferior to those of the Westerner.

The salient factor in the building of racial character is climate. Climate more than religion (which after all arises to a great extent *from* character) creates sensibility, from which a spiritual conscience grows. No climate in the world is more varied than our own. Our organism must be attuned to every kind of abrupt change. It cannot but respond, emotionally, spiritually, intellectually, to the quickening life of the spring, the glow of summer, the luxurious melancholy of autumn, the harshness of winter. In Europe a thousand shades of change in nature develop parallel shades of sensibility in man. How can you sit and contemplate your navel when the buds are bursting or the storm-clouds are gathering, when each variation of climate and natural environment is a potential spiritual experience?

But in the tropics nature is for ever the same. Tropical landscape is like a backcloth which never changes, as in the meagre scenery of an inferior touring company. For four months in the year there is rain. You can tell to a day when it will come and when it will go. You can often tell to an hour what time of the day it will choose. For the rest of the year there is no rain. That is all. The face of nature alters little from the rainy season to the dry. After a few months of heat she begins to fade a bit, to wither and dry up, but she has not the grace to shed her leaves and die nobly. She is stagnant. And the Oriental, emotionally, intellectually, spiritually, is stagnant as his natural surroundings.

The change and decay in all around he sees cannot but make the European ponder on change and decay in human existence. It must make him conscious of time, and time is not a thing to scorn, for it is an incentive to creation. When someone told Ibn Saud that by having an air service across Arabia he could do in two days a journey normally accomplished in thirty-six he said, "Yes. But what should we do with the other thirty-four?" In Europe each one of those thirty-four days would be different, affording a different stimulus to the organism, calling some different faculty into play.

The combination of the greater number of talents in nature's repertoire, in other words the greater complexity, makes the finest landscape. And so it is with man. Nature in the tropics is simple. She can be summed up in the one word, growth: growth, crude and unvarnished, violent, promiscuous growth, without economy and without form. In the West nature is complex, for a wider variety of climatic elements directs her growth. Western man is directed by these same elements: thus he too is a complex organism, and it is a truism that the most complex in art or humanity is potentially the highest. The Westerner, in whom climate develops so many more faculties, has many more needs than the Oriental. He needs love, a home, friends, occupation, intellectual activity. The Oriental needs none of these things. His wife is a chattel, he is nomadic by instinct, personal relationships mean little to him, he is passive, mentally as physically. The lotus-liver will argue that the Oriental is superior because his demands on life are more modest. But this is a pernicious doctrine; for the greater a man's spiritual needs the greater his spiritual potentialities.

Action, by which the Westerner sets store, may not be in itself a virtue, but action at its best is creation. The Oriental, because inactive, is uncreative. One cannot conceive of him sweating blood for six years of unrelenting toil to produce a *Madame Bovary*. Except where it has been stimulated by the complex Aryan, as in the great Hindu temples, you find culture and art in the East only north of the Tropic of Cancer: in China, for instance, and Persia, where a greater climatic variety produces a finer sensibility. But even there it belongs to the past: in modern times creative power in art, thought, poetry or music thrives only in the West.

Granted, then, that each is the creature of his climate, what have we to learn from the East ? What is the much-advertised "mystery of the Orient" if its inscrutability conceals only a bemused and vacant spirit ?

Morally and physically, we can learn a little. Crime and vice in an organized form belong only to the West, born of our social system and our religion. (It is doubtful whether the evils of opium-smoking in the East exceed those of drunkenness in the West.) Nor does the Oriental crave, as we do, for amusement (despite our efforts, with cinemas and so forth, to develop this taste in him). But a craving for amusement, even at its lowest, may have a spiritual and not a sexual motive.

The Oriental is relatively (but only relatively) uninterested in money. His worldly ambitions are modest and do not lead him to "pant with the money-making street". He can teach us a lesson in frugality, for he is in no sense a violent materialist.

These, however, are but negative qualities. Positively the Oriental is credited by the Westerner with mystical tendencies. Certainly his preoccupation with religion induces in him a predisposition to mysticism. But saints are peculiar to no race or persuasion, and I should doubt whether there were more genuine mystics in the East than there are scholars (or even mystics) in the West. The Divine Light penetrates the sluggish fog of the Oriental contentment as seldom as it does the agitated tumult of Western materialism, and the meditations even of a Buddhist priest are not as a rule such as lead him towards mystical experience.

The attraction of the Oriental is in his philosophy of life. He can hardly be other than a fatalist, since Nature moves for him in so relentless and indomitable a fashion. Even when on occasion she goes to extremes it is on a gargantuan scale, with earthquakes, hurricanes, typhoons, inundations such as man cannot stem. In the north man cherishes the illusion that he is superior to Nature, who dies each year while he remains alive. He can usually govern her caprices, and combat her extremest instruments. He can deflect her lightning, shelter himself from her winds, strengthen his banks and irrigate against her floods. Her advance is neither so violent nor so regular as to induce in him an attitude of fatalism.

Yet in her essential march of progress she is as ordered as in the tropics. Spring follows spring, summer summer, autumn autumn and winter winter till the end of time, and may not the course of our own lives be similarly ordained? It is commonly argued that the fatalistic attitude makes for listlessness. But this is to put the cart before the horse. The Oriental is fatalistic because listless, not listless because fatalistic. The tropical climate causes him to be both. Our fate is our character. We, as a people, are not listless, because our climate animates us to a greater variety of physical, emotional and intellectual activities. But we go to the opposite extreme from the Oriental: we strive too hard: we are led away too far in the belief that we can control our own destiny. The introduction of a certain element of Oriental fatalism into our character would not reduce us to aimless lethargy, for it is not in our nature to be lethargic; but it would save us from misspent energy and futile strife. It would bring us resignation, patience, tranquillity, and a philosophic attitude.

This is the wisdom of the Oriental, these the possessions which some part of us envies in him. But it is all that he has. We could possess this wisdom too, and very much more besides. The European who falls beneath the sway of the East and succumbs to its philosophy is acquiring a certain completeness which he never acquired at home. On the other hand, in surrendering to it entirely, he is sacrificing many potentialities. He becomes a lower creature, not than he might in fact have become, but than God gave him the power to become. He allows too many of his natural faculties to atrophy, too much of himself to die.

Love, the highest of all spiritual experiences, ceases to mean anything to him. Authors would have you believe in dramas of tropical love and adulterous passion. But such stories are untypical of the East. It is impossible to feel deeply in the tropics. Here a man may experience fleeting passion or habitual attachment to a woman, but with the diminution of his physical and emotional instincts he loses the power to experience love in its profoundest sense. Perhaps for this very reason, because the emotional standard is lower, marriages among Europeans in the East are generally successful and infidelities rarer than the novelists and dramatists would have you believe.

With the need of love other needs diminish. The intellect decays. The Englishman in the East who reads and preserves his intellectual interests is the exception. He grows oblivious to his surroundings. His senses are dulled by the insensibility of his climatic environment. For the price of an animal contentment and freedom from spiritual responsibility he sacrifices his spiritual conscience.

The casual traveller in the East observes this process engulfing his fellow-Europeans, and determines to flee before it has time to engulf himself. I had been accustomed to sneer at the typical Colonial who went East only to hanker after Surrey. But now I began to see that such hankerings are not to be despised: they represent a last desperate (and probably unconscious) effort to cling to the remnants of that superior sensibility which Western nurture has given. It is not the villas and the golf-courses of Surrey for which such men long but the smell of dead leaves in autumn and the daffodils in spring, the finer shades of feeling such as only a Northerner can experience, the germ of poetry which is hidden, perhaps subconsciously, in every European until the tropics eradicate it for ever.

The East is like a drug. As you reach Port Said on your voyage home you begin to "come to" as from an anaesthetic. Your benumbed spirit thaws, your heart begins to beat, your conscience, your emotions revive; the Mediterranean mistral recharges your sensibility as with an electric current. You are alive again. But for those who have been long in the East this process of awakening is an agony and its effort becomes too much to bear. They have been addicts of the drug too long. They must return to its narcotic ministrations.

To romanticize the East is an insidious habit: it could do with a bit of "debunking". For myself, the more I travelled in the "glamorous Orient", the more I realized the infinite superiority of Western civilization. Nor do I mean the phrase in a material sense. I mean the art and the culture and the beauty, the richness of intellectual and emotional life which the East never knows.

Chapter XII

INDO-CHINA

LAOS

TOWARDS evening we reached a village of some size.
"Pimouln ?" we enquired.
"No," they said. "Pimouln."
"Boat go Paksé ?"
"Yes. Motor go Paksé."
We packed into a ramshackle bus and rattled off across unfamiliar country. The road was orange and we crossed streams which were black and bottle green. When it grew dark a small boy was sent to sit on the mudguard and hold on the headlamps. We had no idea how far we were from the frontier, and the road seemed interminable. Suddenly, in the darkness, we passed a signpost, *"Ralentir"*. The driver accelerated. It was French territory. The road petered out at a ferry. Here was the Mekong at last, and we could see, even through the darkness, that it was a fine, wide river: so wide indeed that it took an hour and a half, sitting in a huge hollowed tree, to get across it. We approached Paksé with some misgivings. From its lights it looked disconcertingly small. It might be no more than a native kampong, devoid of French officials, unvisited by Europeans. We had passed no frontier post and seemed to be at the back of beyond. As we drew nearer, the lights appeared to vanish, and such as remained were only those of sampans moored against the bank. We pointed incredulously into the night.

"Paksé ?" we asked.

They nodded their heads vigorously, indicating a bank where the darkness was impenetrable. "Paksé! Paksé!"

A shabby floating jetty projected, empty but for a limp French flag. There was no sign of life. We clambered up a steep mud bank, stumbling, groping our way in the darkness, feeling like smugglers. This was a fine way to arrive in French Asia. From the top a few lighted shops beckoned reassuringly; but it was the worst-lit town I ever saw. We murmured "Hotel" to the coolies, but they understood nothing. From an inhabitant we gathered by signs that there was no hotel. Then, to our relief, a French voice emerged from the darkness. It belonged to a man in black silk with a bun at the back of his head. He was in the service of Monsieur le Résident. There was a bungalow, he said, for Europeans. He would take us there. We felt our way along pitch-dark boulevards and with difficulty routed out an ancient concierge in flannel pyjamas. His wife expostulated violently at the interruption of their matrimonial bed (it was only nine p.m.), screamed imprecations, shook her fist at the coolies and pushed them away from the door. She went on exclaiming shrilly, angrily, helplessly for the next two hours, while her husband cooked us a meal.

Meanwhile our guide indicated that we should call upon Monsieur le Résident, who would probably receive us in audience if we "lancé'd" our "cartes de visite". The idea of lancé-ing a carte de visite on a perfectly strange French official when in a state of hunger, ill-temper, dirt and exhaustion after a long day's journey appealed to us as grotesque; but the guide further indicated that it would be necessary to obtain the Resident's authorization to stay in the bungalow. We set out once more along the pitch-dark boulevards. In course of conversation we let fall that we were tourists. At this our guide was highly disconcerted. If we were only "des touristes" very probably Monsieur le Résident would not receive us in audience. Perhaps he had gone too far in suggesting such a thing; after all it was not *really* necessary to get authorization. This aspersion, of course, made it doubly essential for us to lancer our cartes de visite without more ado. Our guide melted nervously away: he would wait outside. Perhaps the great man would receive us: if not, then "il va m'engueuler". Much to our relief, and to his, there was no sign of life in the Residency. Not even a servant responded to our batterings. Evidently French officials keep early hours. (Poor things, they are at such a loss to know what to do in these outlandish parts that they can only go to bed.)

Next it was necessary to visit the shipping agent, to discover if there was a boat down the river in the morning. Fortunately he, almost alone among the French inhabitants of Paksé, was not in bed. He and his wife and another fat little bourgeois Frenchman were sitting stiffly round a table in a hermetically sealed salon, talking over coffee and cakes. He was civil, told us that the boat left at seven a.m., and let us depart. To our admitted relief there was no question of inviting us in. How different from a British bungalow with its salaaming servants, its comfortable chaises-longues and its cheery "Come in! Take a pew! Whisky-and-soda?"

We returned to the rest-house for our meal. There was a bottle of red wine to dilute, a delicious omelette, haricots verts au beurre and a tender côtelette de porc, with pommes frites. There was a little bridge on which to rest our knives and forks between courses. The meal tasted good at ten-thirty p.m., after three days of native rice.

Turning the pages of the Visitors' Book I could not help being struck with the pathos of the French, marooned in these distant countries where they are so little at home. These spindly signatures, these Pierres and Jacques and Andrés, these avocats and ingenieurs and fonctionnaires spelt the epitome of French provincial life. Next morning, as our steamer left the quay I observed, standing like a dummy at the top of the steps, the typical Frenchman. There was something ludicrously pathetic about his white-clad, urban figure : his false spade beard, his portly tummy, dumpy legs and abrupt, punctilious little gestures, among the slender Lao with their graceful movements and gay silk clothes. No Englishman, no other European, could have looked so utterly out of place. The British are said to be an insular race : but the Englishman will adapt himself to alien surroundings in a way that a Frenchman never can. France is the most insular of all countries.

We had expected much of the Mekong River. On the map it is a broad black snake, like the Ganges and the Yangtze-Kiang. Many thousand miles long, it rises in the great Central Asian plateau of Tibet, with the Yangtze and the Salween. The Mekong did not let us down : it exceeded all our wildest expectations. Winding through the lovely scenery of Laos it stands out in my memory among the finest things that I ever saw, almost (but not quite) equalling that great white snow-line of the Himalayan Range. However inadequate tropical scenery may be in the aggregate its masterpieces reach heights of beauty undreamt of within the more modest proportions of European landscape. The Mekong must, I am convinced, be the loveliest river in the world.

Some rivers sweep through the land, broad and swift and majestic but standing no nonsense, not to be trifled with, permitting no obstacle to interrupt their path. Such is the Loire. Other rivers seem to be preoccupied solely with the idea of reaching the sea with as little delay as possible. Such is the snow-green, rushing Rhone. Some, like the brown Tweed, are mountain creatures, farouche and wild, ill at ease amid the gentle civilization of the plains. Others, like the Thames, are amicable old lowland gentlemen who browse through water-meadows. There are savage rivers and intimate rivers, rivers which are gay and rivers which are intense, sociable rivers which welcome man, rivers which are cold and aloof. The Tigris has a touch of the sinister. The Niger spreads itself clumsily over wide tracts of country, like a gigantic and cumbersome slug. The Ganges, sanctified beyond reality, seems to have lost interest in anything at all.

The Mekong is like none of these. It is a broad, generous, expansive river. It permits the encroachment of the land on its waters like a nobleman who throws open his park. Islets, stretches of inviting sandbank, piles of rock abound on the Mekong, so that often it has the appearance of an enormous, island-scattered lake. Ahead a reef of low, smooth rock, stacked like packs of cards, apparently bars your path. Until you are quite upon it you think there can be no way through. But at the last moment the reef parts graciously, as a crowd before a royal procession, to allow the passage of its lord and master. That the Mekong *is* master is never in doubt, and for three months of the year, as if to confirm his prerogative, he rises thirty or forty feet to sweep quietly over all that lies in his way. The Mekong's right of way is closed, as it were, to visitors. But now, in the low season, he was in hospitable mood. Islands scampered playfully across his path. Birds skimmed across his glassy surface like débutantes fluttering across a ballroom floor. He was smooth and opalescent. His waters were blue as the sea on their clean, sandy bottom.

Moreover the surrounding country was worthy of such a river. The Mekong reflected mountains: mountains,

Market Scenes at Chiengmai, Northern Siam

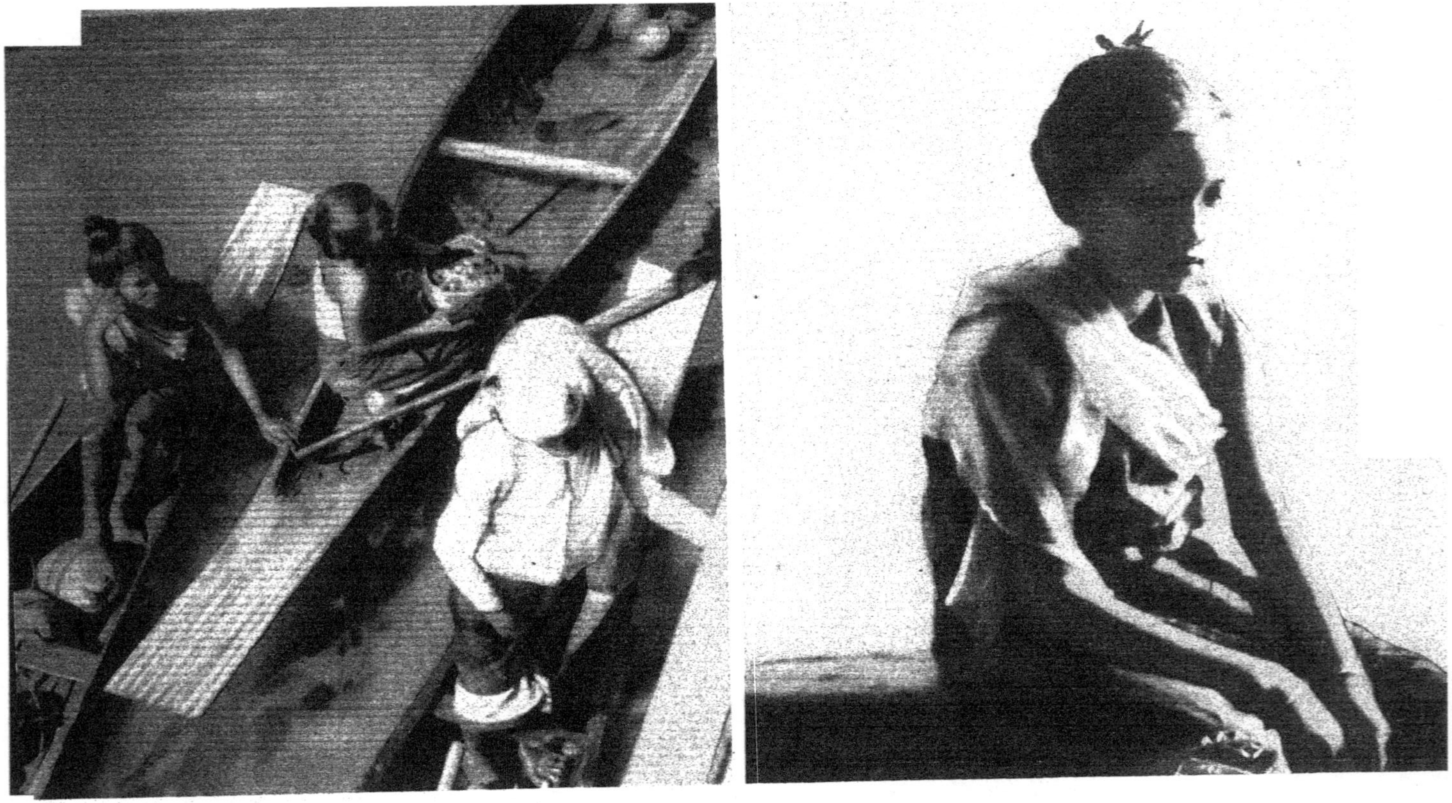

Lao Women on the Mekong River

moreover, whose vegetation was never so dense as to obscure their form but permitted the bare rock to emerge; mountains recalling in shape and colour the grey-green coastline of the Côte d'Azur, but on an infinitely nobler scale. The banks were high like ramparts, and the Lao had lost no time in planting them with vegetables and grain; the soil released for their disposal during a few short months of the year must be rich. Sometimes vegetation which looked almost autumnal varied the colour of the jungle, and here and there was a white-legged, leafless tree, thick with a flower of flaming orange. We passed three fishermen in sampans, throwing their nets. They did so in perfect unison and symmetry: one to the left, one to the right, one to the centre, as in a scarf dance. But on the whole there was not much river traffic. The French have developed the interior of Indo-China with roads, not railways, and the population is shifting away from the rivers towards them.

Occasionally, when we stopped to pick up passengers or put them down, a steep staircase of some fifty steps led from the water's edge like a Jacob's Ladder to a village perched on top of the bank. Up and down it passed, a gay-coloured Lao crowd. The sleek, dark hair of the women was gathered back into a bun, like a door handle, on which some of them hung the jewellery which you might have expected to see around their necks. They wore black Chinese trousers or sarongs of a kind of batik, with an embroidered silk border at the foot. Most of them were hatless but some wore great wide Chinese hats of straw, like lampshades. Their breasts were covered, but not with the indecently European camisoles which the Siamese wear (in conformity with a recent decree in the interests of decency). The men wore bright cotton loincloths, like tartan prints, or little Chinese shorts, sometimes striped like deckchairs. The superior ones had suits of silk pyjamas. Women and children carried bowls and trays of all kinds of food: chilis, melons, bananas, curious roots, dried fish, rice, sugar-cane and little sponge-cakes which they hoped to sell to the passengers. At one stopping-place two primitive Kas, natives of the mountain country, regarded the boat with childish amusement. They were short, muscular creatures, dark-skinned, almost naked, with long, matted black hair like that of Red Indian women.

Though the Mekong here is navigable to steamboats

all the year, it sometimes cuts things pretty fine. The channel everywhere is marked by huge stone pylons (a remarkable feat of French engineering) and often it is very narrow, passing within a few inches of partially submerged rocks. To steer a course requires the utmost accuracy and skill, particularly as the swiftness of the current implies a speedy rate of progress, and our boat was fitted with an especially sensitive apparatus enabling it to make sharp and sudden turns. When the channel was very restricted a boy sounded its depths with a long bamboo pole. As he raised it into the air the water dropped from it in silver stars and he shouted a number. The helmsman would turn his wheel a fraction to one side or another in answer; but deviation of a single inch might have meant disaster. Often rocks and islets encroached so far upon the river that we had to execute a hairpin bend to pass through pylons behind us, to right or left, and the stern swung round as fast as a swing-boat at a fair.

We were the only European passengers on board and ate our meals with the captain. A fat little Corsican, he was genial and hospitable and his cuisine was excellent. For lunch we had turnovers filled with sausagemeat, fresh fish "garni", petits pois à la française, chicken, fresh green salad and cheese, with as much wine (red or white) as we wanted. It was a joy to eat real French food again and the fresh green vegetables which the colonial Englishman is usually too unenterprising to grow. The captain liked to talk politics, demolishing our colonial policy and the entire political system of Europe: his conversation contained more than its share of racial hatred—of the English, the Germans, the Siamese. Nevertheless he was thoroughly contented with his lot and spoke with enthusiasm of the (to me questionable) joys of life on the ocean wave, which apparently included the Mekong's inland stream. His most likeable quality was his appreciation of the scenery.

In the evening we arrived at Khong. Here the course of the Mekong is interrupted by impassable rapids and a five-mile railway takes passengers overland to join another steamer below them. We were to spend the night where we were, but decided to walk through the jungle to have a look at the rapids. The bamboo groves were dead and the trees were grey and fluffy. We failed to find the rapids, discovering only a stagnant green pool and some rocks in a sandy clearing. Returning in that grey twilight which is darker than night, we lost our way. There was a stuffy stillness in the jungle which gave it a sinister feeling: we started at the slightest sound and believed the excreta of a cow in the middle of the path to be a coiled black cobra. It was a relief to get back to the lights of the boat away from that oppressive, dead jungle. All the native passengers had left, so we had it to ourselves. We had a shower-bath, and sat down to an enormous dinner with the captain.

Early next morning coolies started unloading the ship. Lazily each carried a sack up the steps, ambled back again and sat down for a rest. Lazily I lay in my bunk and watched them. They were muscular, sculptural figures of even, brown complexion. Their movements were graceful and they were beautiful as animals to watch. The range of expression which you might expect from them was limited. That face could register primitive feelings: fear, rage, lust. But you could never play upon it the infinite variety of tunes which you can play upon the face of the more sensitive European. It would have been as absurd to read Oriental mystery into its fixed expression as to credit a spaniel with the power of metaphysical speculation. There could be nothing enigmatic about that face: it could hide no subtle shades of feeling. It covered a superb independence of the need to think, and here lay its beauty. Here was the completeness, the directness, the confidence of an animal to whom it does not occur to question the world and its ways. One thing only removed these coolies above the well-bred spaniel: they could laugh. The Indonesian peasant is like an animal who can see a joke.

Later in the morning we transported ourselves and our belongings across to the other boat. She lay in very low water, amid rocks and islands which had a fetid submarine air, as though they should never have been uncovered at all. But we found a clean stretch of sand and clear water, where we bathed, not daring to strike out far for fear of crocodiles. We sailed in the afternoon.

Though built on a similar plan, this boat was as different in atmosphere from the other as two in an identical row of London houses. The first was spic-and-span. One felt the iron hand of the Corsican captain, demanding the respect and submission of his crew, and there was an air of ceremony about its routine. But the second was entirely French and haphazard, like the difference between the Empire and the Republic. We had most of our meals alone, because the young captain was gadding about on shore at every port, as our Corsican would never have done. There was a confused litter in the dining-saloon. The food was good but often cold, and there were laxities in the service.

Some Frenchmen came on board. There was a blowsy lady, caked with powder, a terai hat perched on her coiffure: the wife of a commerçant, taking her son back to Saïgon, where he was in business. "La vie est chère," she wailed, after the manner of her kind. The principal expense was that of transporting herself and family to and from Europe, on leave. The company paid only her husband's passage, whereas the "fonctionnaires" could bring their entire families out for nothing, including their mothers, grandfathers, aunts, cousins and so forth. Only by such a bribe can the French Government persuade people to go to the colonies at all. The third passenger was a weedy-looking official with bloodshot eyes who clicked his heels and announced himself, "Monsieur Doumier. Officier des Douanes."

"Monsieur Balfour," I replied. "Homme de lettres."

After every meal he retired hurriedly to his cabin and locked himself in with his opium pipe. Whiffs of the drug assailed us as we paraded the deck.

We had left the mountains behind and the banks were jungly. The trees were strangled with growths and many had tentacles which stuck out behind them like a woman's matted hair blowing in the wind. But never for an instant was the scenery boring. Translating the water into terms of land one saw the river as a park, with neat clumps of trees dotted about on it at regular intervals. Sometimes it would be a wide prairie. Always it was broken by some kind of vegetation. Outcrop of rock and scrub, with stretches of yellow sand, would give it a Saharan appearance. Further on its surface would be thickly wooded, trees growing straight from water level so that the water was like a clearing or a smooth glade in the middle of a forest. Then it became turgid. We charged at speed over mud-coloured rapids, churning the hostile water so that it curled like an angry snake in whirlpools around us. Here was plenty of wild life. I saw my first crocodile, sitting calmly on the bank like a

Head of Siva, Bayon, Angkor Thom

Bas-relief Bapuon, Angkor Thom

Heads of Siva, Bayon

stage dragon, as though it had just swallowed that alarum clock. It might easily have been made of cardboard. There were huge birds, too, of the stork variety, dispersing unwieldily at our approach and alighting on bushes which looked far too small to bear their weight. I asked one of the Frenchmen what this bird was.

"C'est un marabou," he said.

The French are not great natural historians. Whether a bird be big or small, black or white, a finch or a crow their answer is invariably the same: "C'est un marabou."

We stopped for the night at Stung Treng, a featureless line of concrete houses built on the river. They had the solid appearance of villas in a French provincial suburb: hardly the style of building which is suited to the tropics. Squibs were still bursting in honour of the New Year.

Next afternoon we reached Kratié and changed boats again. This time it was a larger boat, for the wider and deeper channel to Pnom-Penh. The change was very much for the worse, like a pretentious bourgeois hotel in a town after two country inns. Meals cost extra, the food was indifferent, the service incompetent, the captain old and fussy and far from amiable—though at dinner he thawed under the influence of his wine and told us proudly how he had sunk a neutral ship in the Atlantic during the war. The Mekong, as it neared civilization, became flat and broad and uninteresting.

Our bunks had no mosquito curtains, so that we were eaten alive. All night long we kept stopping to load cargo, and sleep was impossible. The din was at its most intense between two and four a.m., when we loaded wood. One solitary coolie had been provided for this purpose and did his work in slow motion, a single log at a time. The captain burst into torrents of excitable rage. Monsieur Doumier emerged from his cabin in a cloud of opium and protested shrilly, shrugging his shoulders: "*Un* cooli, voyons! *Un* cooli!" He added in falsetto that we would be here, at this rate, till "lundi soir" and returned with a snort to his pipe. The captain said that if no more coolies were forthcoming he would go on without the cargo. He went on without the cargo. I dragged my mattress on deck and attempted to sleep there. But either it was too hot, owing to the funnels, or too cold, owing to the draughts. It was not a comfortable night.

In the heat of the next afternoon we reached Pnom-Penh. (Manfred, throughout the journey, insisted on referring to it as Fom-Fen, and still does so. Names are not his strong point: frequently I would hear him telling people of the wonderful time we had had in "Keloontan", while the names of Persian towns would go in at his ear in recognizable form and come out of his mouth as something strangely different, as through a sausage machine or a game of Russian scandal.) Pnom-Penh is the capital of Cambodia. Apart from a palace and some temples in the Siamese style, it is fast becoming a French provincial town, with its uncompromising villas, its boulevards of trees, its cafés and its Cercle Sportif. It was Sunday, the fashionable evening, and in the hotel a crowd more French than anything one could have believed possible in Asia was dancing to a loud-speaker. It played chirpy little Parisian tunes, to which couples danced jerkily on the stone floor, bowing each other to their tables afterwards with innumerable gestures of politeness. At a table adjoining our own three pale-looking French children ate an enormous and unhealthy meal far later than was good for them.

We arrived in Pnom-Penh too late in the day to see the museum, which contains the finest examples of Khmer art in the world. Moreover, to our mortification, it was closed next day, so that, rather than curtail our stay at Angkor, we had to leave without seeing it. As we were returning overland from Angkor to Bangkok we missed out Saïgon from our itinerary. But we obtained a vivid impression of that city from the French guide-book:

> Is it not an amazing scene, that of light and smart "rickshaws" driven by their speedy man-horse running along altogether with motor-cars, without troubling each other ? Unique streets scenes which tourist can seize here for the first time with such an intensity, on his way from Home . . . : Small portable native shops selling unknown things, crowdy tiny markets, unknown fruits, a far Eastern fragrance and sight which no one can forget. Besides, the splendid shady trees protecting streets against the sun's ardours, all that explains the charm of this City.
> The elegance of the feminine Society will be another subject of amazement for the tourist who will see there—15000 kilometers far from Home—a thing that only Saïgon can offer to its visitors. Milliners and dressmakers have realized here that miraculous thing to have all

ladies wearing the latest fashion dresses and hats and thus allow tourists, after leaving Paris or London 30 days ago, to find again here the same "silhouette" which they met over there before leaving Europe.

It is a "smile of Paris" which greets all our visitors.

Those crowdy hours—5 to 7—will remember tourist the alive Boulevards of our French cities.

I should like to have seen the Plain of Tombs, "that desolated region which under moonlight has a dreadfull looking. Numerous french tombs-graves lie there." I would have benefited from Dalat, whose "European climate suits to anemied, week or depressed people". Nor did I encounter the Moïs tribes, who "live quite bare as well as their wives" and are "generally splendid specimen of human creatures". One cannot see everything.

I rose at four-thirty a.m. to catch a native omnibus for Angkor. I would hardly dare to speculate as to when Manfred left his bed. Manfred has this idiosyncrasy: that it invariably takes him two and a half hours to get up in the morning. He is not unpunctual: on the contrary, if I said to Manfred the evening before, "We must start at seven," there he would be, all ready, on the stroke of the hour. If, on the other hand, I woke him at six and said, "We must start at seven," it would be quite out of the question for him to do so. He could be ready by eight-thirty sharp, but not a moment before. How exactly Manfred spends those two and a half hours is a bit of a mystery. He always says that, if cash failed, he could get an excellent job as a valet. His neatness, in this respect, is certainly unrivalled. Whenever we arrived at a place in the evening Manfred would spend half an hour unpacking his suitcase, unrolling all the tidy little parcels in which everything was wrapped, arranging his brushes, his bottles, his manicure set, his medicines, his washing and shaving apparatus with impeccable neatness. Even in the mud hovels of Persia or Afghanistan, devoid of any furniture, where we slept sometimes six in a tiny room, Manfred would continue so to arrange his corner, on a window-ledge or on the floor itself, as though it were a dressing-room in a gentleman's chambers in the Albany.

In the morning Manfred would rise long before anyone else and start valeting himself. He would ask himself what suit he would wear to-day, take his trousers from beneath his mattress, where they had been pressing, brush the suit, fold it neatly, and arrange it beside his bed. Then he would brush, fold and put away the suit he had worn the day before, select tie and handkerchief, put his shaving things ready, turn on his bath (if so be, as happened rarely, that there was such a thing), give himself his morning dose of Andrews' Liver Salt, and inform himself that his bath was ready. Then he would begin getting up. Of the hour and three-quarters set aside for this purpose he would spend ten minutes folding and putting away his pyjamas, half an hour shaving and tending his face, with punctilious care, a quarter of an hour preparing his beautifully curled hair and manicuring his nails, twenty minutes washing, twenty more minutes wrapping up his things in tissue paper and fitting them into his suitcase, and the remaining ten in the actual process of dressing. For this, curiously enough, took him relatively no time at all. Then he would emerge, punctual to the minute, neat as a new pin, putting my tousled, unwashed appearance thoroughly to shame.

But if the ritual of *getting* up occupied two and a half of Manfred's hours he invariably *woke* up with a bang, and from the moment he had called himself would be chirruping and chortling as gaily as at a children's party. I, on the other hand, would awake laboriously and irritably, grunting like a cantankerous raven to Manfred's lark. It would take *me* two and a half hours to *wake* up, and I could rarely count on being fully awake till an hour or so after our departure. But the process of *getting* up, of washing and dressing and packing I took at full speed, since I regard it as the most unpleasant part of the entire day. Medical science has still many refinements to give us. We have sleeping draughts, but why not waking draughts, to soften the agonizing business of waking, so that it becomes pleasantly gentle instead of the cruel, rebellious business that it is? Why not a draught that would paint the grey light of morning in roseate colours, that would make you *want* to wake up instead of cling to sleep? For it is bunkum to talk, as the poets do, of the joys of greeting another day.

To-day, however, was an exception. It was still pitch-dark when I rose. It is always said that in this hour before dawn a man's vitality is at its lowest. But to me there is always a pleasant touch of farce about getting up in the dark, and my spirits, this morning, were unnaturally high. Darkness is an emollient at whichever end of the day you take it, whether like sherry at the beginning or like brandy at the end. It is always soothing, and if you are going to start early it is better to start while it is still dark, before the arrival of that cruel grey glare which strikes you so coldly and inimically in the twilight of dawn. Besides, it varies the monotony of the journey. An hour of darkness, an hour of daybreak, two hours in which the colours of the day are slowly blossoming forth, before the glare of the nine o'clock tropical sun begins to put them out: four hours are gone even before you realize it.

Even at five o'clock there was life in the native quarter of Pnom-Penh. Market stalls were open, people were eating and talking and letting off squibs as at any other time of day. Orientals do not depend on continuous hours of regular sleep: they sleep like animals, for an hour here and an hour there, when they feel inclined: there is little distinction in the East between day and night.

For an hour we rattled along, still in darkness, in our dilapidated bus. Then greyness began to dawn and my spirits to ebb. But suddenly there was colour in it and to the east the sun became a circle of red, to the west were pale green meadows, with scrub that looked like an English hedge, stretching flat to a remote and misty hill. The sun rose, but the air remained cool and fragrant. We ferried across the Mekong, and began to be aware of our fellow-passengers. The bus has taken more of the glamour from modern travel than any other means of locomotion. The ship is an Arandora Star, the train a Golden Arrow, the aeroplane a Flying Cloud. But no one has attempted to glorify the bus with poetic titles. Its very name precludes such canonization: it is an ignoble, ridiculous object: even the prefix "omni-" is merely a bit of pretentious clownery. In fact, however, you will find more of the atmosphere of a country in its buses than anywhere else. Packed to bursting-point with natives, echoing with their clamour, ours was a gay and ramshackle bus. The yellow robes of the shaven Buddhist novices exactly matched the petrol-pumps by the roadside (I offer the advertisement gratis to Mr. Shell). The chauffeur wore a pyjama suit of patterned black silk, with a moth-eaten white zip-fastening singlet and a filthy tweed cap. His assistant crouched on the mudguard in front and made jokes. The women, with their yawning red gaps for mouths, prepared their betel-nut. First they took the nut from a little box and put it in their mouths. Then they spread a red paste on a green leaf, mixed it with shavings from a dirty cube like a bit of old billiard chalk, folded it, and put it between their teeth like a bit of tobacco. For a couple of sous we breakfasted on steaming cobs of sweet corn which they were selling by the roadside.

To passers-by the bus must have presented an odd and unwieldy spectacle. Its roof was piled high with all sorts of luggage: baskets, sacks, bundles of sugar-cane, pedlars' show-cases full of collar studs and combs and mirrors and other cheap trash (the pedlars themselves were always deposited outside a town, so that they might approach it, as pedlars should, on foot), Chinese suitcases and, incongruously enough, a pair of swivel chairs. We stopped continually, so that the journey was never monotonous. At one time as many as nine passengers were travelling (strictly against the law) on top, and the cackles of the women and jokes of the boys enlivened the proceedings considerably.

We went along straight roads through muddy tracts of flat country which in the rainy season is under water. This was a playground for all sorts of birds, and the birds of Cambodia seemed brighter in plumage than those of Malaya. Herons, bitterns and countless varieties of cranes predominated. These long-legged birds never seem at home in their native element. They pick their way fastidiously about on their spindly legs, like women of the town in high heels and silk stockings, inappropriately shod for the country. Their chief concern is not to get their feet wet. They flap unwieldily on to trees too small for them, where they perch like large, smart women on small ladders in a flood. The kingfishers, on the other hand, like gaily clad typists, seem quite at home in their bright colours, and fly briskly about with a businesslike air. After a bit we came into jungle, where monkeys scampered across the road. Here there were rakish areca-palms and kapok-trees like telegraph poles, with horizontal branches and blobs at the end.

We lunched at a European tourist hotel, where hors d'œuvres, vegetables and a bottle of vin ordinaire cost us much more than our entire twelve hours' bus journey to Siemréap. After lunch it became intolerably hot. Twenty kilometres from our destination an enormous Frenchman in a passing car stopped us and stormed at our driver in French for allowing passengers to travel on the roof. Knowing no French, he could not reply. A funny figure in khaki canvas boots and an ill-fitting uniform, he took particulars of our number and so forth, raged, snorted, promised a procès verbal and drove off. To our joy we noticed, as he disappeared, that one wheel of his car was about to come off, and there were shouts of delight from driver and passengers. I wondered vaguely if the magistrate in charge of the procès verbal could speak the native language : if not it would be an odd sort of justice. Never in Indo-China did I meet a Frenchman who could (or would) talk anything but French, while it would have been rare to find a British official in Malaya who could not talk Malay. The result of course is that very few Indonesian natives are without a word or two of the French language, but the Malay who speaks English is the exception.

    We reached Siemréap at tea-time, eleven hours and two hundred miles after our departure from Pnom-Penh. The whole fare was five shillings.

CHAPTER XIII

INDO-CHINA (*continued*)

ANGKOR

THE ruined cities of Angkor are probably the most wonderful in the world. Hence the French have decided that only the rich may see them. Angkor, since its discovery in the jungle seventy years ago, has become a vast tourist racket. The hotels, indifferent and monstrously expensive, have been built at Siemréap, five miles from the Angkor Wat and seven from the Angkor Thom, and visitors must hire a car at the minimum rate of two pounds a day in order to visit them. This policy is short-sighted. Hundreds of people who wish to see Angkor cannot afford to do so; and the hotel proprietors were wringing their hands over empty rooms. But every racket can be undermined. After one exorbitant night in a pretentious tourist hotel I moved to a primitive Chinese establishment nearby, and here I lived for five shillings a day, including admirable meals and wine. It was a curious place, almost devoid of privacy, since the windows of the rooms gave on to the passage. But it was clean, and its inhabitants were a perpetual source of amusement. Huge families would pack into a single room, they would squat in the passages, cooking their meals, and kept up a permanent, raucous chatter.

Only once did I see a European in the hotel. He was a young German, bicycling round the world, exponent of one of the most formidable rackets of modern times. These penniless globe-trotters, on foot, bicycle, or even on horseback, are to be found all over Asia. Germans more often than not, they begin by offering to work or selling postcards to pay their way. But very soon they discover that this is quite unnecessary, and that they can get on perfectly well by

Towers of the Angkor Wat

Above: Cambodian Peasants   *Below:* Bridge at Prah Khan, Angkor

begging. They pester Europeans, of their own and other nationalities, trading on the "brotherhood of the white man" for charity by a species of blackmail, flourishing testimonials, not from officials in their native country, but from gullible consuls en route whom they contrive to impress with their courage and enterprise. They rarely fail to get money, by means which, in Europe, would see them in prison for begging or worse. An ex-British Consul in Siam, of charitable tendencies, told me how he had twice collected an audience for such creatures, that they might sing or do acrobatics or conjuring tricks to earn their money. On the first occasion the man arrived so drunk that he was incapable of performing, and all the box-office money had to be returned. The second time the performer, in the course of a trick with a revolver, shot himself accidentally in the leg. But this time the Consul contended that the audience had had more than full value for their money and refused to return it.

The German youth had reached such a pitch of presumption that he almost regarded free board and lodging as his right, and complained with righteous indignation that the Alsatian proprietor of the de luxe hotel in Siemréap had refused to put him up for nothing. His proudest boast was that the Governor of Herat had given him a hundred rupees. English officials in India had proved equally amenable, and in Bangkok he had had a grand time with Siamese women on money extracted from German residents. He was a German of a particularly stupid and tiresome type, with the wrong reactions to everything. He was highly suspicious, for instance, of the friendly Siamese and Cambodians, expecting a knife in the back at any moment, but trusted the Arabs and Afghans implicitly. He was quite uninterested in anything he saw, had no intention of visiting the Angkor Wat, but remembered precisely what each night's lodging had cost him in every country and reeled it off pat. He was thoroughly insular, disapproved of the Chinese trousers which we wore in the evenings, and refused to eat anything but European food. I hope he may come to the bad end that the majority of his kind deserve.

To visit Angkor, rather than submit to the fantastic charges of the motor-hirers, we adopted the means of transport used by the natives. This consists of a trailer attached to a push bicycle, which we could hire for sixpence an hour.

After a bit we were glad to notice that other Europeans followed our example. Sometimes Manfred, when he felt in need of exercise, would put the coolie in the trailer and ride the bicycle himself, to the hysterical amusement of the natives.

The Angkor buildings, relics of the Khmer civilization which disappeared with abrupt suddenness about the end of the fourteenth century but was at its height during the two hundred preceding years, can be roughly divided into three groups. The most famous is the temple of Angkor Wat, dating from the fourteenth century and surrounded by a moat of water four miles square. Despite much that has been written to the contrary this temple was never swallowed up by the jungle but has been in more or less uninterrupted use as a monastery since those days. Hence it is to all intents and purposes intact. The reason why it remained so long undiscovered was its inaccessibility to travellers. Next comes Angkor Thom, the great Khmer city of the twelfth century, containing eight important buildings (of which some belong to a more ancient city) in varying stages of repair. The whole of this city, ten miles square and surrounded equally by water, was hidden by the jungle until its discovery by Mouhot, a distinguished French naturalist, in the 'sixties. Outside its walls are a dozen or so other temples of varying dates, scattered over a considerable area.

But perhaps most romantic of all is the earliest of the cities, dating from the ninth century, whose existence was unsuspected until 1932 and which was in the act of being unearthed at the time of our visit by Monsieur Victor Goloubeff, of the Ecole Française d'Extrême Orient. Its discovery, in fact, was still undivulged to the world at large. Monsieur Goloubeff formed a theory that the Pnom Bakheng, a large, early temple on top of a steep hill (the only eminence in the immediate neighbourhood), commanding a wide sweep of country, might be the centre of the undiscovered city. By flying over Angkor in an aeroplane at a considerable height he was able to confirm his hypothesis: for there, far below him, almost hidden by the jungle but intermittently traceable, were the lines of the square moat which surrounded it, at a nearest distance of two miles from the centre. Two years of unremitting labour were now beginning to disclose further evidence in the shape of foundations of temples, houses, bridges, and a quantity of ponds; but little that is intact remains of the ancient city.

From the Pnom Bakheng, a large Siva temple with many images of the lingam, guarded at the foot of its steep hill by stone lions, you look down upon the tops of trees, stretching as far as the eye can see. Though it looks a jungle of velvet, you know that it conceals elements of iron hostility: a jibbering insect and animal life, tentacles of vegetable growth whose solitary object is to destroy these cities of man but which man has arrested and defeated in their evil design. The trees grow to a prodigious height but the towers of the Angkor Wat soar above them with a lasting dignity: a haven of stone civilization amid the sinister vegetable forces of nature, a grey rock in the midst of a coiling green sea.

The most striking memorial of this epic struggle with nature is the Bayon, in the centre of Angkor Thom. It is easy to imagine these earlier temples as a conscious experiment to create the supreme work of art. The Khmers went on building, century after century, until in the Angkor Wat they achieved perfection. The Bayon, by its very roughness and imperfection, emphasizes the immensity of the later temple, which its air of consummate facility almost obscures. In the Bayon the labour of its creation is portrayed.

Before you, as you enter the city, is the synthesis of Khmer architecture, in all its sculptural essence. In the West we are accustomed to architecture which is decorated with sculpture. But the three-dimensional sculpture of Angkor is no mere extraneous decoration. The architecture of Angkor *is* sculpture in itself: the two are inseparable. In place of a bridge with conventional pilasters and rail you have pilasters, forty on either side, each of which is a gigantic kneeling statue of a man, glaring inwards, supporting no ordinary rail but the body of a snake which rises at the entrance of the bridge into a naga: a hood of seven heads. Beyond is the gate of the city, carved into a huge four-headed Siva. A mile further on the Bayon rises before you in the forest. At first it looks more like a work of nature than of man: a great mountain of rock which man has attacked and moulded into a temple with thirty-seven towers. But as you approach it you see that the mountain itself has been built by man, by the gigantic labour of piling great hewn stones one on top of another. Imagine the most prodigious works of nature in rock: Fingall's Cave, the Giant's Causeway, vast overhanging cliffs, huge rocks balancing on the face of mountains; imagine these, but made by man. When you stand beneath the central, hollowed cone, a hundred and fifty feet high, you look up to a patch of sky, far above you, and the effect is as though you were at the foot of a mountain chimney or a cave with a cleft at the top. The stones jut out irregularly, they seem to totter, they overhang so that you think they will fall. But though men piled them up without mortar they seem to have been welded together by time into a homogeneous mass of rock, while shrubs and plants grow out of them as from a cliff.

In the ancient wars between Burma and Siam the opposing forces used to vie with one another as to who could build the highest pagoda, and the result of the competition would decide the battle. But these temples of the Khmers were built in an uncompetitive era of peace and prosperity, in the heyday of a great empire. They recorded in their bas-reliefs the wars which were over and done with and had made them what they were. It was not to outdo any human adversary that the Bayon was built. Was it not perhaps to outdo nature itself, so vast, so cruel, so impregnable a force in the country of the Khmers? Man resolved to build, by his own sweated labour, works of masonry which would be greater than the great rocks and trees of the jungle, their towers carved with menacing images of Siva the destroyer to keep nature at bay with a challenging smile. To this end was combined the joint artistic inspiration of a great religion before its decadence and an imperialism worthy of ancient Rome. All Hindu architecture is fashioned in nature's image, but only at Angkor do you feel the force of a struggle between man and nature's hostile elements, giving to these buildings a suggestion of the primeval. Never again can there be such stupendous works of man, for to-day we fight nature with machinery.

The empire of the Khmers decayed with abrupt rapidity. In a very few years their cities were deserted and forgotten. No sooner had they disappeared than nature pounced on their presumptuous creations. Quick as lightning the Angkor Thom was covered up, and for four hundred years it was lost. Now it is unearthed and proves, for the most part, to have defeated nature. The trees around Angkor are the biggest and finest I have seen in any jungle. They had to be if they were to do their work of concealing this prodigious human handiwork. But the Bayon, though worn and battered, is miraculously intact. She had won her battle. Man-made, she has the might of nature's work.

Behind the Bayon is the Bapuon, which is more than ever a mountain made by man and is called "Mont d'Or" by the French. It is one huge mound of terraced masonry, with an unbroken prospect of steps, and the horizontal cornicing gives it the appearance of a broad stack of timber, turned to stone. At the back, where the earth is forcing its way through, its slabs of stone bulge out as in a badly loaded lorry. Opposite, another temple steps high above the trees like a gigantic man-made ant-hill and as mystifying in its purpose. The exquisite little Pimeanakas beyond, with its regular steps as in the plinth of a Nepalese temple, but higher, is a gem by comparison.

But there is one group of buildings over which nature has decidedly won the battle: the Ta Prohm. Here her destruction has been deadly and the spectacle is as horrible as that of a human being in the grips of an octopus. Apparently inert, the great monster stretches out tentacles with which to throttle and destroy. Trees grow out of the buildings, on top of them, underneath them, sideways from their walls, levering them apart until the ground is heaped high with the wreckage of masonry. The roots of a tree have entwined themselves round the gate of a temple, which in time will be crushed to bits until there only remains a tree shaped like an arch. Opposite, the root of another tree is crawling like a serpent along a wall, forcing the masonry up as it crawls, shooting out limbs to strangle it. Roofs are encircled by gigantic arms as of some infernal Samson. On walls is a criss-cross pattern of slender grey roots, pretty enough in its suggestion of silken network; but slowly it is forcing its way between the stones, where it will swell and cleave the wall in pieces. There are trees with broad, flat trunks, like walls themselves, standing where walls once stood. The atmosphere is dank and hideous in its manifestation of nature's diabolical power (Wordsworthians please note), twining, tugging, tearing, tightening on the works of man, locking them in a fiendish embrace. But occasionally on a fragment of frieze a group of Cambodian dancers still flouts the elements or a row of Buddhas stares nature out of countenance.

It is a relief to pass into the courts of the Benteai Kedei, with its corridors and vistas of square doorways still intact. There is a strong suggestion of Roman influence here as in all the Angkor buildings, in general conception, in the formalized, scrollwork carving of plinths and lintels, and in the pilasters of the square windows. It is curious to find sometimes the figure of a Buddha as the central figure of a decorative motif entirely classical in its effect. There must certainly have been commercial contact between East and West in the time of the Roman Empire, and this would bring with it artistic influence. The Romans had silk but no silkworms, and we may assume that they imported it from the East. What more natural, then, that some of the architectural inspiration of their Great Empire should filter through to inspire afresh the Khmers?

The moat of the Angkor Wat is 250 yards wide, and thick with mauve lotus on which elephants graze. A stone causeway crosses it, passes through the cloister which forms the outer square of the precincts, and proceeds for a quarter of a mile across the inner, grass-grown park to the steps of the temple itself. You begin to mount the building, by a covered way, past deep stone tanks which must once have been filled with water. Then you emerge into the inmost courtyard, and the central block of the temple is directly above you. Its height is terrific; its walls are so steep, the space which divides them from the cloister is so narrow, that you have to crane your neck in order to see the top. Here is none of the soaring ease of a Gothic cathedral: the Khmers had no arch and the doorways and the colonnades of the cloisters are square: the building piles itself in horizontal stages by infinite labour but with the effect of an infinitely civilized grace towards the skies. Ever-steepening steps lead upwards in an unbroken progression and the cornices too are like steps. The barrel roofs of the cloisters ascend steeply towards the central building, and here, with some architectural ingenuity, a stretch of roof has been lowered to make the ultimate ascent appear steeper. From the summit the five great towers grow skywards: flower-like cones of a wonderful delicacy with petals of grey stone flame licking up them. The upward urge of the petals is repeated in the curling snake-headed pediments of the doorways and roofs.

These five stone flowers which crown the Angkor Wat grew more and more beautiful as the days went on. At first, when the weather was sultry, they were heavy and black and still; but after rain they soared alive into a sky which no longer oppressed them and turned to a light, diaphanous silver grey. I would see them at the end of a vista, from some other part of the jungle, or reflected clearly in the waters of their moat at sundown. I would come upon them unexpectedly from a hundred different angles, and always with a fresh shock of delight. They were ever-present, watching over all the forest. Sometimes I would see all five at a time, sometimes four, sometimes three. Sometimes two would seem to grow together and then, as I moved, detach themselves, the smaller opening out like a Japanese flower in water. As I walked away more towers would grow up and hide themselves in turn behind their fellows. My favourite view was from the north. From here the temple seemed too steep to be credible; its three cones rose immaculate, unhidden by the jungle trees. I would sit and watch them in the evening by the water-gate as the young priests came down to bathe and wash their yellow robes and the grey buffaloes wallowed in the muddy water.

The wonder of the Angkor Wat is not in its towers alone but in its sculpture, in the bas-reliefs which cover its walls, extending for miles along its corridors and galleries. A mighty war frieze covers one side, and though the attitudes of the figures are entirely stylized they vibrate with movement. You feel the force of the opposing armies sweeping along the wall, and when they meet you almost recoil at the clash, which sends figures of men and horses and elephants flying pell-mell in all directions. In other corridors there are religious processions and processions of state, and high up on the outside walls of the temple are static figures of Khmer women in the semblance of Vishnu. Elsewhere are medallions of dancers, often in mere outline as though drawn on the wall with a sharp, cutting pencil. They have the mastery and economy of consummate pencil sketches, alive with the poetry of motion. It is curious that the art of a people so lethargic in movement should be so instinct with energy and life in its representations. Sometimes the designs grow so stylized that the conventional Khmer figure, with his legs apart and knees bent, becomes a leaf or a flower, traced as delicately as the imprint of a bird's claw in powdery, soft sand. But still it remains vivid and alive.

The Bayon too (as indeed all the Angkor buildings) is covered with bas-reliefs, contrasting in the refinement of their workmanship with the ruggedness of the temple as a whole. Many are unfinished, and you can trace the outline of further carvings, just begun, like a child's rough drawing on stone. Here hunting scenes and the everyday domestic activities of the Khmers prevail over the more martial and ceremonial subjects of the Angkor Wat. I was looking at this frieze one afternoon; then I looked out towards the road, and there was a human frieze which might have been its model. A line of peasants was proceeding through the forest. They had the same features, they wore the same loincloths as the Khmer peasants carved in stone on the wall beside me. They carried the same household utensils, the same baskets hung like scales on rough branches. Even their bullock-carts had not changed in eight hundred years. Here, before me, was a living example of the axiom that time, in the East, stands still. I turned a corner, and at the end of a passage, with its back to the light, was a cross-legged figure of a peasant. Only when I drew near did I see that he was made of stone.

I wandered to the centre of Angkor Thom, a delightful open space where the terraces of the imperial palace remain. Their rough, high walls are carved in deep relief with life-size elephants and figures both human and animal. I sat on the grass and drank the milk of a coconut, idly watching the thin stream of peasants which filed beneath them. Here there was no such thing as past or present. In Europe one tries in imagination to people ruined places with their ancient inhabitants. But the effort is often too great, so remote from to-day is the life even of the eighteenth century. Here at Angkor life has changed so little that it is easy to connect these palaces and temples with the people who built them. They seem perfectly natural and in place. To-day they are dead; but life could at any moment be resumed in them and it would be neither incongruous nor a pantomime.

That night there was a performance of Cambodian dances before the floodlit façade of the Angkor Wat. The dancers were women, few of them over twenty, since the effort of training is so great that it exhausts them prematurely. Their faces were dead white masks, and they wore elaborate costumes, heavily embroidered in gold, with rich bracelets round their

Cambodian Dancers, Angkor Wat

Above: Moat, Angkor Wat   *Below:* Funeral Procession at Angkor Wat

wrists and ankles. Their epaulettes curved upwards and on their heads they wore crowns with gilded spires, so that their shadows were like pointed pagodas, their shoulders curling at the ends like the Cambodian roofs. There was none of the rhythmical energy of the carvings. The dance was purely plastic in character; odd half-movements of unaccustomed muscles caught up and stylized into a pose with an awkward, childlike grace. Though it lacked the passion of Western dancing it had an extraordinary beauty of its own. The faces of the dancers were expressionless, with a touch of that sulkiness which appeals to the Oriental. All their expression was in their hands, which bent right back like the seven-headed hood of the naga, twisting and turning in sinuous motion. There was little variety in the dance but its monotony was fascinating and there seemed to be no indication that it would ever come to an end. Concentration is not an Oriental gift. The native audience talked and their attention wandered. Just so must it have been when the Cambodians danced these same dances here six hundred years ago before the emperors of the Khmers, less as a spectacle than as a continuous accompaniment to some feast.

There are still two monasteries in the precincts of the Angkor Wat, so that the place still lives, and the yellow robes of the priests enliven the grey of the stone like marigolds. High up on the cliff of masonry you see them standing in a doorway or flitting through the cloisters. Moreover we were fortunate in our visit for it was the occasion of a feast. The body of a priest, who had died a year before, was to be cremated on a pyre with many junketings and funeral rites. Thousands of priests and peasants from every part of Cambodia were encamped in the grounds in an improvised village, round a huge artificial pagoda. At the edge of a moat a primitive bamboo scaffolding, such as Heath Robinson might have drawn, pumped water for the campers. It was drawn up through bamboo pipes by suction into a rough wooden trough, which conveyed it into a tank in the compound. Thence it was baled in coconut-shells by those who required it. The people lived in the open and in bamboo huts, while the priests of the various neighbourhoods each had their communal pitch, where they entertained. There were booths and cookhouse stalls and amusement enclosures, and the atmosphere was as gay as an Elizabethan fair. In the evenings crowds squatted on the ground at a simple shadow-play like a Punch and Judy show. There were Cambodian dances, primitive compared with those we had seen, cheaply dressed and crudely lit but with an atmosphere all their own. Now and again men in shabby peasant clothes joined in the dance with a sinuous feminine grace of movement curious to see in their rugged, half-naked forms. Sounds of music filled the air: of xylophones and drums and gongs. In the paper cloisters of the pagoda a boy played a pipe to companions who had fallen asleep, and presently fell asleep too.

One morning gamblers were assembled in the shade of a big tree in the temple precincts. They gambled in sous, on mats marked out with numbers, the croupier spinning his dice like a top in a porcelain saucer.

Siemréap was en fête on the morning of the funeral procession, and overloaded buses clattered out to Angkor every few moments. The wide stone causeway was dense with spectators, and a yellow group of priests with white umbrellas made an agreeable splash of colour on the steps of the temple itself. A rough orchestra of drums, gongs, and reed instruments led the cortège. The high priest followed, small and wizened, cross-legged on his litter like a miniature Buddha, with a gay-coloured canopy above. Behind him were other litters with offerings to be laid on the pyre: bundles of priests' robes, fruit and vegetables and sugar-cane, porcelain cups and teapots, fans and straw hats. Next came the dead priest's empty throne, with some of his simple possessions: robes, a fan, a teapot. Dancers, their faces smeared with ash, capered curiously behind it.

Then the procession took a decidedly secular turn. There followed two comic dummies of French policemen, made of newspaper and papier mâché, with moustaches and official-looking bands on their arms. They swayed stiffly and idiotically, to the amusement of the crowd. There were more musicians, more dancers, then two huge papier-mâché horses, ridden by minute human mahouts elaborately dressed, expressionless and plastered with white make-up so that they looked quite as unreal as their ridiculous mounts. Two white elephants, with trappings of wallpaper, followed, and then came the catafalque itself. It was like a huge, over-decorated quintuple-decker tram and its wheels groaned and shrieked in a dozen cacophonous keys like a harmonium gone mad. Decorated with garish, painted panels of glass and an incredible quantity of gold tinsel, it was dragged along by a human equipage, hundreds strong. A man stood where one would expect to see the conductor, beating a gong, and priests crouched chanting on every tier. The coffin was perched on top, and where the panels were disintegrating they had been patched up with newspaper. I could distinctly read a Peugeot advertisement and a heading, "La Vie Théâtrale".

It was absurdly like a gala week carnival organized by some provincial municipality, perhaps to celebrate the anniversary of its tramways. If we were to bury our bishops in this fashion the Church would surely have more converts. Or perhaps the ceremony would be more suited to the obsequies of town councillors.

After a complete tour of the grounds the catafalque was lodged beneath the sham pagoda, built of newspapers, bamboo and bunting. We walked round the edge reading old bits of the *Petit Parisien* and the *Echo de Paris* on its walls. That night it rained. The rainy season was over, but the natives took the downpour as a matter of course. The rain would continue every night for a week, they said, until the cremation of the priest. And it did.

The morning after the rain there was a lovely glistening freshness in the jungle. We visited other temples. There was the Prah Khan, much covered by jungle roots, but with lovely carved tympana, many fine nagas and two huge stone figures guarding its entrance. A naga bridge approached it, guarded like the Angkor Thom by gigantic busts: ranks of Horatii with the truculence and the coiffure of Edwardian dowagers. There was Neak Pean, a tiny shrine in the centre of a tank, almost covered by a magnificent tree, with a pleasantly fantastic, Wagnerian effect. There was Ta Som, with some fine carved elephants. There was Pre Ru with its tall wats of rose-apricot brick and a broad terrace overlooking the surrounding jungle. There was Ta Keo, the nearest approach in design to the Angkor Wat but in the rough, devoid of decoration. There was Pra Kravan, a small, early brick shrine with a huge bas-relief reminiscent of Epstein.

In the evening we decided to go to the Barai Occidental, a great formal lake ten miles away, and bathe. We set off gaily on our bicycle trailers; but we had forgotten the rain. It broke in a tropical deluge when we were half-way there.

There was no shelter, nothing to do but strip and treat the rainstorm as a bathe in itself. Manfred rode his bicycle. Mine developed a puncture and I walked or ran the last three miles. The rain poured over me like a shower-bath, harsh and invigorating. Underfoot the puddles were incredibly warm to my bare feet. As we reached the swimming-pool the rain cleared. Three Frenchmen, sitting in the bungalow, were astonished at the arrival of a very wet, mad Englishman in nothing but a topee and shorts, riding a bicycle with a coolie in the trailer. No sooner had they overcome their surprise at this apparition than a second Englishman appeared, equally mad, equally wet, walking alone and clad only in a towel. They shook their heads at so irrefutable a proof of the long-suspected insanity of the race. The water of the pool was so warm that it affected us like a hot bath : just what we needed after our wetting.

The time had come for us to leave Angkor. We were to take the bus early next morning to the Siamese frontier at Aranya and proceed by train to Bangkok. The moon was all but full as I went to take leave of the Angkor Wat. I fancied that by moonlight it would be at its grandest and most majestic. The moon was behind a cloud as I approached, and the temple reared up ahead of me, dark and frightening. Only a light like a star, far up in the topmost shrine, relieved the darkness. Not a soul was inside, and I groped my way amid the fetid smell of bats. Someone has described the Angkor Wat as a splendid nightmare. I had disagreed : it had not struck me as sinister. But now that I saw it unmasked by the darkness it seemed to take on a different character. An awful gaunt, huge emptiness reigned : it was like the unbeliever's conception of death. It was no ghost feeling that frightened me, as in a funeral vault which is inhabited by the spirits of the dead ; here were no spirits but a void, a vacuum. The place was dead, like an untenanted house. It was as though it had been built for certain gods but those gods had never taken possession : not from displeasure but simply because they did not exist. Its nothingness, its monumental futility seemed to symbolize the tragedy of a people who had backed the wrong god.

I sat at the top of the temple for an hour, quite alone in its emptiness. The jungle below seemed to mock at the Angkor Wat, invisible now in the night, which had flaunted itself so nobly by day. The bats made play in its belfry. The crickets tittered. The moon smiled sardonically. A beetle croaked at it like a cuckoo in blasé cynicism, now from one tower, now from another, and his laugh was hollow, like the devil's. The distant music of drums and gongs called me back to the park, and even the grotesque, sham paper pagoda seemed more real; for at least it was impermanent.

The Cambodian dancers on the terrace had finished their performance and the Central Gate was flung open. Beyond the causeway was a line of car-lights as at a London party. Tourists from the *Empress of Britain* were streaming in, ludicrously caparisoned in mosquito boots, veils, topees like pagodas and all the other paraphernalia of tropical kit which they had been gulled into buying at Port Said. I passed them hurriedly and went out. The Angkor Wat was better dead. Thus at least it had the haunting beauty of desolation.

Chapter XIV

SIAM, SUMATRA, HOME

THERE comes a psychological limit to every journey, a saturation point beyond which it is unwise to proceed; for the mind cannot absorb an indefinite sequence of change. My perceptive faculties had come to the end of their tether: the battery of my powers had run down, and I knew that it could only be recharged in a different atmosphere. I was tired, and longed suddenly for a magic carpet to transport me back to the West. How nice to wake to-morrow to the patter of cold March rains and the damp, grey smell of a London square with but a month of winter to go!

But the Dutch boat in which I had booked my homeward passage did not sail for a week. I said good-bye to Manfred, who was completing his tour of the world with the mosquito-booted harpies of the *Empress of Britain*, and left Bangkok to fill in the intervening time at Chiengmai, in the north of Siam.

The hot weather was well under way in the north. The air was stifling and dusty, and a thick haze so obscured the landscape that although we were in mountainous country we seemed to be on a plain, so dim was the outline of the hills. This phase of nature coincided with and aggravated my mood. I grew dull, listless, uninterested in my surroundings. Whereas a week before I would have encouraged any proposal to visit a temple or look at a view, now the prospect of neither tempted me. I was arriving at that psychological state of bored indifference which is, disconcerting to relate, the permanent condition of half the Europeans in the East. In such a frame of mind I should not write of Chiengmai at all, save that in retrospect some definite impressions do emerge from my mental fog.

The market, for instance. Here was all the colour which

one expects in the East and so rarely finds. The market of Chiengmai differs prominently from other markets in that it is populated so largely by women. As a rule men predominate in an Eastern crowd: not that the Oriental male dresses much less gaily than the female, but in a woman's costume is always some extra touch of colour, some peculiarly happy juxtaposition of shades such as a man does not achieve. Chiengmai is a town of Lao women in gay colours, each with a flower in her hair, a garland coiled round her neat doorhandle chignon or petals sprinkled on her head as from a pepper-pot. The Lao women, traditionally impassive, have a chic, an elegance, an allure such as I saw nowhere else in Asia. In the market they squat beneath wide, transparent umbrellas, thread their way sideways like shying horses between the stalls with that awkward, quick amble which the balancing of their basket scales necessitates, but always with a graceful movement of the hips. I felt like a clumsy colossus as I walked though this market, since the umbrellas only reached my chest and the doorways were built for a smaller race than mine. But the Lao are so beautifully proportioned that I had not before observed them to be small.

They have a rich country, to judge by the quantity and variety of meats and fruits spread out for sale on the ground. To their north there stretches away towards China a great conglomeration of mountain races: Shan, Lawa, Kaché, Chong, Meao, Muksö, Kuwi, Yao and Kaw. Many of them come down over the old Chinese caravan roads to Chiengmai, as Scottish highlanders of many clans come into market from the remoter crofts and villages. You see them with the hills in their eyes and in their limbs the expression of mountain men, moving darkly amid the coloured throng.

The handicrafts of Northern Siam are of a superior kind. The pottery is good, and at a place rejoicing in the name of Lampoon a special cloth is woven under the direction of a Lao beauty known to all Europeans as the Rose of Lampoon. In the grounds of her small native house she has developed a thriving industry, where all kinds of cotton cloth are woven on handlooms. The Rose of Lampoon has even obtained the latest European patterns and you can buy cotton for shirts such as you see in Jermyn Street but for next to nothing.

The Europeans in Chiengmai are for the most part in the teak trade, and spend long, solitary months in the jungle working the timber with elephants and floating it down the rivers (it takes seven years to reach Bangkok). Their life is probably the loneliest of any Europeans in the East, but it is real and contents them abundantly. I met one old stager who had recently returned to England on leave but had only been able to stick it for a month. He returned to spend the rest of his leave among the hill-tribes of the Shan States.

Chiengmai is a hive of gaiety during the weeks that the men are in from the jungle. The elephants had ceased working by the time of my visit (they need several months' rest in the year, for they are sensitive animals, prone, I gather, to nervous breakdowns) and Chiengmai was full. I was somewhat nervous as to the nature of my reception, since authors too frequently seek out the jungles of Northern Siam in search of "copy"; nor did the inhabitants lose much time in telling me of their various gaffes. One had gatecrashed a native wedding, another had published a tale of how the elephants are tormented by butterflies, another had earned ridicule by going off into the jungle swamps in a pair of light suède shoes, yet another had been hit on the head with the drumstick of a goose. But my nervousness was unjustified, for I was treated with great hospitality, even to the extent of being lent a suit of the evening dress peculiar to the Europeans in Chiengmai: a pair of black silk Chinese shorts with a white silk shirt. (The shorts, to my shame, I accidentally took away with me in my baggage, thus presumably adding to the Chiengmai saga of authors' misdemeanours.) The older residents of the place in particular (men for the most part who have settled down there in retirement with Lao wives) did everything to make my visit an agreeable one.

I saw the ancient thirteenth century walls of the city. I saw a thirteenth-century temple with remarkable reliefs in stone, different from anything I had seen in Siam or Cambodia. I was shown over the American leper asylum, like a garden city with its numerous little villas for the inmates, and formed a milder estimate of the dangers of leprosy than the Bible had led me to believe in. (Only by continuous contact can infection be transmitted.)

On the train which took me back to Bangkok was an important Siamese official, who was presented with bouquets

Racial Types

Above: Siamese *Below:* Italians

Racial Types

Above: Tibetans (in Nepal) *Below:* Afghans

of roses and received an ovation from a crowd at every station. Next evening the International Express took me down to Penang, and it was pleasant to wake up in a country which was still green, with refreshing pools of muddy water among the trees. After a night in Penang I took a boat to Belawan-Deli, in Sumatra, where I was to join the mail-boat of the Rotterdam-Lloyd.

I spent the afternoon at Medan, one of the principal towns of Sumatra. Here, for the first time in the colonies, I saw good modern buildings. The market at Medan is worthy of Corbusier. The East is an admirable field for modern architecture: virgin soil with no architecture of its own, nothing to desecrate or destroy, ample planning space and a landscape well suited to modern forms. Yet only the Dutch have realized its possibilities. The whole town was clean and well planned, like a town in Holland itself. The difference between Sumatra and Malaya in this respect is psychological. The Dutch make of their colonies a home: the East Indies are a second Holland, to which they have expanded from a country too small for them. When a Dutchman first sees their shores on his return from leave he rejoices as at a homecoming. The Englishman groans at the prospect of another three years' sentence.

The hotel where I lunched might have been in Amsterdam. Prosperous business men sat in its modern kunst surroundings and sipped delicious gin drinks. The curry, I must confess, laid me out. But a Dutch companion laughed me to scorn. It was nothing, he said, to the reistapfels which are the speciality of the place. On half-holidays the Dutch put on bathing-dresses for lunch. They drink quantities of gin pahits beforehand. (The record individual consumption is a hundred and seven gins before dinner, achieved by a Dutch archaeologist in Batavia.) Then they settle down to the reistapfel and tankards of beer. When the perspiration becomes intolerable they go out into the garden in their bathing-dresses and are hosed by a servant, after which they return to more reistapfel and more beer. The proceedings end when every guest has been carried off to bed in a coma. Such is the Dutch idea of a really good meal.

We sailed that evening. The daily news bulletin reported 18 dead and 2291 injured in Paris street riots; 60,000 workers causing upheaval by a General Strike in Madrid; threats of war in Vienna; Labour sweeping the L.C.C. elections in London. This was the Europe to which I was returning. No matter. For the time being I had had my fill of the stagnant East and Europe, even in a state of revolution, seemed preferable because alive. After Colombo we had nine long days across the Arabian Sea. I fretted with the restless boredom that only a ship can bring. I scratched off the days on a calendar like a schoolboy awaiting the end of term. Suez, one stage nearer home, seemed a haven of beauty. I saw the Suez Canal for the first time and was astonished at its narrowness. From the centre of the deck I could see water on neither side, and it was as though we were bowling through the desert on wheels. At Port Said the first chill of Mediterranean air set my dormant faculties reviving. The mountains of Crete seemed like home. Sicily, Corsica followed in blessed succession. I disembarked at Marseilles, spent a night in Paris and arrived in London in time for Easter, three weeks to a day since I had left Bangkok, twenty-four weeks since the Pall Mall pantomime.

PERRY GREEN.
1934.

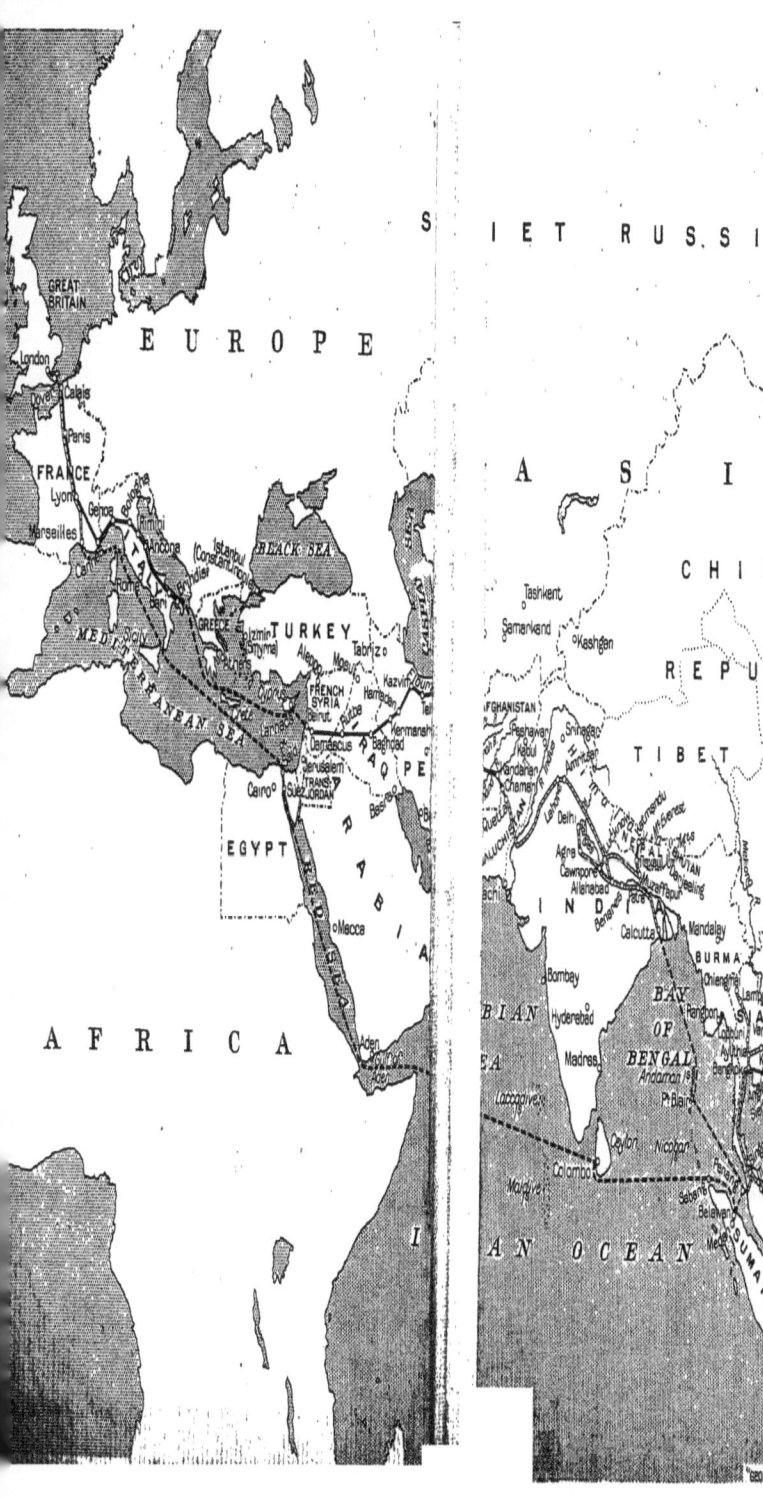

www.ingramcontent.com/pod-product-compliance
Lightning Source LLC
Chambersburg PA
CBHW032000220426
43664CB00005B/84